THE LIES OF MONEY:

Who Are You Being?

LIES OF MONEY
© 2016 by Live Your Roar! LLC
ISBN: 978-1-63493-120-5

All rights reserved.

Reproduction and distribution are forbidden. No part of this publication shall be reproduced, stored in a retrieval system, or transmitted by any other means, electronic, mechanical, photocopying, recording, or otherwise, without written permission from the publisher.

This publication is designed to provide accurate and authoritative information with regard to the subject matter covered. It's sold with the understanding that the author and the publisher are not engaged in rendering legal, intellectual property, accounting, or other professional advice. If legal advice or other professional assistance is required, the services of a competent professional should be sought.

Dr. Lisa Cooney and Live Your Roar! LLC, individually or corporately, do not accept any responsibility for any liabilities resulting from the actions of any parties involved.

Testimonials

I did it. I finally made it to a LIVE Dr. Lisa Cooney class called the Lies of Money. But the funny thing is, it wasn't really about Money, so much as it was about all the limitations we hoard in our bodies that keep us from moving forward, creating our lives, and receiving.

I am an energy critic when it comes to facilitators and their skill with commanding a class, connecting with their audience and creating actual change. Basically, I'm asking... How good ARE You?

The performance I saw and experienced last night with Dr. Lisa Cooney was worth a standing ovation. I have never seen or heard that level of expertise, ease, and contribution in the way that she BEs.

It is almost indescribable, but the one thing I can tell you is that if you're asking for change and you really desire it, Dr. Lisa Cooney can take you there in a magical, kind, humorous, and potent way that is like nothing else you will have ever experienced.

Thank YOU, Dr. Lisa for YOU.

~ Amy Cristol, Owner Cedar Haven Stables, Cedar Hill, TX

Working out of the Lies of Money, I got my new job. I can now make in a week what I used to make in a month! My position also comes with a brand new Cadillac to drive with insurance, gas, and toll fees covered! HDIGABTT? My body chose a pair of work shoes that cost $300 and I thought was too much, but asked if they would make me money. I got a big whoosh of "yes a lot!" energy and bought them. I love wearing them. I am more willing to look at where is my money going and how much it costs to run our life. In my eBay store I sold 2 things for $39.99 that I paid $15 for. Cody and I turned in our leased Audi early, and bought a playful jeep. We both had jeeps when we met in the Off-road Club in college, so that purchase is doing wonderful things in our relationship. More please! What else is possible?

~Mandi, Dallas, TX

So far, I've been making the same amount of money at work, HOWEVER, I haven't been stressing about money or paying bills.... PLUS, I have been invited out for dinners and work lunches. I've been offered an awesome trade. I've been told I will be getting a raise at work by the end of the year without asking, and while others are getting fired. Today, I've been offered the opportunity of making some nice bonuses with something I had already started to do. Tomorrow I've been invited to a fabulous restaurant by a fabulous friend who is making me feel very special! You're right! I was not paying attention to all those miracles! WOW! Thank you, Dr. Lisa Cooney!! How does it get better than that!! More of all that, Please!!

~ Laura, Dallas, TX

Today, I acknowledge (thank you, Dr. Lisa Cooney) that I am a powerful creator and my choice to experience money as: all my Bills are Paid and I have more coming in than going out. I created this though my choice.

Ok today was a fantastic breakthrough. I cannot wait till I listen to all those potent processes again. Oh, my gosh thank you for today!

~ Nancy, Denver, CO

Acknowledgements

Thank you Amy Cristol for showing me the ease of having money; the pleasure of being with what you have financially; and the possibility of allowing yourself to have and never needing anything or anyone.

To Donna Hildebrand for always having my back and showing me how to lean in and show up bigger, better and more real than I could have imagined possible.

To London, my youthful playmate, that always makes me smile, home or abroad, with her unique being-ness that lights up my world.

To Sara Wilson, your unyielding care and kindness for me, my body and my well-being, partnered with friendship and personal assisting beyond measure. Words can never express how dear you are to me.

To Gary Douglas and Dr. Dain Heer, I am extraordinarily grateful for your dedicated commitment to consciousness, change and personal empowerment. Thank you for always honoring me with knowing I can create so much more by being more and more and more of me.

Dedication

This book is dedicated to all of you out there struggling with money.

To all of you feeling like the debt or financial worry you are in is a big black hole that you will never climb out of or get beyond.

For all of you feeling lost, confused, immobile, terrified and impotent with changing your financial reality, I share these words with you as a beacon to see you through. You can make a different choice.

You can have the living you desire.

You can create the money, cash, currencies, investments and vacations you like.

Choose You

Commit to You

Collaborate with those conspiring to Bless You

Create

You being free and living joyously with your financial reality is a real possibility but you must demand of you to have it no matter what it takes, who you lose or what you let go of.

May all of Life Come to you with Ease, Joy and Glory®

Dedication

Table of Contents

Who does this belong to?

Introduction

You've now got your hands on a gold mine.

At the very least, a whole pile of cash and money – whichever you want (because, as I've found out with thousands of clients around the world, there is a difference).

But this book isn't just about money...

It's about the lies of money.

And, quite frankly, if you don't get to the bottom of them, they will keep you tethered like a ball on a string tied to a pole, circling around in the same orbit again and again.

It may surprise you that these lies of money have nothing to do with actual cash or money, yet have everything to do with what you use to create your 'money flow' – or lack thereof – in your bank account, portfolio, investments, checkbook, and in your pocket book right now.

In other words, it all actualizes as your financial reality.

Does this sound like a massive undertaking or a bit overwhelming?

If it does, then you'll be pleased to discover, like the people who attended these workshops in person, that all it takes to begin creating a new financial reality for yourself is a 1°, or 1%, shift.

And anybody can do that, including you.

As you'll see, once you get in there and look, the cage of lies and limitation starts to rattle and then collapse.

And then the truth starts to be.

So how does this relate to money?

Because money is an energy, just like everything else. We are energy. We have ATP in every cell of our body, Adenosine Triphosphate. That's the spirit energy, our soul print energy.

We come in a form. Money comes in a form. We're all energy, though, and we make it separate with these lies.

Money is not the problem – we are.

It has nothing to do with anything outside and everything to do with what is within yourself, and what your belief systems are. It has to do with what you think about it, what you project on it, what you make it mean to you, what you define yourself by, and whether you have it or not.

This book is a compilation of transcripts from five workshops, or "Tasters" as I called them, that I held in various parts of the country. Each one is a whole workshop in and of itself yet, while the concept and tools are the same throughout, they're all uniquely different.

And there's a good reason for this...

Because people are unique.

At the same time, there are similarities that make up the lies of money and float insidiously through individuals, their families, and their cultures, passed from generation to generation.

In over 20 years of private practice, group practice, international practice, money is one of three main reasons people come to me (the others are health and relationship).

I started noticing that there was a pattern in my clients who had the same 'presenting problem,' where they could create money, but they never kept it or had it.

Others felt they couldn't create money – and, therefore, they couldn't create it and they couldn't have it.

I suspect that if you're reading this book, you'll find your own experience somewhere in these pages and, as a result, begin to have to your own 1° or 1% shift. And when you do, I will have done my job.

Because, at the end of the day, the lies of money are really about confronting these three questions:

- *Who am I being?*
- *What am I being?*
- *What lie am I buying into that I've made true?*

Trust me, it's not work for the weak.

But it is for those of you who are ready to live your ROAR – what I call your Radically Orgasmically Alive Reality.

It's work for the wicked ROAR inside of you that's says, "No more. It's not worth hiding behind those lies anymore."

And, you know, it really isn't.

So, come get your money…

Because money in your hands will change the world.

Maui

Speaker: It's my pleasure to introduce Dr. Lisa Cooney tonight. She is among other things, a therapist, an Access Consciousness® facilitator, and radio show host who facilitates classes internationally and changes lives. She's changed mine extraordinarily and I'm grateful to have her here.

She'll be here for the next five days, so if you'd like to delve in and shed layers and layers of old trauma, holding patterns, judgments, self-judgments, whatever limits you, tomorrow has no prerequisites. The next two days are called *Embrace Your Roar, Your Radically and Orgasmically Alive Reality* and you're so welcome to join us.

It's going to rock worlds.

Dr. Lisa: I'm going to give you just a little taste of the Lies of Money tonight. It's so interesting when we talk about money because it brings this energy of stuckness.

There are three main lies of money and, if you take a look at them, you'll find that it is these assumptions within you that create the financial reality that is actually not you.

But you believe that it is you.

Now, that might sting your mind for a moment and feel like, "What is she talking about?"

I hope that your mind will expand, reading this, because what we've all done to ourselves around this topic of money is actually a radical elimination of our creative phenomenal brilliance.

You are the people that could change the world. Do you know that?

So, what does money give you in this reality? Does it give you freedom? Does it allow you to make you a good choice? Does it give you something luxurious? What else does it give you? Laughter?

Participant: Entertainment.

Participant: Security.

Dr. Lisa: Yes. This reality functions by money, yet there are so many people who have kept money away from themselves for many different lies. I'm going to address three.

Here is this thing called money. I keep my money literally, in my wallet, and then I use it. I love one-hundred dollar bills. And I keep it in a 14-karat gold money clip. It's pretty heavy – even the wind doesn't sweep it away.

When I look at it, it makes me happy. When I hold it in my hand, I feel powerful. I feel creative. Today, it felt very good because I did do a little bit of my shopping and used some of the money.

When I hold this in my wallet, I know that anything's possible. When I look in the mirror, I know that anything's possible. When I look at the ocean, I know that anything is possible.

However, most of us look at money and choose to believe that everything is impossible unless we have it.

So, this is the first lie of money: Many of us believe that this piece of paper has power over us, that it's stronger than us, more than us. It has authority over us. It owns us.

Look at how you're looking at it right now. Look at what's coming up in your body right now as you look at it. Listen to your mind and what you're actually saying as you see it:

- *What are you thinking?*
- *What are you judging?*

- *What have you decided?*
- *What have you concluded?*
- *What have you computed?*

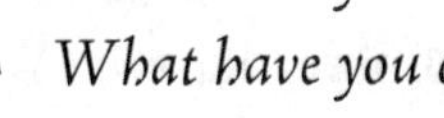

And…

How perhaps have you configured that money is a god of this reality that you must bow down to and pledge allegiance to, in order to have it?

That's a lie.

There's nothing you need to do or be to have this right here.

You just simply need to choose to be or do what's right for you.

So, that's the first lie of money.

The second lie goes something like this: Let's say you took your money to couple's counseling. You put it in the chair – and you have your chair – and the therapist directs you and your money to have a conversation, using "I" messages.

If it would speak to you, what would it say to you? How well would it be treated by you? Is it the lover that sleeps on the couch and, therefore, is really not the lover?

Is it the one that walks out on you and would rather go to the bar to hang out with his friends, instead of being with you? Or are you the one that walks out and go to the bar to be with your friends and not want to be with it? Could you even entertain that money would be your lover?

That's the second lie we'll talk about, that money is your perpetrator, your jailor, and you are its slave. And that, unless you have it, you can't choose beyond what you're choosing right now. That it will never give you what you need.

In this lie, you'll always criticize it. You'll always be skeptical of it. You'll never trust it. You'll want to cheat on it. You'll want to binge with it. You'll never save it. You'll never have it. You'll always spend it. You'll never choose to surround yourself with it.

Are you noticing there's a theme to all of this?

The theme lies within each of us, within each of you.

So the first lie is that money is god and you are less than. The second lie is money is your perpetrator, your eternal jailor, and you can't have it.

And the third lie is what?

Can anybody guess? Because there are like 8,000 lies, so you can't be really wrong.

Participant: You're never going to have enough money.

Dr. Lisa: That you're never going to have enough of it. Sure. Anybody else?

Participant: Money is evil.

Participant: You have to work hard for it.

Participant: Money can't buy me love.

Dr. Lisa: Yes, so all of these are 100% accurate for what's true for you and what's true in this reality. They are belief systems. They are judgments. They are things that we have decided, judged, concluded, computated, and configured our reality around, our bank accounts around, our relationship around, our body around, our job around, our chores around, our clothes around.

They determine when we can go to Hawaii, when we can't, what we eat, when we can go to Whole Foods or Safeway or whatever it is. That's all true...

But they're all belief systems.

The third lie is that money is a problem.

Money is not the problem – we are. What we think about it, what we project on it, what we make it mean to us, what we define ourselves by, whether we have it or not.

These are not all the lies of money, but they're the three lies of money that came very clearly to me and throughout my personal journey.

Now, whether you've seen me speak or never seen me speak, you probably know that I usually start with a structure or an outline for what I'm going to talk about, and then about ten minutes before the class I throw it in the garbage because I connect with the energy of what and who is coming in and showing up.

I listen to what the bodies, beings, you – the energy of all of you here together – may hear and may wish to hear. That's more important than any outline, to me at least, that I could come up with. And then I always, even though I threw it out, tie it back in somehow.

Now how do I do that? Well, part of it comes from my license and titles as a doctor of psychology and therapist, and being a trauma and somatics practitioner. I travel internationally, have a radio show, and I do workshops – body work, energy work – all over the world.

But there's a couple of other things that have distinguished me to be able to come in to a class, throw out my outline, and talk and speak to what's here in the room – and that's based on the energy.

So I can go all the way back to when I was seven years old or I can just tell you a couple of really quick things:

One, about 15 years ago, I was diagnosed with a life-threatening illness. This is when I really got clear that I had big problem with money. If you get sick, you'll find out that your health care in the U.S. doesn't cover your naturopathic

choices. You could easily cash in your retirement, your house, your investments, your portfolio, and on, and on, and on, and on.

And that's exactly what I chose to do consciously and I'm still here.

When I was first diagnosed, the doctor said that the best I could do was live on medications for the rest of my life and I'd have to cut out an organ or two, maybe three or four once they got in there. Who knew? So they gave me three options: kill it, live on medication, or have it taken out.

At the time I was just about 30 and I said to the endocrinologist, "Well, there has to be another option."

I will never forget him because he was one of the main reasons for my going to energetic means to cure, change, and make different choices in my life – different possibilities – in my life physically, emotionally, spiritually, financially, energetically.

He said there was no other choice.

Nothing else was possible.

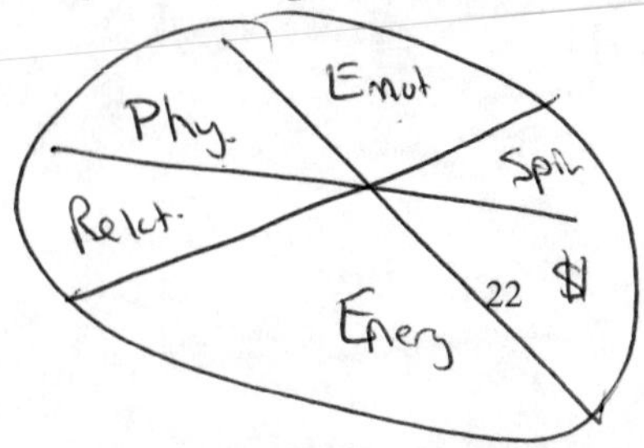

So I walked out and never saw him again, and that led me down the path of going to Theta Healing® Institute (now in Montana) where I stayed for three months.

Within three weeks, I cured the disease. It took a little longer to cure the whole body of all the issues. Energy healing and natural medicine actually looks holistically, meaning the whole body.

On the other hand, the endocrinologist uses allopathic medicine to look through the endocrine system, and those couple of different organs and systems of the body. I'm not necessarily talking bad about endocrinologists or allopathic medicine. I still use them. This is just my experience.

When I made that choice and I saw what could happen with energy, I knew that, energetically, there was something else in this life going on. And so I made the choice to change my entire practice over from being a traditional therapy doctor of psychology and weekly sessions to a more group facilitation, energy work, energy healing, and getting into the belief systems and the limitations by what we think psychically and psychologically that creates the dis-ease and disease in the body.

Okay, so how does this all tie back to money?

Well, I needed to make more money. It cost me about a million dollars to heal myself. I was pretty sick. I was in the naturopath's office probably two or three times a week, eight hours a day, getting tested for this, that and the other thing. Shots, IVs, everything. And, at same time, I was traveling to the institute to get my master's degree – because, of course, I needed another degree.

But, all the while, I saw this bill keep building up and my retirement going down. I saw the house and land I wanted to build, the plan and everything that I set for my life start to fall away at 30. I thought that that was the end.

And then the real end came…

Zero.

You may know what I'm referring to.

Participant: Your bank account?

Dr. Lisa: My bank balance, yes.

I hit that 'zero' point and I was terrified. I grew up in New York. My father worked really hard when he was in real estate. He put us through college. We always had a job. We always worked. We always had our own money. We always learned. He taught us how to save, what to do, all of that stuff.

I wasn't familiar with 'zero'…ever.

I've been working since I was nine years of age. I loved my little paper route. My mom had a panel station wagon and she would drive us. Anyway, it was fun. And I loved Christmas. You know, Christmas tips.

I love the smell of money. I love the taste of money. I would literally taste it and smell it. In my summers in college, I worked in the bank and every Friday, we'd get into the vault. I'd sit in there and just smell and breathe in the money.

My father was an entrepreneur. I'm an entrepreneur. I haven't worked for anybody since I was 20 something years of age. He told me very young, "Lisa, it is not just a man's world. It's a woman's world. Do only what you love. Always work for yourself. Be your own boss and go out there and make some millions."

He was a poor boy from Brooklyn. He got a football scholarship to college, then went in to the army and got an education that way, too. He was a 2nd generation Irish immigrant. My mother was a 2nd generation Italian immigrant. Working hard was part of the culture. Education was part of the culture. They all worked on Wall Street in New York, that sort of thing.

I actually went to California and put on my Birkenstocks, instead, but money was a love of mine. I had a love affair with money. Do you know what it smells like? Tastes like? There was something about it. And I really attribute this to my father. He was great with it.

He had 16 or 17 different apartment buildings at one time and my job was to count the money and put it in stacks of cash across the table in his office downstairs in the basement. I didn't want to do anything else. I didn't want to go anywhere else. People can go play. They can go play dress up. They can go to the mall, do whatever the hell they want, but I wanted to be by the money. I wanted to smell it, taste it. If I could put it around myself, I would have.

Then I hit 30 and I have zero in my bank account.

Where was I going to live if this kept going? What was I going to eat? What was I going to tell my mother? How was I going to tell my father?

More particularly, how could I look in the mirror at myself?

I mean, at that point I did have my master's degree. I was the therapeutic coordinator of a treatment center in Arizona. I did have my shit together a little bit.

Then I got sick.

And when you get sick, your whole world changes.

So I had to really look at that '0' over and over and over and over and over and over and over and over and over and over and over again – and really make a choice because I could die.

I could go home, which was going to kill me but I could go home.

I could go to a friend.

I could sell everything.

I could keep going to work. I could work harder, but it was kind of hard to work when you're sick.

So what was I going to do?

This is when I started to ask, "Okay, how does somebody who's so healthy all of a sudden get so sick?" I must not have been that healthy. Disease doesn't just show up overnight. You may get a diagnosis overnight, but disease builds for years and decades. That's when the universe said many things to me but, in that moment, I needed to change my reality, including my financial reality.

There were lies that I was living by that were somehow creating this disease, actualizing as a disease in my body – really a choice point to live or die. And it was all because the one thing that I never, ever, did not have was taken away.

If money wasn't taken away and that 'zero' didn't come, I want you to get this: I wouldn't have listened. I would have kept going with how I was living because there was no problem, right?

Well, apparently there was a big problem.

To be honest, I was little bit of a money hoarder. I love it. Truthfully, I really do. And I believe when I have money and spend money, I'm changing the consciousness of something.

When I sit and do work all the world is real – India, Hong Kong, Taiwan, Hawaii, California, Colorado, Florida, and wherever else I haven't mentioned and done classes. When you guys get an awareness, an 'aha,' that's money well spent in me getting here. That's contributing to seeds of consciousness. I don't even know what's going to happen, but it's going to increase my bank account somehow.

In fact, it's going to increase me on all levels: energetically, psychically, spiritually, psychophysiology, as well as financially. I want it all. But I want it all for myself and I want it all for all of us.

As I said earlier on, you are the people that we require on this Earth and that I require to have money. I require for you to have money. I desire for you to have money. Not just to spend it, but to have it, to change the consciousness on this planet because I have a larger target than you just popping in for two hours and then never seeing me again.

My target is to eliminate and eradicate all forms of abuse off this planet, and that all individuals are radically and orgasmically alive.

Do you know how much financial abuse is on this planet? How many of you have been financially abused? Even though my father taught me all these things, there was also a big lie in my family.

I was a child model in New York, and there were unspeakable acts and events that I was forced to participate in at that very young age. People were paid for the acts that I was forced to participate in and I wasn't paid.

But it cost me a lot 30 years later.

You don't have to have an extreme story. Some of you will resonate with what I said and some of you will have no clue about what I'm talking about. I'm not saying, "Hey, come over here and have these experiences."

But the money thing, yes, I'd like you all to bathe yourself with money. Put it on and wrap yourself around it. Actually, that's your home play: Go get as many hundred dollar bills or $50 bills, crisps are better, as you can. Put a little glue on it and paint yourself with the money.

Okay? Just do it and have fun with it. You can invite somebody, whoever you want. Hopefully, if you're married, it's the person next to you, but maybe you want someone else next to you.

You want to invite something else in – that's what I'm talking about – a radically, orgasmically, alive reality. Money doesn't have to be such a heavy topic. In my extreme situation, believe me, it wasn't fun.

However, this is what it looks like when one has turned and looked, gone in and cleaned out. To be able to stand here and speak and think that I have something to share. I have to turn and look.

And you know what? What it comes down to these days, with these eyes, it's like my father gave me a gift. He taught me that money wasn't about gender. It wasn't about having, or coming from. It wasn't about education. It wasn't about training. It wasn't even about having to work hard.

It was choosing to be what he wanted to be.

My father worked hard and he played hard. I've been to more Super Bowls and more sporting events than I could ever tell you about. My father was a Yankees fan, so every Wednesday,

Friday, and weekend we were there. He was a New York Giants football fan. On Sundays, we were there. Hockey, New York Rangers, Monday, Wednesday, Friday. And he would drag us to Madison Square Garden, New York Knicks, the Madison Square Garden. That's what we did.

He told all of my friends. My brother and sister and I would each have to invite two or three friends with his tickets. He'd go out on the street to buy a $5 bleacher seat, so all of his kids and their friends could go to the games. Why? Not because he had the money necessarily, but because that's how he wanted to live. He's no longer here, but that is something I'm so grateful for because in 25 years of practice, internationally, nationally or locally, that's not something I've ever found with anybody about money. No one has been parented like that. No one comes from that reality.

Well, I've met one person. Some of you know him. Gary Douglas from Access Consciousness.

So, when I got sick and I hit that zero point, it took that brilliance, that fun, that smile that I'm talking about here, that energy that kind of lights up the room – it took that away when I saw that zero.

And I could have been the abused victim, sick and desperate, letting go of everything, no longer desiring to help anyone, not even help myself, and I could have chosen to die.

But I chose to live because no matter what our story, no matter what our past, no matter what horrific things have transpired and all of us have our story, it still doesn't take away our choice.

Our choice is: lies or truth? Which reality do you want to create? Abundance or scarcity?

Which reality do you want to create?

Now, I know that that seems really simple. Believe me, I know it, especially when it's like you're in quicksand and you're in a lie. You think it's so real, you keep creating it over and over and over again. It becomes more real and gets harder and harder to look at something different.

The question is, are you smiling?

Are you happy when you're believing the lies of money?

And if you're not, then find that molecule in your body, that childlike innocence that my father kind of implanted me with, if you will, around creating and business and working and fun and joy and choosing to be my own boss.

This doesn't mean you have to be your own boss, but you could be your own boss even if you work for somebody. Choosing to see what's possible instead of what's not possible.

What if 'impossible' is just I'm possible?

So that's a little bit of my story, but what are your lies of money?

What could you be choosing that you're refusing with the lies of money you've been telling yourself… that you are choosing? And how much is it costing you to continue to believe the lies of money that you've been telling yourself are true? What would you be doing if you weren't sitting at your computer like I was that day, staring at the zero, freaking out, and worst-case scenario, planning your plan B, your exit strategy, if you will.

What could you be choosing or creating with whatever financial situation you're in now?

And here's my favorite lie – and the question – who's financial reality are you living?

Participant: Are we going to reprogram our lies today?

Dr. Lisa: Yes.

So how many of you are familiar with Access Consciousness? Let me explain a little bit about what I'm going to share with you, even though I haven't been saying it out loud.

When I'm asking you questions and I'm talking, I'm actually running what's called the 'Clearing Statement' in the back of my mind. It's an energy clearing statement that sounds like you're speaking in Mandarin. If you want to know more, look it up online at TheClearingStatement.com.

You can liken it to a computer and a hard drive being updated. Your belief system gets stuck on that one thing, going round and round and round and round and round. So, just like when you restart a computer, you boot it up again and everything works, that's what the clearing statement does. We can reprogram with the clearing statement.

The clearing statement and any energy technique only works if you choose to own what the benefit of that belief system is and why you love doing it.

I literally had to ask myself when I was at zero, "What do I love about being at zero? What do I love about being in the state of drama and catastrophe? What do I love about being sick? What do I love about dying? What am I dying to get out of? What am I sick of?"

And it's not, "Can you take me out for coffee because I have no money and I'm really freaked out and my boss is a bitch and I can't go to my parents because you know they hate me and they'll use it against for the rest of my life... and, and, and, and..."

None of that.

You've got to get really, really, really honest with yourself and ask yourself what are you doing to create this? What are you doing to keep choosing this? What are you doing that you actually want to die? What are you doing that actually you want to lie? What are you doing to limit yourself?

That's the hard work. That's what creates lies and inventions.

The invention that we're living by is like denial-colored glasses. We'd rather be superior and right than look behind a curtain about what's going on.

Personally, I would actually rather look at what's going on and be able to look at myself in the mirror and say, "Yes. You're being genuine. You're being authentic. You're being real. You're not inventing things."

When I'm inventing things, I really am one of those crazy people that really like to own it. And it's not that I have to get on the microphone and proclaim it to the world, but I really like to own it and be like, "Okay." For example, when I get mad at somebody I'm like, "Where have I been that? Where have I done that?" When I judge somebody I'll be like, "Wow! Where have I been that?"

I want to actually create beyond that and I'm going to pay attention to that. I use the things that people do and that triggered me to my advantage, and it always makes me more money. I'm going to talk a little bit about some techniques for that, too.

The clearing statement, basically, is this:

Right, wrong, good and bad, POD and POC, all nine, shorts, boys and beyonds®.

Right, wrong, good and bad, POD and POC, all nine, shorts, boys and beyonds®.

Right, wrong, good and bad, POD and POC, all nine, shorts, boys and beyonds®.

Right, wrong, good and bad, POD and POC, all nine, shorts, boys and beyonds®.

Right, wrong, good and bad, POD and POC, all nine, shorts, boys and beyonds®.

Right, wrong, good and bad, POD and POC, all nine, shorts, boys and beyonds®.

Now, given the licenses and titles I have in the health community, to actually stand up around the world and say that to 205,000 people on my radio show weekly took a lot of guts. I wanted to hide from the world for quite some time with it. But before I was even in Access Consciousness®, I was doing Theta Healing®.

Theta Healing® is the whole thing. It's working with the creative energy of all there is. Some people would even say the big G-O-D word, right?

So, again, I'm kind of this person that goes outside of the structural box, even though I have licenses, education and training of this reality which I'm very grateful for. They've been a valuable commodity in my life in business because, when people see the 'Dr.,' they want to come overseas. When they see a book proposal, they'll look at that. I'm not saying this to pat myself on the back. I'm saying that whatever you have got and whatever you have in your bag of tricks, use it to your advantage.

Everybody has something.

Each of you are neat and brilliant. I wrote my dissertation on this, so I know it. It's called *Soul Printing*, just like our fingerprint is unique to each and every one of us. That's your soul print. Each of you have a unique soul print to impress on the lips of reality.

Mine happens to be part of what I'm doing here today. Yours is whatever you do or be – or what you refuse to do or be – but you have it.

So whenever the clearing statement is run, essentially, whatever you were talking about gets dissipated. You're freed up from the decision, the judgment, the conclusion, the computation, the configuration, the algorithm. You've freed up whatever age you made the decision; whoever's it was – your mother's, your father's, your sister's, your brother's, your boss'; whatever gender it belongs to; whatever lifetime it belonged to; whatever nationality it belonged to; whatever culture it belonged to; whatever earth it belonged to; whatever land it came from or came to; whatever food you ate that was energetically flipped with something; whatever air you breathe; whatever radiation you were exposed to or not exposed to.

It's an all-encompassing statement.

Let me tell you a personal story about it...

I was over in Australia teaching when my father was dying. I couldn't get back to say goodbye to him, so I said goodbye on the nurse's private cell phone in his ear. It was the first time he was able to move and raise his eyebrow, and after that he died.

He was waiting for me, and as much as I hated him for it for a moment, he died like that for a reason because he knew that I would come back and he didn't want me to.

He wanted me to do what I love and that's what I was doing. It was hard to get the moment, but I made it back to the funeral and did the eulogy.

I still had six weeks of teaching to continue. It was a fair amount of money and there were people that were counting on me. I couldn't say, "I'm sorry Australia I got to go. I'll be back tomorrow."

But it was hard.

A friend of mine, who I didn't know at the time had gotten into Access Consciousness®, offered to run the clearing statement. I said, "Sure," and, when she did, I felt these bubbles inside. There was coolness going through my body where before there was grief, heaviness, pain, density, trauma, drama, and the bad daughter stuff like, "Did I say everything on that phone call?"

And, after, the teaching I did in those last few weeks in Australia was just amazing.

About a month after I got back from the Australia trip, I went to Access Consciousness®. That's been about four or five years now because it really works. I had never seen a clearing statement before that was so comprehensive and detailed energetically and physically – and makes changes so quickly on things that people struggled with for decades.

At first, they couldn't see beyond the problem. Run the clearing statement, they could start to see it. Run the clearing statement again, they could start to see a little bit more. Pretty soon the problem is, like, over here. But they lived for 40 years with it. To me, that's gold.

I'll face the board. I'll put myself out there and use it because it works, but I'll never do anything that I don't try myself first.

I'll show you how the clearing statement works and you can actually literally be, know, receive and perceive some energy about deprogramming you, undoing your inventions and moving past your own lies.

Participant: Hello.

Dr. Lisa: Yes. How can I contribute to you?

Participant: Well, I was just thinking about the subconscious problem behind the money, not to say that I have money problems. You can always get more money, and I could easily, so I was thinking what might just hold me back, even if I would ask those questions and stuff.

How would I do that?

Dr. Lisa: The first step is by asking a question. I'm going to work with you and the group, too. Is that okay?

Participants: Yes.

Dr. Lisa: Okay, so let's start with this. Every decision, judgment, conclusion, computation, and meaning that you've made about money – would you be willing to give that up right now just 1%.

Participant: Yes.

Participants: Yes.

Dr. Lisa: Right, wrong, good and bad, POD and POC, all nine, shorts, boys and beyonds®.

Every conclusion, computation, oath, vows, fealty, comealty, commitment, agreement, binding, and bonding contract and the lifetime, dimension, body, or reality to any person, place, situation, event, culture, organization, institution regarding money male or female, would you like to destroy and uncreate it a little bit of that now.

Participant: Yes.

Dr. Lisa: Right, wrong, good and bad, POD and POC, all nine, shorts, boys and beyonds®.

Everywhere you have vowed the oath of poverty or struggle around money – would you like to rescind, revoke, recant, renounce, denounce, destroy, and uncreate the forever commitment throughout all of eternity to that.

Participant: Yes.

Dr. Lisa: Right, wrong, good and bad, POD and POC, all nine, shorts, boys and beyonds®.

And truth, whose financial reality are you all living?

Participant: My father's.

Participant: My parents.

Participant: My talent.

Dr. Lisa: Ow, that hurt.

Right, wrong, good and bad, POD and POC, all nine, shorts, boys and beyonds®.

So whose financially are you all living?

Participant: My mom's.

Dr. Lisa: Right, wrong, good and bad, POD and POC, all nine, shorts, boys and beyonds®.

Whose financial reality are you all living?

Participant: My parents.'

Dr. Lisa: Right, wrong, good and bad, POD and POC, all nine, shorts, boys and beyonds®.

So everywhere any of you are living another's financial reality, you, your spirit, or spirit or another you or your mother or your father or the land or the culture you're from. You know that Irish people have their own police about money and so do Italians and so do Scotts and so do Australians and so do Indians and so do Germans and so do Dutch and so do and so do and so do.

Everything that brings up and lets down, can we destroy and uncreate it?

Participant: Yes.

Dr. Lisa: Right, wrong, good and bad, POD and POC, all nine, shorts, boys and beyonds®.

Now notice in your bodies light or heavy right now?

Participant: Light.

Dr. Lisa: Lighter now.

Is it getting heavier for some of you?

Participant: Yes.

Dr. Lisa: Anybody get hotter? Yes, okay. Any of you getting cooler. Okay, good. There's a lot shifting all at the same time, but I'll tell you, nothing brings a good bunch of chutzpah than talking about money.

Okay, so whose financial reality are you living?

Participant: My uncle.

Dr. Lisa: My uncle.

Right, wrong, good and bad, POD and POC, all nine, shorts, boys and beyonds®.

So whose financial reality are you living?

Right, wrong, good and bad, POD and POC, all nine, shorts, boys and beyonds®.

So just notice what that brings up for you because a lot of times we're taught by our school systems, by our mother, by our father, by our bosses, about what it means to be a man in this reality, what it means to be a woman in this reality, about what our financial reality is. So if your financial reality is yours, great. And everywhere that your financial reality has a limit or a cap to it, that is all you can have, and no more. Where you have decided, "It is mine. It is mine. It is mine. It is mine. It is mine. It is mine. And that's all it can be". Let's destroy and uncreate it.

Participant: Yes.

Dr. Lisa: Right, wrong, good and bad, POD and POC, all nine, shorts, boys and beyonds®.

Now why would I want to destroy and uncreate the mine?

Participant: Because it's a limit.

Participant: We limit ourselves by owning something as ours and that fixes it to all it can be and nothing more. This becomes a limitation with creation

Dr. Lisa: When I was saying it, is it light, is it airy, is it expansive, or was it more dense, constrictive and heavy?

Participant: Dense. Dense and heavier.

Dr. Lisa: What if I were to tell you that your financial reality is light and expansive and bubbly like really good champagne.

Participant: Oh, yes, it's lighter.

Dr. Lisa: That's your financial reality.

Right, wrong, good and bad, POD and POC, all nine, shorts, boys and beyonds®.

When I say this stuff, I like to know your answer. It's just my point of view, but what I'm doing is paying attention to the room. There are different people having different experiences about this financial reality question, and it's a hot-button topic. I would have never guessed this group would have been pushed on just the financial reality. I don't mean pushed as in 'triggered.' I just mean it's hitting something that isn't going *woosh*.

It's more like *floomp*.

It's like, "We're not moving. It's mine and that's it."

Well, anything that is yours and 'that's it' has a little bit of superiority to it. And anything with superiority could look a little bit like Donald Trump.

Right, wrong, good and bad, POD and POC, all nine, shorts, boys and beyonds®.

So everywhere that Donald Trump is your financial reality, would you like to destroy and uncreate that?

Right, wrong, good and bad, POD and POC, all nine, shorts, boys and beyonds®.

Did you feel the judgment in that right?

Participant: It's super judgment.

Dr. Lisa: Super judgment, but here's the thing:

Donald Trump had millions of dollars and lost it. Millions of dollars and lost it. Millions of dollars and lost it. No, I'm not voting for Donald Trump when I say this, okay? This is where I stretch myself that I can look at that man and be like, "Are you kidding me? Did he just say that?" And then think, "Okay."

And I think about his business. I don't know him, but I'm like, "What can I learn from someone that I do not aspire to be like, emulate anything about, or even like to look at. What can I learn from him? There's something that he has brilliance with about money and business."

I don't need to have money and be like that, but I can actually receive molecularly and cellularly something that I don't know. He's better than me at money somehow, and I want to be better for me so that I can change the world from my financial reality.

Everybody's financial reality – if you have something to teach me about it, I will allow it and receive from you.

Or if you don't like somebody, look at where you shut off and, therefore, push it away. Do you know every judgment that you receive and every judgment that you allow through you increases your bank account $5,000 a month, I'm going to say?

Would you like that?

Participants: Yes.

Dr. Lisa: So every person that you've ever judged from this moment forward, all the judgments you have about me that get unsaid. It's okay. It's what happens.

All the judgments you've had about me, about this taster, about everything you thought about that I should be saying, I shouldn't be saying, or I'm not saying, and not doing. And, "This is what it's about and why am I going? Why am I here? Everything she's saying doesn't make any sense, and nothing she should be saying should make any sense. And sometimes she's saying exactly...and it's still a waste of my time..."

All of that stuff that you do with me, that you do with everybody else, that you do with yourself, that you do with your body, that you do with your business, can we destroy and uncreate that?

Participants: Yes.

Dr. Lisa: And how much more money could you receive if you weren't holding up all the energy and the judgments that you perceive, disavow, disown you, the potency of who you truly be.

Everything that brings up and let's down, can we destroy and uncreate it?

Participant: Yes.

Dr. Lisa: Right, wrong, good and bad, POD and POC, all nine, shorts, boys and beyonds®.

Dr. Lisa: What did you get? What changed for you?

Participant: I think I'm most awful to myself. I'm really nice to everybody else, but not to myself and that's where it opens up.

Dr. Lisa: Well, you just talked, so right there is the somatic release. You've just uncovered a lie and it's breaking apart psycho-physiologically. Congratulations!

Anything that doesn't allow you to go and be and do and receive energetically with more ease, can we destroy and uncreate that?

Participant: Yes.

Dr. Lisa: Right, wrong, good and bad, POD and POC, all nine, shorts, boys and beyonds®.

Now let me ask you a question, how much do you judge you?

Participant: More than anybody else.

Dr. Lisa: What is any one judgment you have of yourself?

Participant: I'm not good enough.

Dr. Lisa: Right.

Participant: I can do better.

Participant: I'd feel like a failure.

Dr. Lisa: I'm a failure.

Participant: Yes.

Participant: Yes.

Dr. Lisa: Okay I'm not good enough, I can do better and I'm a failure. Say it again.

Participant: I'm not good enough, I can do better and it's hard to say that sometimes.

Dr. Lisa: Good.

Right, wrong, good and bad, POD and POC, all nine, shorts, boys and beyonds®.

Say I'm the best at failing.

Participant: I really didn't feel anything.

Dr. Lisa: No, I said say, "I'm the best at failing."

Participant: I'm the best at failing.

Dr. Lisa: Say, "I'm the best I know at failing."

Participant: I'm the best I know in failing.

Dr. Lisa: Great. Now just notice the energy: "I'm the best I know at failing" versus "I'm a failure."

And why have you used being a failure to your advantage?

Participant: I guess to keep me small you know. To not stick out too much and not stand there in a spot like right now right here.

Dr. Lisa: Right, yes.

Participant: It's for you.

Dr. Lisa: Is it weird or is it just what you've never chosen until right now?

Participant: Yes, I've chosen to do that.

Dr. Lisa: Right.

Right, wrong, good and bad, POD and POC, all nine, shorts, boys and beyonds®.

There's the attention, right? So all the ways you think you want to hide, but you really don't want to hide and you really like to be seen. But you would like to be seen by you. Can we destroy and uncreate all of that?

Participant: Yes, that's awesome.

Dr. Lisa: Right, wrong, good and bad, POD and POC, all nine, shorts, boys and beyonds®.

Now you said you have a good life, right?

Participant: Pretty much.

Dr. Lisa: Right, right there. Notice when she said, "Pretty much." Did you believe her?

Participant: Not really.

Dr. Lisa: No, so there's a lie of money.

How much more money can she receive if she actually said, "Yes, I have a life." Instead of "pretty much," the universe will conspire to bless you.

How you ask is what you will receive.

"I pretty much have a good life." Basically what I heard was, "I'm okay. I am not happy." That's not a creative or generative energy you're putting out in the future. That's saying, "Yes, keep going as is…c'est la vie." Yet there's a burning inside of you that desires something more.

Participant: Right. You know, I don't want to say it because of other people, because they're jealous of my life. And I've had too many people being jealous of what I'm doing.

Dr. Lisa: So right there is another lie. I'm not going to say everything that I desire inside of me to be.

Participant: Right.

Dr. Lisa: Because someone may get disgruntled with me or someone may feel bad.

Participant: Oh, yes.

Dr. Lisa: Right. Everything that is, can we destroy and uncreate it?

Participant: Yes.

Dr. Lisa: Right, wrong, good and bad, POD and POC, all nine, shorts, boys and beyonds®.

What if what you say inspires someone to make a different choice? What if you showing up as you inspires someone to make a different choice? How much more money will that make you and how much more money will that give them and spread the seeds of consciousness on the planet?

You are the people that can change the world.

You are the people that money needs to be in the hands of because with your consciousness you will change the reality on this planet, just by one person next to you and one person next to you and one person next to you from the 1° shift you make right now, which is moving from invention and lie to the truth of opening light and happy and fun and free.

Like my dad said, "Be your own boss. It's not just a man's world. It's not just a woman's world. Do what you love. You're going to work for someone, love it. You want to be your own boss? Be your own boss."

So what's one thing you can choose right now that you've never decided to choose? What's something that you would choose to do out of your comfort zone?

Participant: To present the work, the services that you do to create an audience, not just to a few people, but to a bigger audience.

Dr. Lisa: Great, I kind of see you on TV.

Participant: Having a website that's more.

Dr. Lisa: Exactly.

Participant: Right now.

Dr. Lisa: Stop where you are.

Before I had a full practice, I didn't have one client. I had an office, so what I did was go to my office and set up my appointments in my calendar. There were no people and I would just write "Amazing Clients" in the 60 or 90-minute schedule. I'd sit in my office for that period of time, take a break after the 60 or 90 minutes, then go back in. I'd create my business cards or create flyers or create my packages or make a phone call and tell people what I was doing.

Sometimes I'd visit a bookstore, put a group workshop thing out, take another class, or go for training. And every time somebody called me, I would fill in the slot with the person's name and that would be the session.

I just kept going and going and going because I chose to not buy the lie that if I get out there somebody's going to feel bad. Instead, I bought the truth that if I get out there, someone else is going to get out there. Something is going to collaborate, to inspire them to collaborate with me and with them, for and of themselves.

That is moving past the lie.

To move past the lie, you have to act. You have to do it.

I can do a lot of clearings in here that will free you up, but until you actually take one foot forward and then the other to follow and choose what you're going to do that's light and right and fun for you, you'll never move.

Action is the key.

Participant: Can do you do the clearing statement on all of that stuff you were just talking about.

Dr. Lisa: Absolutely. So everywhere you've attended every workshop including this one and believe that that one clearing statement, that one energy clearing, that one person is going to be the one that clears everything for you, that's going to make the difference and a million dollars is going to show up in your bank account tomorrow and you don't have to do anything because you're special and it should just be that way for you gosh darn it. Let's destroy and uncreate it.

Participant: Yes.

Dr. Lisa: Right, wrong, good and bad, POD and POC, all nine, shorts, boys and beyonds®.

And then it does occur, how does it get any better than that®? Right? Come with me now. I have to charge the 10% finder's fee. No, I'm kidding.

Right, wrong, good and bad, POD and POC, all nine, shorts, boys and beyonds®.

Now I know how to get you guys laughing, money jokes.

Right, wrong, good and bad, POD and POC, all nine, shorts, boys and beyonds®.

And everywhere you used the lie that you don't know what to act or what to choose or you don't know where to start. Let's destroy and uncreate that.

Right, wrong, good and bad, POD and POC, all nine, shorts, boys and beyonds®.

Participant: I just feel like I have a little headache. I keep feeling the energy vibrate.

Dr. Lisa: Yes, so is it a headache or is it the change that you've been requesting showing up in a different way than you expected?

I usually ask the question with the two pieces right? It's a fact or is it this? When you smile, that's usually the truth. It's lighter, it's freer, it's more expansive.

Did you know that when it's dense and heavy, it's usually a lie, but most of us don't believe that? The dense and the heaviness is our reality and we believe that is true. So everywhere you've been lying to you and believing the lies about you and embodying them as you when they have nothing to do with you and they're certainly not fun for you, and you call that you. Can we destroy and uncreate it?

Participant: Yes.

Participants: Yes.

Dr. Lisa: Right, wrong, good and bad, POD and POC, all nine, shorts, boys and beyonds®.

Is your headache better? It's not?

Everybody, take a moment, close your eyes, expand your energy of space 500 million miles up, down, right, left, front, and back. Let's expand the space, and then also breathe energy in through the front of you, in through the back of you, in through the side, up through your feet, and down through your head. Hi body, hi body, hi body, hi body, hi body, hi body.

What energy, space, and consciousness can me and my body be to be my own embodiment of a financial reality beyond this reality that only grows what's light and fun and bright and airy and free and creatively for me, contributing to the Earth and this reality in a way that no one has ever seen before? Anything and everything that doesn't allow that to be, can we destroy and uncreate it for thee.

Participant: Yes.

Participants: Yes.

Dr. Lisa: Right, wrong, good and bad, POD and POC, all nine, shorts, boys and beyonds®.

And what energy, space, and consciousness can me and my body be to receive all of the abundance from all the other lifetimes that is coming to me if I just open up to receive. Everything and anything that that brings up and lets down, can we destroy and uncreate it?

Participant: Yes.

Dr. Lisa: Right, wrong, good and bad, POD and POC, all nine, shorts, boys and beyonds®.

And every lifetime, dimension, body, and reality where you were brilliant with money, where you actually created money, where you were wrapped in gold, creator of the world, wherever, whoever that was, can we bring that acumen back to you now?

Participant: Yes.

Dr. Lisa: And anything and everything that doesn't allow that, can we destroy and uncreate it?

Right, wrong, good and bad, POD and POC, all nine, shorts, boys and beyonds®.

Expand your energy of space again 500 million miles up, down, right, left, front, and back. Breathe energy in through the front of you, in through the back of you, in through the right of you, in through the left of you, up through your feet, and down through your head. Hi body, hi body, hi body, hi body, hi body, hi body.

Now, notice, lighter or heavier in the room?

Participant: Lighter.

Dr. Lisa: Lighter or heavier in your body?

Participant: Lighter.

Dr. Lisa: Are you embodying your body in a way you haven't before or is there a lie you're buying into. Truth?

Participant: A lie.

Dr. Lisa: Great, what's the lie you're buying into?

Participant: I feel like I'm stuck.

Dr. Lisa: The lie you're buying into is that you're stuck. Great, say, "I'm stuck, I'm stuck, I'm stuck."

Participant: I'm stuck, I'm stuck, I'm stuck.

Dr. Lisa: Everybody always laughs. They say, "I'm stuck," and they're sad faced and then I say, "I'm stuck, I'm stuck, I'm stuck" and they stop and they smile. Okay, you're healed.

Participant: Aha.

Dr. Lisa: Say, "I'm stuck, I'm stuck, I'm stuck."

Participant: I'm stuck, I'm stuck, I'm stuck.

Dr. Lisa: Say, "I'm the best I know at being stuck."

Participant: I'm the best I know at being stuck.

Dr. Lisa: And you are, aren't you? How good are you at being stuck?

Participant: I'm pretty good about it.

Dr. Lisa: You're pretty damn good at it, aren't you?

Participant: Yes.

Dr. Lisa: Tell me how good you are? Tell us all how good you are because I bet some of you know that she's the best stuck-er regarding creating catastrophes with money there is?

Right, wrong, good and bad, POD and POC, all nine, shorts, boys and beyonds®.

Participant: I'm really good at being stuck.

Dr. Lisa: Yes, tell me how good you are at being stuck with money. What major catastrophes have you created for yourself?

Participant: Oh, I couldn't take a test for this.

Dr. Lisa: Oh great, see, she's the best. She doesn't just have one catastrophe, she's got all kinds of catastrophes.

Okay, wait, where's the Oscar?

We just had the Oscars. How about we give you the Oscar for being the best catastrophic stuck-er around the lies of money. Thank you, how creative are you? How creative and brilliant do you have to be to create all kinds of catastrophe?

Everything that brings up and lets down, can we destroy and uncreate it?

Participant: Yes.

Dr. Lisa: Right, wrong, good and bad, POD and POC, all nine, shorts, boys and beyonds®.

And everywhere you all judged, decided, concluded, and computated that all kinds of catastrophe actually isn't creativity, can we destroy and uncreate that?

Participant: Yes.

Dr. Lisa: Right, wrong, good and bad, POD and POC, all nine, shorts, boys and beyonds®.

It takes quite a phenomenal brilliance to be a catastrophic nightmare. Seriously it does. You went counter-clockwise instead of clockwise, but it's still creativity. I bet if we could just sit here for a little while, you could tell us some pretty good conundrums of your catastrophe, right?

Participant: Yes, but I don't really want to.

Dr. Lisa: Good, you don't have to.

So what's the 1° shift that you could take right now that you'd really like contribution of to interrupt this?

Participant: Like for me I'm stuck.

Dr. Lisa: Well, that's what we were talking about.

Participant: Right.

Dr. Lisa: So, yes. See how good she is?

She's even dancing around the stuckness by asking, "Oh, you need to get unstuck to get unstuck?"

This is how good you are.

Participant: Yes, I'm the master at it.

I'm a master at the wrong stuff, too, like backwards. I need to get going forward.

Dr. Lisa: Okay, so how do we get going forward? What do you love about your catastrophes? Give me three things you love about your catastrophes.

Participant: I guess I create drama.

Dr. Lisa: What do you love about drama? So you were just bored?

Right, wrong, good and bad, POD and POC, all nine, shorts, boys and beyonds®.

So you love the catastrophe because you love the drama because you're bored. You're even bored with the Oscar-winning brilliance of the catastrophe you're creating, I get it. What else do you love about the drama?

Participant: But I think it doesn't do that much for you – it's not really supporting me.

Dr. Lisa: Okay, when you want to facilitate yourself, do that there.

Participant: Okay.

Dr. Lisa: Let me keep you focused here now. Just entertain me for a minute because I have to keep all these other people entertained.

Participant: Yes, yes.

Dr. Lisa: So tell me three reasons that you know you love catastrophe. You said "I'm bored" and "I love the drama," too.

Participant: I think it gives me something to do.

Dr. Lisa: Totally.

Participant: But what do you think it would be? I don't know. It's just kind of like I have something to do.

Dr. Lisa: Wait, I'm getting something, I'm psychic remember, are you bored?

Participant: Yes.

Dr. Lisa: Okay.

Right, wrong, good and bad, POD and POC, all nine, shorts, boys and beyonds®.

Say "I'm bored."

Participant: I'm bored.

Dr. Lisa: Say, "I'm bored."

Participant: I'm bored.

Dr. Lisa: Say, "I'm so fucking bored."

Right, wrong, good and bad, POD and POC, all nine, shorts, boys and beyonds®.

Participant: I love that part.

Dr. Lisa: Thank you. Thank you for lightening up the room. I'm laughing because so is everybody else. You know, it takes great courage to really own that you're bored.

Participant: Yes.

Dr. Lisa: Now, I'm just going to take a stab at this, but how brilliant are you really? Are you an artist? Are you a creator? Are you a dealer? What are you?

Participant: I've got a little bit of all that.

Dr. Lisa: Right. You have so much brilliance you don't know where your focus is.

Participant: Yes.

Dr. Lisa: So all you do is put your toe down over here, and over there, and a little over there, right?

Participant: Yes.

Dr. Lisa: And none of it is satisfying for you.

Participant: Right.

Dr. Lisa: So what's the lie that you're buying and the lie that you're assuming that's actually destroying you? Truth.

Participant: I'm fine that I'm uncreative.

Dr. Lisa: Right, wrong, good and bad, POD and POC, all nine, shorts, boys and beyonds®.

You're so creative that you're uncreative.

Participant: Yes.

Dr. Lisa: Right, wrong, good and bad, POD and POC, all nine, shorts, boys and beyonds®.

So who or what told you that you were uncreative?

Participant: I just want to see my mom for some reason there or something.

Dr. Lisa: Sure, bring in your mom, why not?

Participant: Yes, yes. It's like a go to.

Dr. Lisa: It's an easy go to.

Participant: It's like that.

Dr. Lisa: Okay, so the truth for the moment. Everybody blame their mom for anything.

Right, wrong, good and bad, POD and POC, all nine, shorts, boys and beyonds®.

Especially their money issues. Can we destroy and uncreate it?

Participant: Yes.

Dr. Lisa: Right, wrong, good and bad, POD and POC, all nine, shorts, boys and beyonds®.

All of the lines in the world, I bow down to you.

Dr. Lisa: Right, wrong, good and bad, POD and POC, all nine, shorts, boys and beyonds®.

And everywhere you obligated your body to embody your mother's judgment of you as uncreative so that you can never be the brilliance of who you truly be, can we destroy and uncreate that?

Participant: Yes.

Dr. Lisa: Right, wrong, good and bad, POD and POC, all nine, shorts, boys and beyonds®.

And everywhere you've made her the lock and your body the key, and you the lock and her the key, and her the lock and you're the key, you're the lock and her the key, and the lock and the key and lock and the key, you put all those locks and all those keys and all that catastrophe and all that insanity together and begin to unwind it and set it free.

Right, wrong, good and bad, POD and POC, all nine, shorts, boys and beyonds®.

Everywhere you decided to duplicate and mimic her reality of you as uncreative, can we destroy and uncreate that? Can we return that to her with consciousness attached so that she can wake up, too? Can we dissipate and release it to the Earth?

Participant: Yes.

Dr. Lisa: And can we send it back from whence it came never to return to this dimension, reality, body again.

Participant: Yes.

Dr. Lisa: Right, wrong, good and bad, POD and POC, all nine, shorts, boys and beyonds®.

And whatever lifetime, dimension, body, and reality that you and your mother decided to do this crazy dance that you're so bored with now that it's come up right here, right now to end forevermore. Can we just say that you've done a really good job, here's your damn severance package, go home.

Participant: Yes.

Dr. Lisa: It's done now.

Participant: Yes, completely.

Dr. Lisa: Because you can't stand one more day of this boredom anymore. Your creativity is dying to be unleashed as the soul print on the lips of this reality, isn't it?

You've got bodies to touch, people to heal and a brilliance to get out in this world that's going to plant seeds of consciousness and change in your way – just you walking as the symphony of possibility.

But I could be wrong.

You know you're going to ask yourself, "Why is she saying all of that stuff?"

I'm looking right into her consciousness and into her molecules and pulling it out of her body. If that's what is dying to come out and that's what she's trying to do with that catastrophe, which is why it's not uncreative, it's actually very creative. You've just been waiting for someone to see it. And how many people have been paid to try and see this that you have successfully navigated them around.

Participant: Not too many really.

Dr. Lisa: Oh, okay good.

Right, wrong, good and bad, POD and POC, all nine, shorts, boys and beyonds®.

Just everybody.

Participant: Right.

Dr. Lisa: Right, wrong, good and bad, POD and POC, all nine, shorts, boys and beyonds®.

Now, I'm making a joke because I'm really only looking at anything – a 1° shift – but as you can see with you and everybody else who's been talking, as you start to get in there, the cage of lies and limitation starts to rattle and then it starts to collapse. And then the truth starts to be.

How does this relate to money?

Well, money is an energy. Sexual-ness is an energy. Beingness is an energy. Embodiment is an energy. Brilliance is an energy. Phenomenal-ness is an energy.

Fantasm is an energy. Magic is an energy. Soul print is an energy. We are energy.

We have ATP in every cell of our body, Adenosine Triphosphate. That is the spirit energy. That is our soul print energy. That is us unleashing our soul print, our lips of reality.

We come in a form. Money comes in a form. We're all energy, though, and we make it so separate with these lies.

Right, wrong, good and bad, POD and POC, all nine, shorts, boys and beyonds®.

Better, worse, or the same?

Participant: The word sameness is popping up in my mind, but I don't know if that's really true to be honest with you.

Dr. Lisa: So is your head part of your body?

Participant: Yes.

Dr. Lisa: Okay, is your body part of your head?

Participant: That's what's up.

Dr. Lisa: There's a reason I say, "Hi body, hi body, hi body" when I do that to expand anything.

Actually, your head is on your body. So body connect to my head. Head connect to my body. Body and head connect with the Earth. Earth connect with the body and the head. All of us commune as one.

What energy, space and consciousness can me and my body be to have my head and my body and the Earth be one within me. Everything and anything that doesn't allow that to be can we destroy and uncreate it with me?

Right, wrong, good and bad, POD and POC, all nine, shorts, boys and beyonds®.

Does that help comfort anybody else?

Participant: Cool.

Dr. Lisa: So how much more can you receive and how much more money would you be able to perceive and how much more energy and joy would you be able to be?

Right, wrong, good and bad, POD and POC, all nine, shorts, boys and beyonds®.

Still the same?

Participant: No, it's different.

Dr. Lisa: Yes. Say, "I'm different."

Participant: I'm different.

Dr. Lisa: Can you say it louder?

Participant: I'm different.

Dr. Lisa: I'm sorry, I couldn't hear you.

Participant: I'm different.

Dr. Lisa: So now, I double dog dare you to be the walking, talking earthquake that alters reality simply by your mere presence, be your ROAR (Radically Orgasmically Alive Reality).

I have no idea what that looks like. I have no attachment to what it is, but you all got the energetic song of light bulbs go on.

So where you can start that 1° shift is to ask every day, "What's my ROAR? What's my rumble?" And move. It may feel good for half a second and you'll be like, "Damn, I'm doing this. That feels pretty good. I think I'll do that a little bit more. Keep going. Nah, done with that, I'm going to go over here."

That's okay.

We're taught in this reality that's not okay.

Trust me, I was kicked out of every class I was in, including the principal's office, because they thought I was retarded. They thought I was slow and retarded and autistic and needed a whole lot of help and whatever, but I was just different. I couldn't focus the way they wanted me to focus in school. My mind went a thousand million miles a minute. I was so bored in that reality.

So just keep going, keep choosing 'instead of this.'

Participant: Yes, I don't know how to go there.

Dr. Lisa: You may get there again. Embrace it.

How much more can you receive if you embrace what you're actually being and be like, "Oh, here I am again. Damn, I haven't been there in a while. This sucks. What else can I choose?"

Here's a different example:

I work with a lot of people who trade in the financial markets. Sometimes they get stuck and they keep going for the same trade or whatever. They don't want to leave it or they lose. They think it's a failure instead of moving.

It's really high stakes, a lot of money.

If it's not working and getting heavy and dense – move, move, move. Cut your losses and move. They'll get it and you'll gain it in the next moment, somewhere else, but it will never show up how you think it will. So you can't use your head.

Yes, now that your body is connected to your head, I think you can have a lot of freedom. That's probably a lot of our fun. Thanks for sharing.

Participant: Sure.

Dr. Lisa: You're welcome. Thanks for not staying the same. She did great. I'd like everybody to give her a clap. Thank you.

Participant: I am choosing, choosing, choosing.

I'm in the midst of getting my home built for the last month or two. I've turned things around incredibly in 30 days.

Dr. Lisa: So how can I help you?

Participant: It's about the business.

Dr. Lisa: You're stuck with the business?

Participant: Well, I'm stuck in terms of do I go more towards the creative or do I go towards the corporate where I know I can make the money.

Dr. Lisa: Okay, pause for a second.

Is she in her head or is she in her body?

Participant: Her head.

Dr. Lisa: Is she in conclusion or expansion?

Participant: Conclusion.

Dr. Lisa: Can you create anything in conclusion?

Participant: No.

Dr. Lisa: Repeat it. Can you create anything in conclusion?

For all of you that say yes, let's destroy and uncreate it.

Right, wrong, good and bad, POD and POC, all nine, shorts, boys and beyonds®.

And all of you that say no, let's destroy and uncreate it.

Right, wrong, good and bad, POD and POC, all nine, shorts, boys and beyonds®.

Conclusion relates to superiority, conclusion and being right relates to expectations, conclusion relates to limitations and results.

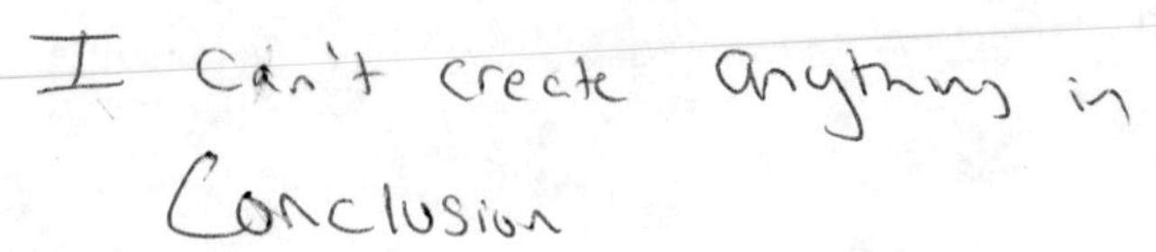

If you're trying to receive contribution about your business, where it's stuck, and you're stuck in your head about the stuckness of your business, where are we going to go?

Yes, to yawning… exactly, to unconsciousness.

So all the unconsciousness we all have about where we can go in our business, and what do we do in our business to create the result we think we should have, can we destroy and uncreate that?

Participant: Yes.

Dr. Lisa: Right, wrong, good and bad, POD and POC, all nine, shorts, boys and beyonds®.

Because there's really something magical if you listen to this phrase. It never shows up the way you think it will. It always shows up better. I know this so clearly every moment.

What I do in my own life and business is I listen. I listen for the lightness – and that's the rightness for me. When it's dense and heavy and hard, and when I'm getting it up against something, I don't keep hitting my head against the wall.

I say, "Oh, I need to ask more questions. I need to go somewhere else." Then I ask, "Who or what can make this easier right away? Where do I need to go? Who do I need to talk to? Who can help me? What other information do I require? Who has that information?"

And I don't know how it happens, but somehow I get an email. I get a text message. I see something on the computer. I read something in the mail or I talk to a friend and they say, "Hey, this person is looking for that," and it's exactly what I need. That's how I found my CFO for my business.

Participant: That was just amazing.

Dr. Lisa: So should I go here or should I go there? No, you require more information.

Participant: More information about work.

Dr. Lisa: Exactly. That's the question. The first thing you should require is more information. Truth?

Participant: Yes.

Dr. Lisa: Great, now here's where I want to start. Have you ever apologized to your business?

Participant: No.

Dr. Lisa: Okay, so every morning I wake up and I destroy and uncreate what my business was yesterday, what it was when I first started it, what it was today, and what it will be tomorrow.

I start with a blank slate every day, every class, every session, every time I get out of a team meeting, wherever it is. Destroy and uncreate.

Right, wrong, good and bad, POD and POC, all nine, shorts, boys and beyonds®.

Your business is its own entity, like it's its own person, similar to a child with its own person. Like you are its own person. You are your own entity. Your business has a purpose.

My business is called Live Your Roar. It has its purpose. I have a target. I've listened to it, and everywhere I move in my business is because I'm asking it.

So you need more information starting right here. That's why we want to go destroy and uncreate results and conclusions and open up to possibilities by asking questions like these:

> *What other information can I add in here?*
> *Who has that information?*

Where can I get that information?
What can I do?

Here are some things you can do:

Destroy and uncreate your business and your relationships every day, even if you have a job and you don't have your own business. Destroy and uncreate it. Take your business, take your job, take your position out for coffee every day and have a 'coffee talk' with it:

What would you like today?
What's your target?
What requires my most attention?
Where can I help to make more money?
What do I need to create to do that?
Who do I need to hire?
Who else do I need to talk to?
Where do I need to go?
How much money do I actually require?

That's another thing. Know very clearly what it takes to run your business every day, every week, every month. Know that number.

Have a target for your business for the year, and every day know how much money that you would like to attract and actualize so that you can have that – whatever it is that you're selling.

I know how much that I need to make every day and what I need to create every day in order to live the way I like to live. That's what I aspire to actualize every day. Some days, I do, some days I don't, but I never forget it. I always keep going and I keep asking questions.

Participant: Okay, the book that I'm writing that I haven't finished. It's time for me to go out and finish those books and get them out there, but then I said, "Oh, but I don't know if I can make money." And I do need to find someone who can help me with the internet and all that.

Dr. Lisa: Great, so you need more information, you need more people.

Participant: I need more people, definitely. I need my own business. But then I started questioning myself again.

Dr. Lisa: Right, so that's the piece of the lie that you're buying into, the questioning of yourself. Do you have your own back?

Participant: No, I don't have my own back.

Dr. Lisa: And does the business have its own back?

Participant: No.

Dr. Lisa: Right, if the business doesn't have its own back and you don't have its own back, you're coming together backless.

Participant: I understand that.

Dr. Lisa: So that's what needs to change.

When you take it out to coffee, ask your business, "How can you have your own back? How can I have my own back?" And create a contract together about having your own back so that you can be the business and do the business and join together.

That's what I call radical aliveness.

There are four C's to radical aliveness: Choosing you, Committing to you, Collaborating with the universe who is conspiring with you to bless you, and then you Creating your living from there.

These are the four tenets of you and the four tenets of the business. Choose for you, commit to you. Collaborate with the universe conspiring to bless you and then create and go forth together.

I do a radio show called Beyond Abuse, Beyond Therapy, Beyond Anything, right? We've been on the air for two and half years now.

When they asked me to do it, I said, "Will you let me do creative clearing statements? I'm going to talk about abuse in ways it's never been talked about before and I could alter the world. If you'll let me do that, I'll do it." And they said, "Yes."

In the first 13 weeks, we were in the top three on the top ten on the Empowerment Channel, and we've stayed in the top five since the inception of the show.

I've listened to the business every day. This morning I got up, did a live radio show, and I listened to the business.

Every week I have to create a live show: new, original content, a show description, social media quotes, and topics. I listen and I say, "Okay, Earth, universe, world, 205,000 people listening, what do you want to hear about?"

Bam.

I don't get in my head and say, "What do I need to do for Voice America?" I ask the question, "What energy is calling to be spoken about now?"

What is the business asking you? Literally. Maybe that's what is spinning your head – to get in touch with what is now outside of you. Outside of you, everywhere you completely are the only source of your business, can we destroy and uncreate it?

Participant: Yes.

Dr. Lisa: Right, wrong, good and bad, POD and POC, all nine, shorts, boys and beyonds®.

And everywhere believing that you're the source of your business which is actually destroying your business from getting off the ground. Can we destroy and uncreate that?

Participant: Yes.

Dr. Lisa: Right, wrong, good and bad, POD and POC, all nine, shorts, boys and beyonds®.

Your business is an energy and entity in and of itself.

Let it soar. Let it roar. Get your head out of results and get your head into possibilities. Draw and actualize the people, places, situations, and events that will correspond to collaborate on your behalf, and it will be easy.

Participant: Thank you, great.

Dr. Lisa: She's smiling.

Participant: Thank you.

Dr. Lisa: Right, wrong, good and bad, POD and POC, all nine, shorts, boys and beyonds®.

Participant: Hi Lisa.

Dr. Lisa: Hi.

Participant: I love your radio show.

Dr. Lisa: Thank you.

Participant: It makes sense when you're talking about if your money likes you.

I have this visual in my mind that it's a relationship where I show up all sexy wearing a $300 cologne. But then we sit down to talk and it's like, "Oh, you're still doing this? Is your mom still like this? Are you still smoking cigarettes?"

Dr. Lisa: So you're judging each other?

Participant: I don't know if it's judging me, but it's like, "I love you, but not if you're still doing this. It's like I love you and you need to show up like this and this."

Dr. Lisa: Well, how about if someone said to you, a lover, "I love you, but you know I would love you a little bit more if you wore your hair like this, and you actually wore this, and if you bend over like that, and if you do this."

What would you do?

Participant: Yes, I know, it's horrible.

Dr. Lisa: Right, so what do you love about doing what's horrible and expecting a good result?

Right, wrong, good and bad, POD and POC, all nine, shorts, boys and beyonds®.

Participant: He's in control of that part.

Dr. Lisa: That sounds like really committing. Maybe it's a control factor – so listen underneath. What do you love about controlling?

Participant: I'm actually not a very controlling person. I don't know if I have attachment to this or not because I'm really free with other things.

Dr. Lisa: So what do you love about what you're talking about? What do you love about conditions?

Participant: It's like a superior thing.

Dr. Lisa: Great, what do you love about being right?

Participant: It's like, "I'm better than that." It's my stubbornness, like I am only welcome to receive 'this.'

Dr. Lisa: How much can you receive if you're only going to receive this? A little, a little less than little, or a little mega ton of little?

Participant: A little less than little.

Dr. Lisa: Yes, so what do you hate about receiving?

Participant: I don't know.

What joy would like to catapult my life into?

Dr. Lisa: Yes, so say, "I hate joy."

Participant: I hate joy.

Dr. Lisa: Say it again.

Participant: I hate joy.

Dr. Lisa: Say it again.

Participant: I hate joy.

Dr. Lisa: "I like to limit it and constrict my joy so I can receive less."

Participant: I think I'm constricting my joy so I can't receive.

Dr. Lisa: Now, I'm crazy or what?

She's laughing hysterically at that – and whenever somebody laughs like that they know that it's right. So how old were you when you limited your joy and started to receive less. Truth?

Participant: I think seven.

Dr. Lisa: Great, and where did that get you in your body? Right in your heart. Yes. Breathe, breathe or I will fall over. Breathe.

Right, wrong, good and bad, POD and POC, all nine, shorts, boys and beyonds®.

Now how much money can you receive from breathing like that?

Participant: None.

Dr. Lisa: Right, because the money is energy, air is energy, sexualness is energy.

So all the ways that the seven-year-old you algorithmically computated and configured your chest, your body, your being, to start beating the joy out of you for whatever reason. Right wrong good and bad. Can we destroy and uncreate it?

Participant: Yes.

Dr. Lisa: Right, can you breathe?

Right, wrong, good and bad, POD and POC, all nine, shorts, boys and beyonds®.

That's like the most painful breath I've ever heard.

Right, wrong, good and bad, POD and POC, all nine, shorts, boys and beyonds®.

So what did you decide about you? What did you decide that receiving means about you at seven? That you were what?

Participant: I stood out too much.

Dr. Lisa: What did that mean about you?

Participant: I don't have power in anything.

Dr. Lisa: Yes, and did something bad happen that set it?

Go ahead, give me your breath. Okay good. Do your thing. We only want 1° of shift, so you're going to have to breathe here, alright?

Okay, so we don't know why. She doesn't have natural memory – although it doesn't actually matter – but, physiologically, something's shifting. That's how we're undoing it and unwinding this lie that she lived by without receiving, right? So she's hiding.

How joyous are you at seven?

Participant: Oh, freaking joyous. I was a happy kid.

Dr. Lisa: And how different was that for you?

Participant: Pretty different. I went to Catholic schools.

Dr. Lisa: I know, I went to Catholic schools and a Jesuit College and I didn't have a choice about any of it. I understand.

Right, wrong, good and bad, POD and POC, all nine, shorts, boys and beyonds®.

So this is really important…

All the ways that at seven you knew you were different, and to be different was bad, so you stuck your joy in a sardine can and never allowed yourself to receive it as you had up until that moment because that would make you bad and you would stand out or you'd be different, which is really terrifying to kids, right? All of us in our formative years, can we destroy and uncreate that commitment now and update the hard drive?

Participant: Yes.

Dr. Lisa: Can we rescind, revoke, recant, renounce, denounce, destroy and uncreate all the impelled judgments about happiness from the church, from the nuns, from the priest, from the kids, from the school you are in, from this reality that to be joyous and happy means you're a freak. Can we destroy and uncreate it?

Participant: Yes.

Dr. Lisa: Right, wrong, good and bad, POD and POC, all nine, shorts, boys and beyonds®.

And all the oaths, vows, fealties, comealties, commitments agreements, binding and bonding contract. The vibrational virtual realities underneath that and all the secret hidden, invisible, covert, unseen, and unacknowledged, unspoken, undisclosed agendas underneath that, can we destroy and uncreate that?

Participant: Yes.

Dr. Lisa: And all the vibrational virtual realities under-neath that and all the implants and explants, secret, hidden, invisible, covert, unseen, unacknowledged, unspoken, undisclosed agendas underneath that and underneath that, and underneath that, and underneath that, and underneath that, and underneath that, and underneath that, and underneath that, can we destroy and uncreate it?

Right, wrong, good and bad, POD and POC, all nine, shorts, boys and beyonds®.

And everywhere to be joyous and free…

Did you hear her breath?

Participants: Yes.

Way bigger.

Participant: Yay!

Dr. Lisa: Everywhere to be joyous and free was the wrongness of thee, can we destroy and uncreate it?

Right, wrong, good and bad, POD and POC, all nine, shorts, boys and beyonds®.

So what energy, space, and consciousness can you and your body be to be the joyous fantasm of inevitable, unrelenting, phenomenal possibility that you truly be.

Right, wrong, good and bad, POD and POC, all nine, shorts, boys and beyonds®.

Better, worse, or the same?

Participant: A lot better.

Dr. Lisa: A lot better.

Thank you…so this is the end of our time.

Does anybody else have a burning, burning, burning, burning, burning, burning question?

Participant: I got really nauseous and felt major heat come up hearing all that.

Dr. Lisa: So, truth. Did what's burning just work to open up something for you?

Participant: Yes.

Dr. Lisa: So is the nausea something wrong? Or is there a cellular shift going on?

Participant: I'm hoping there's a shift.

Dr. Lisa: So "I'm hoping there's a shift." Is it light or heavy when you say that?

Participant: Heavy, yes.

Dr. Lisa: That doesn't mean there isn't a shift.

So, truth. Say, "There's a shift going on in my body right now."

Participant: There's a big shift going on in my body right now.

Dr. Lisa: Is that light or heavy?

Participant: Light.

Dr. Lisa: Yes, so if you take that nausea and you fertilize it to the Earth right now, and you take a little bit more of it and fertilize it to the Earth right now, and you take a little bit more of it and fertilize it to the Earth right now, and you expand your energy – take a deep breath in through your mouth – what do you notice?

Better, worse, or the same?

Participant: I feel a lot of energy with me right now.

Dr. Lisa: Yes, so did what we have been working on this evening or speaking to create a shift for you?

Participant: Yes.

Dr. Lisa: So is what you're experiencing, physiologically and somatically, the effects of the shift showing up in a way that is different than you would like?

Participant: Yes.

Dr. Lisa: So what if, in the next moment, all of you feel something that is called uncomfortable or intensive? In reality, just recognize that it's a shift showing up in a different way than you expected, first thing.

When you feel that nausea you didn't have two seconds ago – or a headache or pain somewhere that you didn't have five minutes ago – because someone was talking, or you bumped into somebody, or somebody called you, or sent you a stupid email, and then all of a sudden you feel sick afterwards – know that's not your energy and say this:

"Return to sender with consciousness attached. Dissipate and release it to the Earth, turn back from whence you came and never return to this dimension, reality and body again."

Better?

Participant: Yes, it's good.

Dr. Lisa: Molecularly and cellularly, we're all made of the same things. So, when somebody asks a question and I run the clearing statement, everybody in the room gets it.

Everyone benefits.

Everything that is asked, you can personalize it for yourself, put a different name in. It's your mother, it's your father, or somebody else. And, then, as I'm running the clearing statements, you get all the clearings.

Everybody is going to get something.

Your body is 90% of you – your head is 10%.

We live up here and limit the other 90%. This has so much information. The pain in your neck has information. Your chest has information. Every part, every organ, in the system has information.

In my case, I went through every system of the body and learned all the belief systems that were in every organ of my body, and then cleared every one of those belief systems in every organ of my body. I cleared out the systems of my body so that I can keep the organs in my body and return them to their function prior to illness.

I was not ill coming into this life.

I got ill in this life with the choices that I chose, so I had to undo that. That's what it takes.

And using this clearing statement makes it much quicker.

You get it when you get it. It shows up when it shows up…and you use it when you use it. All we're looking for is the 1° shift – so, in regard to the lies of money – do you feel you learned something?

Participants: Yes.

Dr. Lisa: With a different perspective?

Ready to make a million dollars tomorrow?

Participant: Yes.

Dr. Lisa: Ready to make a $100 million dollars?

Participant: Yes.

Dr. Lisa: What would it take to make a $100 million a year for the rest of your life every year? You've got to think that big with that big possibility to move in this space of possibility.

Go beyond $5,000.

Go beyond the $50,000 that you desire.

Go beyond the debt and the bills.

Go big or go home.

Go big and allow the universe to correspond on your behalf.

Money is your friend. Money is your ally. Money is your lover. Money is your energy. Money will have your back. Money will change the world and you using it as an

altering of reality, to conspire on your behalf with what you love, with who you be is what I wish for all of us to be.

Thank you for playing.

Thank you for asking questions. Thank you for being willing and courageous enough to look at your own lies and being open to a really crazy clearing statement that can make a world of difference in this life. I appreciate all of you.

You are brilliant and you are a phantasm of possibilities, so go out there, be you, beyond anything and create magic.

Participants: Thank you.

Tiburon

Dr. Lisa: Welcome to The Lies of Money, you are courageous beings. Money is not necessarily a fun topic for people to discuss.

Most people bring their decisions, judgments, conclusions, computations, projections, separations, expectations, oaths and vows, fealties, comealties, commitments, agreements, prejudices and condemnations – all around this topic of money.

Today I'm going to give you a specific number of the Lies of Money and the problem in this reality, and then hopefully a solution to it. But I'm not going to tell you exactly yet what those lies are. I'm going to see if I can trigger you a little bit and, at some point, you'll laugh and bring up what really brought you to be here doing this.

So after 20+ years working in the mental health profession running workshops locally, domestically and internationally, what I've learned is that there are three reasons why people come to do personal work for change and transformation:

1. Health – some crisis occurs.
2. Relationship – a break up or a separation or divorce.
3. Money – struggling in business or not making ends meet.

After a little while, I got really good at working with people in the relationships area and really good with working with people on the health stuff, myself included. But this whole money thing was still gnawing at me and my clients and the world. I decided to focus on this to see what else I can bring to this topic all over the world that people are having workshops and writing books about.

It was kind of a stretch for my branding person. If you don't know what a branding person is, they tell you where to stick your niche and then stick you into a box – and you're supposed to stay in that and not go outside of it.

For those of you who are just getting to know me, it's kind of like that *Dirty Dancing* thing, "Nobody puts Baby in the corner." You definitely don't put me in a box and there's no box that really fits me.

When I started branching out on this money topic, I was doing workshops, tele-calls, my Voice America Radio Show, along with individual sessions and coaching sessions and my 2 or 3-day VIP sessions with people. At the same time, when my father passed away about 3 or 4 years ago, I had my own stuff to deal with personally when a whole different financial situation occurred.

What I was blind to became very, very clear once he passed away, which I'll get into in a little bit because it fuels a lot of what I talk about regarding money. In this Taster, and in some of the offers I have in my business right now, I'll be talking about moving beyond your own constriction and cage of lack and limitation with money.

So I started really, really looking at it and realized, "This is crazy!"

I started looking at the decisions that I have had about money, the decisions that I've made about money, what I've made money mean to me – how I made it so significant, how it was my God, how it was the way that I received love or the way that I felt about myself if I had money. I didn't feel good about myself if I didn't have money.

You're all shaking your head a little bit…these are things you know.

And then I started asking, "What's beyond that? What's beyond that? What's beyond that? What's beyond that?"

What is this money thing that everybody is having some sort of issue with? It runs the gamut.

I've had a lot of money and I've had no money. And I have a very large community of people that have a lot of money – and they have as many issues with money as people that have no money.

It doesn't matter whether you have nothing or you have billions or millions or quadrillions. There are still issues with regards to this thing called money – so nobody escapes it.

Then when my father passed away, I got to thinking, "What is this? What is the meaning of this thing called money that everybody chooses to not enjoy?"

And even when they do enjoy it, they're always in fear of like, "When am I going to lose it? When am I not going to have it?"

There are all kinds of syndromes out there – for example, 'feast or famine,' 'work hard/servant mentality,' or 'work hard, it can't be easy.' Or, 'I'm kind of like a peasant and I'll always be owned by something', and 'I have to work for somebody else because I can't go out on my own because, if I go out on my own, how am I going to actually fend for myself or let somebody else fend for me?'

All these go on in this reality, and they went on within me, too.

When my father passed away, I literally lost all access to everything that I had access to. It was completely taken away from me and I had no access to anything at all.

I remember standing at a gas station putting a card in the pump to get gas like I normally did. I never had to think twice about it before. It doesn't mean I hadn't had money problems or issues or lack of funds in my time on this planet, but at that particular moment there was nothing.

I thought, "How am I going to pay for this? And how am I going to live?"

I'd never had to think like that because I always had my father. He made it very easy for me and was always someone who said, "What would you like?" I never knew when it was going to come, and it was always kind of a joke: "Alright, I'll go down to the basement, I'll get the printing press out and you'll have it in your account." He was my ATM, my debit card, in a lot of ways – no pin code, no passcode, just ask and receive.

It was the easiest thing that I've ever experienced in my life, but it was from somebody else. You guys get that, right? It had nothing to do with me, it was outside of me.

And when he was gone, I stood there at that gas station like that, thinking, "I have no idea what it means to have money, what it really means to save money, or plan for a future with money at the level that I knew I really need to because everything was buffered by someone else."

Was I close to my father? Did we live near each other? No, he was across the country. In fact, there was about a 10-year period of time I didn't see him and we'd talk only when I needed money. That was the relationship and the distance was pretty large, but it was okay. It was what we did.

From a very young age, he told me, "Lisa, it's not just a man's world. It's a woman's world. Be your own boss, do what you love and never settle, make your own money, be happy."

So I did that, and he made it easy for me, although that doesn't mean I didn't work hard from morning till evening. I loved and enjoyed what I did helping people.

Then, fast forwarding, his death really put it in my face that, "Oh, I can only walk people as far as I've walked myself." It was a blind pocket that wasn't uncovered until then. I didn't even know that he was sick, and he passed away when I was overseas without me saying goodbye to him other than on the cellphone, which was perfect. It's actually a beautiful story and was what I know now exactly what he wanted.

He wanted me to be wherever I was, doing what I love, living my life. I didn't need to be there. It might sound like a justification to some, but for me it's been something that I've truly embodied. He was someone who made money so easy for me in a certain way.

The other stuff going on in the household, if you know anything about my story, was not so easy, so I had a little bit of entitlement going on. It was like, "Damn, given the 2 ½ decades of abuse and violence that I suffered in my childhood, from sexual to financial, to physical, to emotional, to psychic, to energetic," having a little bit of ease – a father that didn't require a password or a pin code for an ATM – well…

I felt like I deserved it given what I suffered.

I was really grateful for that experience because he was there for me from the beginning, and then, even in his death he put this in my face, "Once I'm gone, who do you have?"

And then I realized who I had and this is how my money situation changed.

I had me.

Everything was taken away, every bit of money and access to any money that I had ever had in my life through my father was completely taken away with his death. I stood there, having no access to any cash, no access to any bank accounts, credit cards, nothing. At that gas station that day, I knew that my father was gone and there was not one person on this planet that I could rely on to help me financially.

The only person, the only thing, I had was me – and I had to do something completely different. This is where I directly faced the lies of money – everything that I had believed, the persona that I developed around it, the security that supposedly was there through him – all of it.

He used to call me Li-li. "Sure, Li-li, I'll go down to the basement and go to printing press, print you some money and it will be in your account."

I never knew when it was going to come. It could be two weeks, a month, three months or the next day, but I always saw it in my account. That's how it worked with him. Now I had to become that because he was gone, nobody else was going to do it for me.

I was in shock, looking behind me and thinking, "What does it mean to have your own back with money? What does it mean to really, really have your own back and stand up in the world and not depend on anybody, not project on anybody, not pull from anybody, not suck from anybody, not victimize yourself in order to get money, not defend against authority, not even align with the tragedy or the trauma or the drama of your own story? Because, believe you me, if you want to sit around and talk about story, I got one."

I remember thinking, "Wow, this is going to be the first time that I have embodied my own financial reality."

Little did I know that my father's death was going to be the rise of me – that it was going to be me embodying me and knowing what it feels like, smells like and tastes like to have my own back and to completely leave behind the victim story, the trauma and drama story, the catastrophe story.

And little did I know that my abusive background growing up, the 2 ½ to 3 decades of abuse that I put myself through and suffered, would be the shining beacon through which my own lies with money would come through and move me beyond the cage of destruction and death and scarcity, spending but not having, and getting a lot of money because I'd always made a lot of money but never allowed myself to keep it.

Everybody else was more important.

People who were in relationship with me did really well. Trust me, they're still asking. I said no to somebody recently for the first time in a long while. I said, "No, I just gave you some money. Give me that money back through a payment plan and then we'll talk." That's my New Yorker coming out. That's what it feels like to have my own back and to say yes when it actually is a yes, and no when it's a no.

My father's death catapulted my business, my being, my body and the work that I was going to do in the world to wake up financially, and little did I know that it was going to unleash me living my financial reality for the first time.

What developed is what I now call the cage of abuse, radical aliveness, and the bridge for your ease to that aliveness.

The cage of abuse is what I call the "4 D's": Denying, Defending, Disassociating, Disconnecting.

In the story I told you, can you see all the denial that I was living in from what my father so naturally gifted to me? The defending against being and having my own back, the dissociating from allowing myself to have the money for me like I deserved it and created it.

Back then, I was the person you wanted to hang out with. I would put a couple hundred dollars down on the table, and when we finished that money, I'd put my credit card down on the table. Every Thursday, Friday, Saturday, Sunday night, my friends and I would have a really good time. I felt so generous, like my father.

My father was a sporting guy who played football and, as a kid, we skied, and I went to more Super Bowls and World Series than just about anyone. It was fun and he'd always tell my siblings and I to invite 2 friends. No matter where we were, no matter what we did, he would give us his tickets, the good front row seats. He'd go buy a bleacher seat for $10, make friends with people up there, and then come back down to where we were.

"How you doing? You want a beer?" We were about 15, probably a little inappropriate, but at the time it was fun.

It all led to this whole cage of abuse around money, where it was so limiting and so constricting that I could work hard, make money, make a lot of money – but I could never keep it, never keep it.

I'd have it for a little while. It was like the 'binge and purge' syndrome. I'd have a lot of it and then be like, "La-la-la-la-la-la-la" followed by, "Alright, now I've got to do it again."

Feast or famine.

Moving to radical aliveness, I woke up at that gas station. Not being able to pay for anything, I thought, "Oh, I've got to choose for me. I've got to commit to me and my financial reality."

Somewhere along the line, I'd heard, *"Ask and you shall receive."* So the way I think about it, the Universe is conspiring to bless me. It's part of the "4 C's": Commit to me, Choose for me, the Universe is Conspiring to bless me and wants to Collaborate with me, and then Create.

That's what I call radical aliveness, and you move from the cage to radical aliveness by way of the "4 E's" – *for your ease* – Embrace, Examine, Embody and Expand.

Embrace whatever's going on, Examine with a tenacity of consciousness and a truth. Remember, you can only take yourself as far as you can let yourself go and see and you can only take somebody else, if you work with other people, as far as you have gone. They can't go beyond you if you haven't.

So I'm grateful for all the lies of money that came through my father's own very poor, Brooklyn, no education, alcoholic family, and were gifted to me through his death.

I didn't know until then because of who he was. He'd say, "I never had anything, you guys have everything, I want to see you use it and be happy while I'm alive." And that's exactly what he did.

Do you believe that your beliefs create your reality?

Participants: Yes.

Dr. Lisa: Do you know that your beliefs also create your body and the form your body is in? And do you know that your beliefs also create your financial reality?

Participants: Yes.

Dr. Lisa: So how many of you are familiar with Access Consciousness, more particularly, the Access Consciousness clearing statement?

If you're not, let me give you an analogy. Have you ever had your computer get stuck on something and that hour glass comes up, or that Apple computer start spinning?

Participant: Today.

Dr. Lisa: Exactly, probably because your computer knew that you were coming here to talk about the lies of money and to undo some algorithmic computations.

Basically, when it gets stuck, that's like our point of views that are stuck. It gets stuck and doesn't work. You may have made lateral moves and lateral changes, but you never gone beyond that constriction and that limitation.

You get better – but never beyond.

And that's called surviving and thriving, but never living radically alive.

After all the education, training and different modalities that I have taken, this clearing statement has been the most comprehensive to get underneath what's sticking hardware in your brain and in your body somatically – and start blasting it out of existence.

Every time I run it, we're restarting your computer.

Right and wrong, good and bad, POD and POC, all nine, shorts, boys, and beyonds®.

What this does is take the energy and the density that we live with and then call creation, and it says, "Boom! Wake up, take another breath, what is it that you're thinking and creating?"

Right and wrong, good and bad, POD and POC, all nine, shorts, boys, and beyonds®.

I'm not going to go into what that Mandarin-sounding statement actually means here. If you want, you can go to www.clearingstatement.com and learn more.

I'm assuming you're all here because there's some lie of money you know you're functioning from. It's the hub holding what you know in place. What I'm hoping to do in this Taster is give you something to get to that hub and just pull it out.

Will that be okay with you?

Participants: Yes.

Dr. Lisa: And the only thing that I require of you while you're here, if you're willing, is to make a 1° shift with me. Would you all be willing to make a 1° shift?

Participant: At least.

Dr. Lisa: Some of you, at least. Some of you are probably thinking, "I didn't come here for a 1° shift, dammit! It's California! I want to walk out the door and have millions of pennies thrown out right in front of me, I mean millions of dollars, no, pennies, no, millions of dollars. I don't know what I want."

Right, wrong, good and bad, that's what happens with money.

Right and wrong, good and bad, POD and POC, all nine, shorts, boys, and beyonds®.

Why do I say 1°? I know you want more, but all I'm asking of you here is to join me in a 1° shift because, just as I said it, did anybody notice the energy in the room? Did it get denser or did it lighten?

Participant: Lighten.

Dr. Lisa: Totally lightened – because everybody can do a 1° shift, even your body, even your buddy. And even if you don't think you're your own buddy.

Right and wrong, good and bad, POD and POC, all nine, shorts, boys, and beyonds®.

A 1° shift is all we're looking for. And when you think right now and perceive all the judgments, the decisions, the conclusions, the computations, the configurations, the separations, the wars, the traumas, the dramas, the catastrophes in the entire world right now with regards to money, a 1° shift on this planet is huge. It has the capacity to turn the world on its axis.

So would it be okay with you if we just started this 1° shift with destroying and uncreating every decision, judgment, conclusion and computation, known and unknown, that you have made significant, vital and real about money, would it be okay?

Participants: Yes.

Dr. Lisa: Right and wrong, good and bad, POD and POC, all nine, shorts, boys, and beyonds®.

And would it be okay with you if all your oaths and vows, commitments, fealties, comealties, prejudices, condemnations, marriages, contracts to money, having money or to not having money be changed right now?

Participants: Yes.

Dr. Lisa: Can we revoke, rescind, recant, renounce, denounce, destroy and uncreate the forever commitment to them?

Participants: Yes.

Dr. Lisa: Right and wrong, good and bad, POD and POC, all nine, shorts, boys, and beyonds®.

And all the vibrational, virtual realities that you created in your bank accounts, in your wallet, in your investments, in your portfolio, in your non-portfolio, in your non-investments, in your houses or non-houses, in your rent, in your job, could we destroy and uncreate all those?

Participants: Yes.

Dr. Lisa: Right and wrong, good and bad, POD and POC, all nine, shorts, boys, and beyonds®.

Dr. Lisa: And all the secret, invisible, covert, hidden, unseen, unspoken, undisclosed, unacknowledged agendas to keeping them in place because that's the way you know you fit into this reality could we destroy and uncreate that?

Participants: Yes.

Dr. Lisa: Right and wrong, good and bad, POD and POC, all nine, shorts, boys, and beyonds®.

Today I have a whole list of Lies of Money that I want to speak to you about.

So how many of you believe that you have to work hard for your money in order to earn it?

When you have to work hard for your money, and you have to earn it, what's the lie there? Notice that everyone stopped breathing for a moment. How many of you believe that there's no lie there, that it's just true?

Okay, let me ask you this, how many of your bodies believe that there's no lie there – that it's just truth? So truth, raise your hand if your mind knows that that's not true. And raise your hand if your body knows that that's not true.

So your mind knows that you don't have to work hard for your money to earn it, but your body doesn't. Yes, I think so. You're yawning, which means we're on to something. How many of you believe that working hard for your money to earn it is a mind thing and has nothing to do with your body?

Participant: I think I do.

Dr. Lisa: It's a different question.

Participant: So I could have a conflictual reality.

Dr. Lisa: Yes, if your mind believes something and your body believes something else, that's called a conflictual reality.

So, I'm going to ask you some questions and, when I'm asking, I want you to notice what happens in your body. Notice if it's light and expansive and a cool kind of energy, like we felt before when I started running the clearing the statement. That's a truth.

If it's dense and constricted and you feel like a knot in your gut, or your head is thinking about what you're going to do after this or tomorrow, and how quickly you can get out of here – then I'm probably hitting something you would call truth, but it's actually a lie.

So dense, constriction is a lie. Expansion, bubbly, energy, coolness in the room is the truth.

So truth, do you have a conflictual reality around money?

Participant: Yes.

Dr. Lisa: Light or heavy?

Participant: Light.

Dr. Lisa: That conflictual reality is the lie that you're abiding by, and whenever you abide by a lie, you generate and create the abiding of the lie.

So how many lies are you all abiding by and calling that your portfolio?

Participant: Too many.

Dr. Lisa: Too many. A little, a lot, or a megaton mocha-chocolate?

Participant: A megaton.

Dr. Lisa: She's yawning and falling over.

So all the lies that you're abiding by that create the conflictual reality about your money, about having money, about spending money, about making money, about being money, about not being money, could we destroy and uncreate that?

Participants: Yes.

Dr. Lisa: Right and wrong, good and bad, POD and POC, all nine, shorts, boys, and beyonds®.

And how many of your bodies are the hoarding storage container of your conflictual reality around money?

What do I mean as a hoarding storage container? Does anybody have a chronic disease or illness in here?

Participant: Yes.

Dr. Lisa: Anybody have the binging and purging that I was talking about earlier around money, kind of a little eating disorder with money?

If you're laughing, it's kind of true.

How many of you have gotten in conflictual relationships with your partners around money? That's what I'm talking about regarding that.

So all the ways that your body is holding and abiding by your lies, creating your conflictual realities which creates a vibrational reality of you being in a cage, incarcerating yourself to that reality around money and calling that creation, when it's actually destruction and has nothing to do with choosing for you, committing to you, collaborating with the Universe conspiring to bless you, or creating, can we destroy and uncreate that?

Participants: Yes.

Dr. Lisa: Right and wrong, good and bad, POD and POC, all nine, shorts, boys, and beyonds®.

And truth, light or heavy inside of you, how many of you believe that your money flows whether you have it or don't have it? That it has something to do with proving you're good or bad?

Participants: Yes.

Dr. Lisa: That you're worthy or not worthy? Truth.

Participants: Yes.

Dr. Lisa: Truth.

Participants: Truth, yes. Or that you're working hard or not working hard.

Dr. Lisa: Or that you're working hard or not working hard.

Notice the disparity, notice the back and forth, notice the denial, defending, dissociating, disconnecting. And notice that there's a no-choice Universe in that. You can't go anywhere other than over here and it looks like this.

But I'll tell you what, it's never over here, because your belief systems and your interesting points of view about worthy or not worthy, good or bad, working or not working have nothing to do with you.

They are what you hoarded in this reality as you, morphed yourself into, and said, "This is me."

Welcome to your financial reality. I did it too.

Right and wrong, good and bad, POD and POC, all nine, shorts, boys, and beyonds®.

In fact, I did this one today, which was really, really funny.

I was in Fairfax driving my sporty new Mercedes really fast. It's beautiful, I'm taking pictures, I'm on the phone and having so much fun. I'm feeling like I won the lottery! My life is so good, I'm so happy!

Because, when I left California, I was so down and despondent. I felt so poor and bankrupt and heartbroken and blah, blah, blah, blah. And now I felt so rich and affluent and beautiful and happy and light.

Then I see the police car. Here I am doing everything at once and I was just like, "I'm screwed." I knew it. I could feel the radar. So I was asking some questions like, "Can I get out of this?"

"Like, no."

"Alright, how can I make it as light and fun as possible?"

And I sat there. I could feel that police officer's energy. He was not happy. I was going about 25 miles or so over the speed limit I found out, but it didn't feel like that, of course. I felt his energy and think, "Oh, there's something wrong with this person. This person is mean. What will this create? How can I not let this ruin my day, pop my bubble?"

I mean, I'm feeling like I've won the lottery. I'm still vibrating out of this energy. I'm not wishing I won the lottery, I am living as if I did win the lottery. That's what changed for me – and I was driving that way.

Everything felt that way. Every cell of being down to my fascia was feeling that way. Now there's an expensive ticket – $1,000, or whatever it's going to be – and his energy was just like, "Screw you, hate you, screw you, hate you!"

I just handed him my license and he says, "Your hair color and your eye color isn't on here. Can you tell me this?"

I said, "I need to tell you my weight, too?"

"Yes."

"That's a little personal," but he wouldn't have any of it, so I gave it to him and he went back to his car.

I'm sitting there thinking, "I've got to get to this appointment. What will this create? What will this create?" I felt all this tightness inside and then it hit me. I thought, "Oh, I'm going to use this tonight. Okay, what will this create?"

And it was the lie that no matter how good my life gets, no matter how much I experience myself as holistically happy throughout every muscle, ligament, cell, tendon, system of my body –

You guys know what that feels like, right? A little bit? 1°, 1° baby! That's an A.

So everywhere you refuse to know what it feels like, smells like and tastes like to be holistically happy through every muscle, ligament, cell, tendon, organ, system of your body, can we destroy and uncreate that?

Participants: Yes.

Dr. Lisa: Right and wrong, good and bad, POD and POC, all nine, shorts, boys, and beyonds®.

And then could we just ask the Universe and the molecules of the Universe to download to your cells what it feels like, smells like and taste like to live and know what it feels like to live as molecularly, holistically happy, financially, psychically, psychologically, energetically, somatically, physiologically, sexually, sensually, orgasmically?

Participants: Yes.

Dr. Lisa: Orgasmically?

Participants: Yes.

Dr. Lisa: How does it get any better?

Right and wrong, good and bad, POD and POC, all nine, shorts, boys, and beyonds®.

Participant: Thank you for that.

Dr. Lisa: You're welcome, keep talking like that, that was so sexy.

Right and wrong, good and bad, POD and POC, all nine, shorts, boys, and beyonds®.

After the ticket, I get a bill from the IRS, and a letter from an attorney saying something about stealing someone's copyright or something like that. That's never happened to me.

So something happens that puts that rock in your shoe, and you go to that drink or that food or that destructive thing or that cage in your mind where everything sucks and you suck and you're horrible. You think, "No matter how hard I try and work, nothing ever changes, I never get a break, I'm still slapped with a ticket."

But you never say, "Yeah, I was speeding, life was a lottery. I knew I was caught and how does it get any better than that?

I'm going to pay it and nothing is going to change my day because it doesn't mean anything."

We make it to mean something and we live our life with this fear in the back of our head, lies of money, that the shoe is going to drop and there's nothing scarier.

Truthfully, even through the abuse – the rapes that I've been involved in and had done to me – there's nothing more scary than zero in your bank account. There's nobody that you can turn to, there's no way you know where the next whatever's going to come. And when that shoe drops, who's going to be there for you? That's a pretty scary place.

I think that's the real epidemic of this reality that our judgments and our points of view and the impelled financial reality, psychological reality, psychic reality that we adopt as us makes us sick, makes us unhappy, makes us choose relationships, myself included. It's like we just dump things into and dump things into and dump things into, never getting anywhere because we're always contracted somehow to get the ticket.

How many of you believe that, one day, no matter what or, every day, no matter what, you're going to pay? I know it's pretty strong, but just ask yourself that.

Participant: I used to.

Dr. Lisa: I used to, good. Have you paid enough?

Participants: Yes.

Participant: If you live in San Francisco you've –

Dr. Lisa: You've paid enough. I did for 20 years.

Participant: Or maybe not.

Dr. Lisa: Yes, exactly.

Participant: We haven't paid enough.

Dr. Lisa: Right, because in San Francisco, you get a box that's 800 square feet and rents for $3,000. That could seem like a hostage situation to live in a beautiful place. You have to work hard, earn money to live in a beautiful place, and all you're going to get is an 800-square-foot box.

How many points of views regarding that keeps you in that incarceration?

Right and wrong, good and bad, POD and POC, all nine, shorts, boys, and beyonds®.

This money thing is so insidious. That's why I do it in tandem with the Moving Beyond Abuse stuff, because we live in a financially abusive reality.

So, who's the real perpetrator, the reality or us?

It's all a perpetration in a certain way unless we make that 1° shift out of these lies. So, what lies have I talked about?

The first one is: *Money is the proof that you're right or wrong.*

How many of you believe that you would just be happy if you had money? You certainly could believe, for sure, that you'd be happier if you had money because money gives you more choices doesn't it?

Participants: Right.

Dr. Lisa: It gives you freedom, but are you dependent on having money for your freedom and happiness?

Participants: No, not any more.

Dr. Lisa: Not any more. So when everybody's saying no, there's still a constriction that occurs in the room.

Is that your mind or your body?

Participant: Body.

Dr. Lisa: Do you see what I'm doing here? You're answering me from your mind but I'm hearing you from your bodies.

So one of the lies of money that I'm hoping to get across to you is that what you think isn't what you're projecting out there. That what you feel and have embodied as the hoarding storage container of crap – that you call creation – is actually what's creating your money and financial situation, in opposition to what you know.

I know that you're all brilliant. I know you've done a lot of personal work. I know you read things. And I know you're smart – you live here. I get it. I lived here, too.

But what was in my cellular memory, the fascia of my body is:

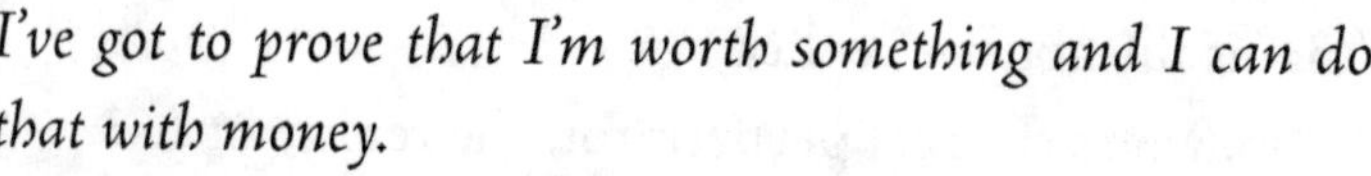

I've got to prove that I'm worth something and I can do that with money.
I'm only lovable when I have money.
I'm only lovable if I'm giving to somebody else.
No one will ever love me for me.
I will never be able to afford or be independent financially.
I will always require somebody else.
A two-income family is better than a one-income family.

These are all lies that your body is embodying and putting out in your reality, while your mind looks at all those things that I'm saying here and says no, but your body's saying yes.

Your mind's saying "No" and your body's saying "Yes." Your mind's saying, "I used to, your body's saying I still do."

Right and wrong, good and bad, POD and POC, all nine, shorts, boys, and beyonds®.

I always do this next thing. Some of you have seen this before.

If your money decided to speak to you what would it say to you?

Participant: You don't think I'm enough.

Participant: What the fuck.

Participant: You don't have to worry about me.

Dr. Lisa: Keep bringing it, what would your money say to you if you went to couples' therapy?

Participant: You never let me in.

Participant: You need to nurture me.

Dr. Lisa: I don't know about you, but I love when someone tells me what I need to do. I'm right there saying, "Okay." That was a joke.

And all of you here would be like, "Honey, there's another way of talking to me, don't tell me what I need to do. How do you like it if I tell you what you need to do?"

You know what happens, right?

They start doing the hand gestures. I've got some good Texan lines, but I don't know if they're appropriate here.

What would your money say to you if you went to couples' therapy?

Participant: You don't trust me.

Participant: With that point of view, I can't give to you.

Dr. Lisa: I love that one, no incarceration there, no hostaging. With that point of view, I can't give to you. How well does that tell you how wrong you are?

Participant: Every day, every minute.

Dr. Lisa: So what is this saying? You are what?

Participant: Wrong?

Dr. Lisa: Yes, which basically is then the embodiment of "I am wrong." That's the biggest lie about money – and it has nothing to do about money.

Participant: Right.

Dr. Lisa: "You need to, you're not letting me in, let me show up for you, I'm not enough for you, I can never give you, we haven't had sex in a little while or ever, you don't love me, you're not touching me, you're not nurturing me, I'm sleeping in the other room, sleeping on the couch, I'd rather go out with the boys/girls than be with you, I'm going to meet somebody else instead of you." These are all the ways you've made your money be a reflection to you about the wrongness of you, the horror of you, the ugliness of you, the disgust of you –so that you can embody those delicious statements and call them your wardrobe, your persona, whatever that word is, can we destroy and uncreate that?

Participants: Yes.

Dr. Lisa: Right and wrong, good and bad, POD and POC, all nine, shorts, boys, and beyonds®.

Dr. Lisa: Let me ask you a question…

How wrong are you?

Participant: I'm not supposed to be alive, that's how wrong.

Dr. Lisa: So, how wrong are you? A little wrong, a mega wrong, or a megaton mocha tapioca pudding with a walnut on top?

Participant: Megaton.

Dr. Lisa: All of that, that's the biggest lie of money.

How many of you believe in the wrongness of you 1°? And how many of your bodies believe in the wrongness of you and embody that 2°, because your mind is smarter than your body.

So you think.

Your body is the smartest around. Your body is the sensory organ of a perceiving, knowing, being and receiving capacity that almost none of us ever really get to embody.

Everything that brings up and lets down, could we destroy and uncreate it?

Participants: Yes.

Dr. Lisa: Right and wrong, good and bad, POD and POC, all nine, shorts, boys, and beyonds®.

So what do you love about the wrongness of you that you're not even supposed to be here? You're still here after 6+ decades on the planet, but you still know that you're not even supposed to be here. What do you love about that?

Participant: I don't know.

Dr. Lisa: It's a good question isn't it?

What do you love about the wrongness of you? What do you love about the judgment you be? What do you love about being wrong and calling that your financial reality?

Right and wrong, good and bad, POD and POC, all nine, shorts, boys, and beyonds®.

Participant: It's an artificial motivator.

Dr. Lisa: Isn't it? It's a gross artificial motivator, and all of us stick our face in it and lick it. I like being crass because it wakes people up. But that's a whole other workshop.

Right and wrong, good and bad, POD and POC, all nine, shorts, boys, and beyonds®.

What do you love about it?

Right and wrong, good and bad, POD and POC, all nine, shorts, boys, and beyonds®.

I want to mention that some of the space – before you can actually say something, feel something, notice something or even say anything – is, in Access Consciousness, called a 'Beyond.'

A 'Beyond' is something that isn't in your consciousness. It's kind of covert, but you felt it before. You can't really put words to it, but it's there. It can bring in some shock and trauma; it makes you search the database, but there's great energy that gets brought up in that searching.

This is her 1° shift. This is what it looks like for her and this tells you a little bit about what it's like for her. It's a great example because you may not be at this level – you're at your own level.

She's still searching for what she loves about it.

Participants: Because it's a place where there's no words, it's not a language.

Dr. Lisa: That's a 'Beyond' she put into words. "I'm not even supposed to be here, that's how wrong I am."

And so underneath, we're still looking. We haven't gotten to that hub yet. It's still in the somnambulant reality of anesthetization. The numbing, the dissociation, the cage – really far back – but if we can get there, we can take that out.

But you've got to choose to live. You've got to choose your own financial reality. You've got to choose that no matter what your story is.

No matter what your ancestors are, no matter what your sickness or illness or disease or your tragedy, your trauma, or your past is – it can never take who you be intrinsically.

No lie can.

And when we buy into these lies of about ourselves and create our life like that, the wrongness, we have to then project it on everybody else. You're seeing through judgment-colored glasses. In fact, I just did a Voice America Show on this called Seeing Through Abuse Colored Glasses.

So everything has to be a judgment of the wrongness of her.

Where are you judging you with money that is keeping your financial reality in a Beyond that has nothing to do with you?

Your ancestors, your mother, your father, your history, your stubbing your toe at the pool when you were five years old and dropping your money and losing it. Who knows what the story is?

We all hold on to that and create ourselves as that.

I double-dog dare you to step out of that and be the one that has so much money because you are the people that show up here and you are the people that are going to change this reality if you let yourself have it, myself included. I never allowed myself to have what I'm allowing myself to have now, I never did.

But I'll tell you…having has been the greatest embodied healing that I could ever say. I don't even know how to put it into words but having, having – being me.

You being you, you having you, committing to you, collaborating with you, choosing you, creating from there, that's the truth.

It's funny. There are all these lies of money, but I change every class. We did this in Hawaii and it was a whole different conversation. I thought I was going to do the same list of Lies of Money and had it very pragmatically lined up. But the entire time, when I'm checking in to this class, I get, "No, they don't want to hear that. No, they don't want to hear that."

So here we are – there's your money talking to you.

When my father got in estate and foreclosures in New York, my job was to sit in the basement with him, where he had his office. He had 16 apartments houses that he'd bought, multi-family units, from flipping houses.

We collected the rent and there were stacks of money. We used the old calculators and green pads then before we had a computer. I would sit down there and put the money in my mouth. I'd smell it and it was all kind of dirty, but I loved it.

Then I got a job at the bank, and every Friday all the lawyers would come in and they'd stack and stack and stack fresh, crisp $100 bills, which is why I love $100 bills. I was like, "Yes, come to my teller station. I want to count your $100 bills."

I had this infatuation and love affair with a financial reality of this reality that just made me happy. I loved counting it and I loved organizing it. In fact, I'd look in all my friend's wallets and make sure they organized their money: ones, fives, tens, twenties, fifties, hundreds.

I know people who would just have it in balls. I can't stand it. I would say to them, "What are you doing with your money? Treat it better, love it and it will come to you."

I'm a little OCD, I guess, but it meant something to me. There was just this happy molecule dance with money for me. I loved sitting in the vault at the bank and I loved when the Brinks would come. Whenever they were driving around in the car, I'd be like, "Yes! What bank are they going to?" I was just obsessed. I don't know what you guys did as a kid but I followed money.

Money comes to the party of happiness.

It doesn't come to the party of depression, constriction and no joy.

And, believe you me, when I got sick with a life-threatening disorder years ago and the endocrinologist said, "Kill it, take medicine for the rest of your life, or make me take your organ out," I said, "There has to be another choice."

"There isn't."

Remember I told you about the box thing – that I can't be put in a box? Don't tell me there isn't another choice because I will find it.

And then I ended up at an Institute called the ThetaHealing® Institute and spent 3 months there. Within 3 months, I had my Master's degree in ThetaHealing®, and, in 3 weeks, I didn't have the disease anymore.

He told me there was not one thing that he could do other than medication, surgery to remove it, or whatever else he told me – and I cured it all energetically.

I used every penny I had at that time to do holistic healing for myself. I let go of my house, let go of my retirement, let go of anything for that choice. I knew I would make it again. It cost me about $1 million to heal myself naturopathically. Not one ounce of pharmaceutical anything, and no insurance. Well, I had insurance, I was paying for it for decades, but when time came, nothing helped due to my choice to go holistic.

Fortunately, I had a disability insurance policy that my aunt had set up, and that's how I went to the ThetaHealing® Institute and got my Master's of Science in ThetaHealing®. Some people would say, "Oh, my God, you should keep that money because you're in so much debt." I thought, "This is going to heal me and this is going to be everything. I'm going to use that money for this."

Use your money to create, not destroy. Judgment destroys.

How much have you been destroying what you actually can, even if you have a good amount of money? Right and wrong, good and bad, POD and POC, all nine, shorts, boys, and beyonds®.

How much have you been using some sort of judgment, some sort of turning your back on money, some sort of being the wrongness of you and not being the rightness of you so that you can keep the struggle going and you can keep choosing to destroy you? Right and wrong, good and bad, POD and POC, all nine, shorts, boys, and beyonds®.

How many of you use money to prove how awful you are, how much you shouldn't be here by not receiving it. Right and wrong, good and bad, POD and POC, all nine, shorts, boys, and beyonds®.

I thought after the ThetaHealing® Institute I would be done, but when I landed in Bali last year, I didn't know that another level of "I think I'm done with life" was going to come up for me.

I'd turned my back on a lot of things, and I also felt that things had turned their back on me very clearly. So when I landed there, I was in that kind of despondent place again with a lot of things, not just money. "What's the point, what's the purpose of this, this, this and that?"

I was lying on one of the tables in the healer's hut, like in the book *Eat, Pray, Love*. They had a special person come in to work on my body, and he was literally pulling out these lies that I was embodying from my body. I did a radio show on it on Voice America called *The Shards of Abuse*. He pulled it out of my body and my mind was like, "What are you talking about? I can't see energy, I can't see anything like that, what are you talking about?"

And then he handed it me to me.

It was actually a shard.

This took something like 8 hours. It was everything I've been carrying about the world, which is how I know about all these lies of money. I got up close and personal in that 8-hour session with this healer pulling stuff out of my body.

And then, finally, once I felt it, my psychic sense opened up even more and I could see the energies, I could see the belief systems. I saw the words and the people. I saw the pictures and my childhood. I saw a lot of stuff. "No wonder why I fucking want to die, I get it. What better way to go than in Bali? It's easy."

Well, something else happened or I chose something else.

In that moment that I said, "I got more living to do because what's coming out of my body are all lies. And there's no way in hell that I'm going to die from lies. I want to fucking live and I'm going to live big and I'm going ROAR!"

And that's what I decided to do, and I changed the name of my business to Live Your ROAR – Live Your Radically, Orgasmically Alive Reality instead of The Beyond Abuse Revolution and The Beyond Abuse Movement.

I thought, "I survived all that. And if I could survive shards coming out of my body and some old grandfather taking a knife and putting it into my breasts saying, 'Sorry, sorry, it's just going to hurt a little, sorry, sorry, it's just going to hurt a little, sorry, sorry, it's just going to hurt a little, then...'"

It hurt, but those lies hurt you, guys.

That density you feel in your body, that's a lie, that is not you.

How many lies are you projecting on your money flows? And how many lies are you projecting on your money flows are you actually doing so that you never get to receive anything from anyone, from the Universe or for yourself? Right and wrong, good and bad, POD and POC, all nine, shorts, boys, and beyonds®.

Because that's what I learned in Bali.

I had a receiving issue. Actually, I had a receiving refusal.

I boycotted it, I holocausted myself from it, I dropped bombs on myself. I had WWI, WWII, WWIII, WWX, I can keep going, but you get the point?

You're laughing because I know you did, too.

Right and wrong, good and bad, POD and POC, all nine, shorts, boys, and beyonds®.

I literally got to this point where I had suffered enough and I had died enough, and then I chose to have everything no matter what. No matter what I had to lose, no matter who I had to lose, no matter where I had to go, no matter what I had to do, the books were going to get out there, the radio show was going to go viral.

I have 205,000 listeners now from 30,000. The first book is going to get published, and then we'll work on the other ones. And, and, and, and, and, and, and completely – even, as of yesterday, firing my entire team that I worked with – 12 people – giving them 30-day notices and starting fresh.

When I say I'm having it, I'm having it.

Go big or go home, that's what happened in Bali.

I was living some of that before, but when your eyes are open and you see all the lies and you make that choice, providence moves too. What did I do? I chose me, I committed to me, I collaborated with the Universe conspiring to bless me and I created.

Not one person is responsible for anything. Not one heartbreak or whoever I was with, had anything to do with anything other than what I chose. Not one problem, not one rape, not one abuse, not one client difficulty, not one law situation, not one family situation, it didn't matter.

I didn't care who I lost or what I lost, I was not going to lose me any longer.

I was going to choose me.

And nothing was going to be like this ever again. Nothing was going to have a projection, a separation, an expectation, a resentment, a rejection, a regret on it. My body was not going to suffer any more, my mind was not going to go down the same route that it had.

Everything that I chose to eat after that moment was different. Everything that I chose to drink was different. Everything that I put in my body was different. Everyone that I shared my body with was different. Seriously, everything was different. Right and wrong, good and bad, POD and POC, all nine, shorts, boys, and beyonds®.

There's a certain food that was always my fallback position and I just loved it: pizza. In California, you can get gluten-free pizza, but it's hard to get in Texas. You can get gluten-free pizza here, though, at Good Earth. They have the best gluten-free mushroom pizza but, when I saw it there today, my body was like, "Greens."

It's just more of a vibration, and when you don't perceive and abide by the lies anymore, the vibration obviously changes. And then what you attract, create, institute and generate changes and updates to that vibration.

So are you willing to give up 1% of your lies?

Participants: Yes.

Dr. Lisa: Are you willing to give up more that 1% of your lies?

Participants: Yes.

Dr. Lisa: Are you willing to give up 33.3% of your lies?

Participants: Yes.

Dr. Lisa: Everything that brings up and lets down can we destroy and uncreate it: Right and wrong, good and bad, POD and POC, all nine, shorts, boys, and beyonds®.

– do me a favor – take the energy with your hands, and I'm going to count to 5. I want you to throw the energy off this way – all those lies, 33.3% of it.

Let's get that heaviness, and on 5, throw it and toss it out.

Ready?

1-2-3-4-5! 1-2-3-4-5, 1-2-3-4-5, 1-2-3-4-5, 1-2-3-4-5, 1-2-3-4-5. Now take the rest of it, and I'll do a 3-count and we'll give it to the earth. 1-2-3, 1-2-3, 1-2-3, 1-2-3, 1-2-3!

And on 4, right out in front of you, let's open the door to a new possibility, 1-2-3-4, 1-2-3-4, 1-2-3-4, 1-2-3-4! Expand your energy as space, 500 million miles, up, down, right, left, front and back. Up, down, right, left, front and back, you're in this room, breathe energy in through the front of you, in through the back of you, in through the sides of you, in through the top of your head up through your feet.

Light or heavy or more space, less space?

Participants: Lighter, more space.

Dr. Lisa: More space?

Participant: Yes.

Dr. Lisa: Okay, so you did you learn anything? Glad you came?

Participant: Yes.

Dr. Lisa: Here's the biggest lie...

When I looked at my bank account, I'll never forget seeing the scariest thing ever.

You know what it was?

$0.00.

I sat there looking at it on my computer and said, "Oh, so that's what that feels like. Did the world end? Did I die?"

I looked in the fridge. There was still food, I had a car, full tank of gas, I could at least survive another day or two.

I was pretty happy.

And I stayed there and I embraced it and then I heard this whisper, "Are you ready to give up being a zero?"

Then I heard, "What is it costing you to be zero? "What are you refusing to be by choosing to be zero?"

Right and wrong, good and bad, POD and POC, all nine, shorts, boys, and beyonds®.

But, you know, that's what most women would do, something like that, right? Shut it down and go do something to numb it or jump off the Golden Gate Bridge or jump off the balcony or go cry to somebody about something, whatever it is, just something to avoid what that was.

How many glimpses have you all got about the brilliance of you and what you need to unlock and do? That if you just did that it, would change your reality immediately, but you shut the awareness on it, turn away and go because you're believing the lie.

I'm not saying it's easy to turn and face, but as somebody that has looked at three decades of abuse – from rape to pornography to abuse every day to being kicked out of my house every day, to being dragged by my hair down the stairs, peeing my pants, being left outside for my friends to watch us on the front porch for hours, to being beaten for dropping milk, being beaten for writing outside the lines when I'm learning to write because I can't see the lines because somebody's smacking me in the head to stay in the lines.

Do you get the disparity?

I had to turn and face everything and look at it.

And look at what I created in every disease, dis-ease, dysfunctional relationship, every choice, every body thing, every this, every that.

I had to look at all the lies because I created my persona or who I thought I was based on that – based on all those stories.

When someone's hitting you, it's like the energetic realization of what they're thinking imprinted on you. When someone's verbally saying something to you, it's an energetic imprint on you. When you say something to yourself, when you see yourself in the mirror, it's an energetic imprint on you.

When you share sexual relations with somebody, you are energetically imprinting you to them and them to you. So even if some of you are not married, you may still be married in a way you might not like.

Right and wrong, good and bad, POD and POC, all nine, shorts, boys, and beyonds®.

Would you like to be energetically divorced from all those past relationships?

Right and wrong, good and bad, POD and POC, all nine, shorts, boys, and beyonds®.

Would you like to destroy and uncreate all your contracts with that person(s)?

Participants; Yes.

Dr. Lisa: In all lifetimes, dimensions, bodies and realities.

Participants: Yes.

Dr. Lisa: Right and wrong, good and bad, POD and POC, all nine, shorts, boys, and beyonds®.

Would you like to return to sender, with consciousness attached, all their stuff, all their points of views, all their points of views about you, all their judgments about you, all their views about money and you?

Participants: Yes.

Dr. Lisa: Right and wrong, good and bad, POD and POC, all nine, shorts, boys, and beyonds®.

And everywhere you've obligated every muscle, ligament, cell, tendon, organ and system of your body to be nothing and to be a nothing and to always end up with nothing and no one and nobody, could we destroy and uncreate it?

Participants: Yes.

Dr. Lisa: Right and wrong, good and bad, POD and POC, all nine, shorts, boys, and beyonds®.

How many of you believe the lie that you need to be humble and not talk about money?

How many of you don't want to talk about whether you have your Mercedes or your Porsche or your BMW or your Saturn?

Participant: I don't.

Dr. Lisa: I thought I saw you post one day how much you loved your car.

Participant: I did, it was tricky.

Dr. Lisa: Interesting, so maybe I have some awareness here that I'm bringing up for some reason.

Participant: Yes.

Dr. Lisa: Okay. So how many of you are not willing to share about your big fortune because people will judge it?

Participant: Well, people do.

Participant: Or try and take it.

Dr. Lisa: So you better hide it, never use it or enjoy it, and be always in fear that the Germans are going to come and get you.

Participant: It's really heavy.

Dr. Lisa: Right and wrong, good and bad, POD and POC, all nine, shorts, boys, and beyonds®.

You may be picking up something else other than yourself.

Right and wrong, good and bad, POD and POC, all nine, shorts, boys, and beyonds®.

It's like believing there's a wrongness in having something good.

So what is that? It's a lie.

Everywhere you believe that everything you have that is good, that is affluent, that is luxurious, that is rich, that is wealthy – or – go the opposite way, the asexual way, and not have it at all.

Either way can we destroy and uncreate it?

Participants: Yes.

Dr. Lisa: Right and wrong, good and bad, POD and POC, all nine, shorts, boys, and beyonds®.

It's funny because my lover now has more money than I do. We talked about this at the workshop recently at Sex and Relationship Class with Gary and Dain of Access Consciousness. They both laughed at me when I asked the question, and said, "Well, I double-dog and triple-dog dare you to out-create her."

I said, "Okay, why not?"

However, what it brought up for me was shame because it was the first time in my life in relationship history that somebody had more money than me because I always took care of everything like my daddy did, like my daddy taught me.

I was in a whole other position now where someone didn't need me for anything. I didn't know what to do, and it was another lie I had to face, because I didn't really have to do anything except perceive, be and receive. And I learned this for the first time at 45 when this particular vibration, that I'm in right now, started.

It's all about me being – and through that I receive everything holistically.

So how many of you use money as a way to be needed, to give love or receive love?

Right and wrong, good and bad, POD and POC, all nine, shorts, boys, and beyonds®.

How many of you are avoiding the money flows you could have by refusing to be a judge-able offense in this reality? How much more money could you receive if you allowed everyone and everything to just judge you and not care one way or another because, as you are in the judgment of you, you are target for judgment?

As long as you stay sick and depressed, you're a target for judgment. As long as you stay victimized and not choosing your reality, you stay a target for judgment. As long as you point the finger on the other side of it, you are a target for judgment.

When you start pointing the finger, you better believe there are going to be a 100 million of them coming to kill you.

Right and wrong, good and bad, POD and POC, all nine, shorts, boys, and beyonds®.

I had an experience at a class recently where my flyers were out on a table and when I came back at the next break, all my flyers and everything about my workshops were gone, completely gone, purposely.

At the time, I bought the lie there was something wrong with me, that I did something that caused somebody to want do that – that I was doing that. And then, when I stepped out of that, I thought, "Wow, what I'm being is a judge-able offense to that person, to those people's reality."

Participant: It's just like the ticket – that was about him needing to do that.

Dr. Lisa: It was totally him needing to do that.

I've realized that the biggest lie I've been living in is that I've created some of these things.

Sometimes I have to realize that what I create is actually creating more for other people, and it's not a wrongness of me. It's a capacity I've learned to step into. I would not have guessed it because it never shows up the way you think it will.

But I knew.

I was a little sarcastic when I said, "Bye. You can have it. I'll happily pay you. I hope I contributed to your quota and you're having a better day."

He said, "You better drive off."

"Have a wonderful day," I said, "I'm glad I could contribute to Marin's County financial problem." That was my last statement.

Here are three questions I'm going to leave you with before we go:

Whenever you get into a money constriction, the cage, ask yourself, "What is this creating or what will this create?"

Let yourself perceive that.

If it's heavy, change immediately. If it's light, go for it and realize that, whatever you choose, there's always another choice 10 seconds later.

Embrace, examine, embody and expand, no matter what.

I do embrace, examine, embody and expand every moment, that's my choice. If it's not working, I'm changing it. And I'm willing to give up every point of view and every way that I think I am right about something.

I don't want to be right, I want to be happy.

Right and wrong, good and bad, POD and POC, all nine, shorts, boys, and beyonds®.

Here's a special question that I really love:

What is it costing you to create your financial reality as you have?

You can actually use these questions for anything, but I'm tailoring it to money right now.

What is this costing you?

I recently asked myself, "What are you refusing to pay that, if you paid for it, would make you money right away? What is it costing you not to do it?"

This was around a big decision I'd made and put into place on Monday about termination, 30-day notice, and flipping the business over.

Lights off, lights on.

When I did it, there was a little bit of emotion that night, and I felt so light and expansive. The next day, when all of this stuff started to happen – the same stuff I've been trying to fix – someone texted me and said, "I'm so glad you didn't try to glue it back together and just try to plug the hole – that you just let it go and started from scratch creating something new."

I thought, "So am I and I have no bad feeling about it."

So what is this costing you?

And remember, if it's light, go for it – heavy, change it.

Next, what are you refusing?

What are you refusing when you get into this whole story, "I've got to pay rent, I've got to do this, I've got to go here, I can't go there, I've got to do this because of that. I've got a wedding coming up."

What are you refusing?

Those are the three questions that I've been using to undo the lies of money within myself, and it's been working successfully with my clients and in my classes. It's like this: Will you choose the affluence that you be or will you choose the effluence, or diarrhea?

Affluence or effluence? It's just one letter.

What do you choose?

It really is your choice.

When I started changing all of this, my financial reality got really wonky. I didn't understand a darn thing that was going on. It was crazy.

I'm giving you a little bit of a heads up that, as you change all this – not that it wasn't crazy before – but as you start looking at all this and really change, the Universe will provide you with exactly what you're looking at. So don't get scared and run away or put your head down or in the sand or whatever. Go in the vault, play with the money. Get naked and lather those $100 bills all over you.

I double dog dare you to pay somebody to lather you with $100 bills.

You know you'd like it.

Go buy some gold coins and have them rubbed all over your body. Go put some diamonds on, some fashionable jewelry that makes you feel good. Go put a dress on or go shopping somewhere. Put something on that you're not going to buy, but man, you know you feel good in it. Go test drive a Porsche or a BMW or a Mercedes or a Tesla or something just because you can. Go rent a yacht with some friends and experience that.

Buy the most expensive bottle of champagne and sip on it. Go eat some caviar. It may be something completely different like swimming with the whales.

Whatever you experience as affluent, give yourself.

Just go do and be whoever you do and be, but be from the affluence and the richness and the receiving energy that is intrinsically who you are.

Would it be okay with you if you left the wrongness of you here?

Participants: Yes.

Dr. Lisa: Would it be okay with you if you left the judgment of you here?

Participants: Yes.

Dr. Lisa: Would it be okay with you if you really left the 1% of lies here or the 33.3% of lies here?

Participants: Yes.

Dr. Lisa: And anything that doesn't allow that.

Would be okay with you if you had some fun with money?

Participants: Yes.

Dr. Lisa: Another thing I did was buy this 14-karat gold money clip from a friend of mine who does some beautiful jewelry. I wanted to put my hundreds in a money clip because, molecularly, it makes me happy. There's weight to this, a density.

There might just be three hundred dollar bills in here now, but sometimes there's $2,000 or $5,000. Sometimes there's just one.

I never let it go to nothing though.

There's something about having in my wallet all the time. No matter where I am, no matter what I am, I always know I have money. On a vibrational level, this has created more money for me.

Every time I look there, I think, "Hi, babies, I love you."

Participant: The gold is worth money.

Dr. Lisa: And the gold is also worth money, a lot more than money.

So practice some of these things. Put them into practice and see them.

Or, you can keep not having sex, not having fun, and keep your back turned to what the Universe is conspiring to bless you with.

Right and wrong, good and bad, POD and POC, all nine, shorts, boys, and beyonds®.

Sometimes people who are spiritual choose to have no money. But no God that I know would ever want us not to have everything, because we are the people, you are the people, and the people are waiting for you out there that could really change this reality by having money.

You could spend it in ways that could consciously change this reality.

People need to hear your voice no matter what walk of life, no matter what you do, and this reality functions on money.

It just does.

You get to choose what point of view, what reality, you want to create with how this reality functions – and not eradicate, die, step away, not join, or keep yourself suffering. Radically, orgasmically, alive reality becomes your radical ally, your orgasmic ally.

Create an alive reality with money – I double dog dare you.

Right and wrong, good and bad, POD and POC, all nine, shorts, boys, and beyonds®.

Be your own radical ally, be your own orgasmic ally. Reclaim that with money, with relationship, with health, with body, everything and live your alive reality.

Right and wrong, good and bad, POD and POC, all nine, shorts, boys, and beyonds®.

Thank you so much for your attendance, I hope you received something from this, and what I wish for each of you is what I wish for everybody in the world, which is to, within ourselves, eliminate and eradicate all forms of abuse and live radically and orgasmically alive.

And I always end things that I do with this:

Be you, beyond anything and create magic.

Thank you.

Boulder

Dr. Lisa: Hello, everybody. Thanks for being here.

Welcome to the Lies of Money. It's a two-hour taster of the Lies of Money. And you're all here because you already know that, somewhere inside of you, you're living some lies with money. True?

How many of you are familiar with Access Consciousness? And how many of you are familiar with the Access Consciousness Clearing Statement? Okay, cool. I'll explain a little bit about that.

You don't have to be a part of Access Consciousness. I use the Access Consciousness Clearing Statement and a lot of the tools that come through their modality, even though they wouldn't call it a modality, to work with the energies of the lies, the points of views, the constrictions, the cage that we live by.

Whether we know it or not, consciously or unconsciously, we all have a limitation and a constriction and a lie that we live by. Sometimes it shows up in money. Sometimes it shows up in our bodies. Sometimes it shows up in our minds. Sometimes it shows up in our jobs. Sometimes it shows up in our relationships.

I'm sure none of you have ever seen that before.

We actually *create* our reality from those constrictions, points of views, and lies, and, then, we live based on those lies.

So is it any wonder why – when you're trying to change something and you're working so hard on it and you're going to another workshop tonight, and another workshop probably tomorrow, and another workshop next week, why these things don't change?

They don't change because you can't change something that's a lie.

Right, wrong, good and bad, POD and POC, all nine, shorts, boys and beyonds®.

One of my favorite things to do is use a lot of laughter when I talk about lies. I also go around the world helping people transition trauma and move beyond abuse. You've got to have some lightness and some fun in you to do that because, otherwise, it could be quite a bitter pill.

What that brings up and lets down just totally brought the room down. "Wait, abuse? This is money! Let's talk about money. Stay on money. Stay on money."

Right, wrong, good and bad, POD and POC, all nine, shorts, boys and beyonds®.

Before I tell you about why I use the Access Consciousness Clearing Statement, I want to mention that I have a fairly significant number of degrees and licenses and education and training, both traditionally and non-traditionally using energetic healing modalities, that I've utilized in this reality to go around the world as an expert, and as a leading authority, to move people beyond abuse, limitation, and constriction.

And what I've found is that the Access Consciousness Clearing Statement takes in everything that we speak to, in whatever facilitation I'm doing with someone.

It's comprehensive and thorough, and gets in places – in your muscles, ligaments, cells, tendons, organs, and systems of the body, your circuitry, your neural transmitters, your conscious and unconscious thoughts, your private, secret, invisible, covert, unseen, unacknowledged, and unspoken agendas – all of those things that are not visible to the naked eye.

The Access Consciousness Clearing Statement takes all that stuff that I mentioned, and all the energy that's in the room right here whether you know it or not, whether you can see it with your naked eye or with your un-naked eye, and wipes the slate clean.

When it wipes the slate clean, it's like when your computer gets stuck and that hourglass comes up and just kind of sits there.

The computer is like, "File not found."

It's like that with you: "File not found. File not found. File not found. File not found," and you keep running the Clearing Statement till some sort of found-ness happens.

It takes that hourglass that can't find the file that you're searching for in whatever the issue is going on in your life, and then it wipes the slate clean so that you can actually come from a space and energy and consciousness of choice and possibility.

We can all come from a space, energy, and consciousness of choice and possibility.

However, we don't usually because we have a lie that we're buying into or a fixed point of view.

For instance, consider your first and last name. That's a fixed point of view. As soon as you claim it – look at it on your passport or birth certificate, talk to people, put your business card out, write it down – you're identifying yourself with a point of view.

It's can be as innocuous as that to something very, very difficult and full of judgments in this reality, like money. The Clearing Statement takes all of those points of views and just wipes the slate clean.

It gives you that space to choose.

That's why I use it in everything I do. I figure why work harder if something works well? Call me crazy. It's just my interesting point of view.

How do I know it works well?

I've seen for myself based on what I've done in my life, what my clients do every day, what 205,000 people listening to me on Voice America do every week. Something is working, and utilizing it shifts our points of view easily and changes these long standing immoveable positions to something of possibility and creation.

My intention tonight is to give something and contribute to you that which is different around this topic of the Lies of Money than what you already know.

Would that be okay with you if you get something different?

Participants: Yes.

Dr. Lisa: Right, wrong, good and bad, POD and POC, all nine, shorts, boys and beyonds®.

Would you just allow yourself to open to what's coming in these next two hours about the lies of money from my interesting point of view? Would you allow yourselves to open just 1% more to receive this really twisted way that I'm going to take the lies of money and present it to you?

Just 1°. Would you like that?

Participants: Yes.

Dr. Lisa: Could you do that?

Participants: Yes.

Dr. Lisa: Right, wrong, good and bad, POD and POC, all nine, shorts, boys and beyonds®.

Would you be willing to let go, just 1% or 1°, whatever one you like better, of everything you've made money mean to you before this moment, everything you defined money to be, concluded, judged, computed, and configured?

Would you all be willing to let that go just 1%?

Participants: Yes.

Dr. Lisa: Right, wrong, good and bad, POD and POC, all nine, shorts, boys and beyonds®.

Everything that you've already done with money that's already changed for you, that's already worked for you, and everything that hasn't worked for you no matter what you've done, would you be will to give that up 1% and 1° more tonight just in these 10 seconds?

Once you leave here, you can do whatever you want, or 10 seconds from now you can do whatever you want, or right now you can do whatever you want.

Right, wrong, good and bad, POD and POC, all nine, shorts, boys and beyonds®.

To go back to the Access Consciousness Clearing Statement, those fixed positions and those lies that we've lived our life by are what we actually create our reality as. Whatever your reality is, or whatever brought you here about the lies of money, the real cruel joke is you are actualizing that lie.

Those lies that you're actualizing have become your financial reality.

The cruel joke about it is that none of it is yours, likely. Most of it is not yours, probably. You keep making it yours.

Right, wrong, good and bad, POD and POC, all nine, shorts, boys and beyonds®.

Not fun. Not pretty.

I'll share some stories myself, too, that will let you know that I join you in this craziness and insanity. How does it get better than this? We have these tools. We have this Access Consciousness. We have this Clearing Statement that works whenever we're stuck in a fixed position or something isn't working.

For instance, I did a radio show on Tuesday with Dr. Dain Heer. The connection wouldn't work and I couldn't hear him, but everybody else on the show could hear him. So I was talking over him, and looked and sounded like a fool.

Please listen to it. It's one of my best shows ever. I just listened to it again this afternoon, and I was cringing for the first 20 minutes, but then it opened up and we got the connection going.

What do you do in those moments in life where the connection isn't going no matter what you've prepared or how excited you are? Here you've got everything all set up and everything all sorted. Then, urrk! Sorry. Doesn't happen. You can't hear. You can't hear the man you want to hear, that you know can give 205,000 listeners the very thing that you brought him there to do out of his very big, busy schedule.

What do you do?

Some of us will jump out the window. Some of us put our fists through the window. Some of us would drink. Some of us would spend money. Some of us eat. Some of us would just let it go, forget it, and stop the show.

What I do is use the Access Consciousness Clearing Statement.

Then, somehow, miraculously, even with crazy phone lines and internet connections, when you run that Clearing Statement, things change. The lines of communication get open. The energy, space, and consciousness within you opens. The possibilities open.

Your solutions show up, perhaps for things that you could do to change whatever is right in front of you.

You get more possibilities, more solutions, whereas before it was just like one way, one choice: Do it this way because that always works. Do it this way, that way, this way, that way.

When you run the Clearing Statement, it opens.

I liken it to when your computer gets stuck on something and you don't know why. All of a sudden, you can't get on Facebook. You can't get that photo of you, that shouldn't be up there, anyway, on Facebook. You can't get it up there. You can't get it down. What's the best thing to do? Shut it off! Restart and hope it didn't post.

That's what the Access Consciousness Clearing Statement does.

When you do those kinds of things and get stuck, and make yourself look like a fool sometimes, or you don't know what's actually going on underneath the surface, run the Clearing Statement. Turn the computer back on, do your restart. Bam!

You don't know what happened, but it changed. You all get this.

I'm doing this Lies of Money taster because it wasn't enough for me to go around the world helping people and facilitating them in moving beyond their abuse, limitations, and constrictions. I have to throw money on top of it, another lie issue.

I also decided to do this before the 2-day class and before the Body Class. I'm just like, "What was I thinking?" but it's actually worked out pretty well. They're pretty heavy topics.

Money is a pretty heavy topic, too.

So many judgments. So much hatred. So many perspectives. So many people struggling. So many people having no fun.

There's not enough of us having fun and creating more possibilities and having, being, doing, knowing, perceiving everything we wish to do, know, be, and receive because of the cash or the money we allow ourselves to have.

Right and wrong, good and bad, POD and POC, all nine, shorts, boys, and beyonds®.

Would you be willing to allow yourself to have 1° or 1% more of the money or cash than you've ever had before right here in these two hours?

Participants: Yes.

Dr. Lisa: Anything that doesn't allow that, could we destroy and uncreate it?

Participants: Yes.

Dr. Lisa: Right, wrong, good and bad, POD and POC, all nine, shorts, boys and beyonds®.

Here's my question to you: What is it costing you not to?

Urk! Vomit bags in the back.

Everything that brings up and lets down, can we destroy and uncreate it?

Participants: Yes.

Dr. Lisa: Right, wrong, good and bad, POD and POC, all nine, shorts, boys and beyonds®.

I would love to take credit for that question, but that's a Gary Douglas question from a personal conversation I had with him.

Basically, I had to make a decision about my business and hiring a new marketing firm – what not to do, what I wanted to do – which would mean I would have to let go a fair amount of people in my business, or keep doing what wasn't working anyway. But I wanted to keep doing it because I've been doing it and because I like the people.

I certainly loved paying them and working hard for them to do the same things over and over and over again that I asked them not to do.

Take a look in the mirror. Where have you done it?

Right, wrong, good and bad, POD and POC, all nine, shorts, boys and beyonds®.

He said to me, "What is it costing you not to choose that?"

Boing!

What is it costing you not to choose?

Right and wrong, good and bad, POD and POC, all nine, shorts, boys, and beyonds®.

Why do we not choose? Because we don't have the money. We don't have the cash. Then, it goes on to, "I'm not good enough. I'm not worthy enough. I don't deserve it. I'll hurt somebody. I'll hurt these people that I like that are causing me more pain than possibility or progress, whatever it is."

We make all these justifications, all these lies.

Then, we don't go to the space, to the place with the choice that would actually give us everything we would desire, the choice of what's lighter and righter versus the lie, which is heavier and denser.

What is it about this reality that we go for the lies, we go for the density, we go for the heaviness? We create our lies and actualize all of that, and then wonder why we want to put a white jacket on or go somewhere and not talk to anybody and hate everybody? Is that just me?

Everything that brings up and lets down, let's destroy and uncreate it.

Right, wrong, good and bad, POD and POC, all nine, shorts, boys and beyonds®.

Everywhere you have chosen to create your monetary, sexual, emotional, psychic, psychosomatic, physical, financial, energetic, business in the density and the heaviness of insanity about what doesn't work for you, can we destroy and uncreate that?

Participants: Yes.

Right and wrong, good and bad, POD and POC, all nine, shorts, boys, and beyonds®.

Dr. Lisa: Everything that brings up and lets down, can we revoke, rescind, recant, renounce, denounce, destroy, and uncreate the forever commitment to that?

Participants: Yes.

Right and wrong, good and bad, POD and POC, all nine, shorts, boys, and beyonds®.

Dr. Lisa: All the vibrational, virtual realities underneath that and underneath that and underneath that and underneath that and underneath that and underneath that and underneath that, can we destroy and uncreate those?

Participants: Yes.

Right and wrong, good and bad, POD and POC, all nine, shorts, boys, and beyonds®.

Dr. Lisa: All the secret, hidden, invisible, covert, unseen and unacknowledged, unspoken and undisclosed agendas to that density and heaviness as your reality, just in case you've disassociated and you forgot what we're talking about, can we destroy and uncreate that because I'm sure none of you did? Can we destroy and uncreate that?

Participants: Yes.

Dr. Lisa: Right, wrong, good and bad, POD and POC, all nine, shorts, boys and beyonds®.

When I'm doing these Lies of Money tasters, sometimes I can't even see the back walls of the room. Sometimes I can't even see you. Sometimes you come through and I can see all your faces.

Other than that, it's like a big, blurry haze.

Everywhere you're creating a big, blurry haze as your financial reality and letting me see it, thank you. Could we destroy and uncreate that?

Participants: Yes.

Dr. Lisa: Right, wrong, good and bad, POD and POC, all nine, shorts, boys and beyonds®.

This is why I do this kind of talk before I get right in to the specific lies of money, to bring the energy up. Are you noticing those of you who are yawning and feeling a little bit unconscious? Ready to knock out?

Participants: Yes.

Dr. Lisa: That's the secret, hidden, invisible, covert, unseen and unacknowledged, unspoken, undisclosed agendas, i.e. a big word for lie or a lot of words for lie coming up.

They're coming up off your body.

Right and wrong, good and bad, POD and POC, all nine, shorts, boys, and beyonds®.

That's why I use the Access Consciousness Clearing Statement. It's how I can facilitate to get this off all of our bodies, so that you can go out and be and do what you be and do and what you are meant to be and do.

I wrote my dissertation on something called "Soul Printing." Our soul print is like our fingerprint. We all have a unique one.

Each of us has a uniqueness that we're here to impress upon the lips of reality.

What I do is mine. What you do is yours – whatever facet: lawyer, nurse, facilitator, acupuncturist, audiovisual artist, massage therapist, Mom, Dad, investor, teacher, police officer – whatever it is, that's yours.

There's something that each of you do uniquely, and you know this. It's so easy for you and you actually love it – so you decide to put it aside and go somewhere else and do something else.

Just a joke because I'm sure none of you have done that.

Right, wrong, good and bad, POD and POC, all nine, shorts, boys and beyonds®.

Your soul print is so easy and effortless for you that it would allow, if you just stepped up in to that and allowed yourself to be that, it would allow the probability of ease and money and cash and joy and fulfillment and embodiment and health and wealth and fun and possibility in to your life.

Would you all be willing to uncloak the 1° or the 1% of you that knows what you are to be and do – that you're refusing to be and do at what cost to you and the world – and that you know to be true?

Everything that brings up and lets down, could we destroy and uncreate it?

Participants: Yes.

Dr. Lisa: Right, wrong, good and bad, POD and POC, all nine, shorts, boys and beyonds®.

Are you glad you're here?

Participants: Yes.

Dr. Lisa: How does it get any better than that?

Right, wrong, good and bad, POD and POC, all nine, shorts, boys and beyonds®.

Do me a favor. Expand your energy and space. All that means is think it, feel it, perceive it, know it, whatever words you want to use. 500 million miles up, down, right, left, front and back, breathe energy in through the front of you, in through the back of you, in through your sides, up through your feet, and down through your head.

Hi, body. Hi, body. Hi, body. Hi, body. Hi, body. Hi, body. Hi, body. Hi, body. Hi, body.

If any of you are coming to the Body Class, you'll hear this over and over and over again from me. If you're not, this will be repeating in your head and you want to POC and POD it.

Hi, body. Hi, body. Hi, body. Hi, body. Hi, body. Hi, body.

Dr. Lisa: What energy, space, and consciousness can we in our bodies be? What energy, space, and consciousness can we in our bodies be to be energy, space, and consciousness of the symphony of possibilities™, the energetic synthesis of being™, the energy, space, and consciousness, the space of no judgment, the space of infinite possibilities that you and your beautiful body be to create your financial reality with ease, joy, and glory™?

Would you like to join me?

Participants: Yes.

Dr. Lisa: Everything that brings up and lets down, let's destroy and uncreate it.

Right, wrong, good and bad, POD and POC, all nine, shorts, boys and beyonds®.

Just 1% more. What are you unwilling to be or do today that would create money right away? I know.

Right, wrong, good and bad, POD and POC, all nine, shorts, boys and beyonds®.

As it happens, every time I've run this class, and I've done this class the last four places that I've been in, I've talked about something different.

It's like, "Damn! There are a lot of lies here."

Little nuggets.

This is what we're talking about. When you all look at it, it makes you very, very happy. God forbid you actually create that happiness in your bank account, in your finances, in your retirement account, in your vacations, in your car, in your cash flows, in your coin, in your sexual-ness, in your awareness, your psychic-ness.

You can create it.

It's being handed out right now. It's handed out in every moment with every molecule, if we choose.

What are you refusing to do and be in order to receive that right away?

I know about receiving. I grew up in a very violent, abusive household environment. I was forced into child pornography modeling from a very young age. I know a lot about monetary abuse. I know a lot about working hard but not getting any of the money.

When I stand up here and say some of these things, believe you me, it took a lot to get here. A lot. A megaton, a megaton, a mocha choco-latte with a little whipped cream and a cherry lot.

Right, wrong, good and bad, POD and POC, all nine, shorts, boys and beyonds®.

I know what it's like to hate money, to not trust anybody around money or the people that were around me in my family at the time, institutions, organizations, standing up, dressing up, taking pictures, smiling but not getting the money and getting something else totally, completely, and horrifically behind the scenes.

Right, wrong, good and bad, POD and POC, all nine, shorts, boys and beyonds®.

Who are you being with money, with cash?

I know that when we do a money taster like this, that some people come and think, "Oh my God! Thank God. They're finally going to give me the answer. All of this is going to be gone."

Then, they walk out and say, "Well, I knew that. Nothing changed."

Or, they walk out and start doing these things. It definitely changed, but it's kind of like a lateral change. They get a little bit better but then, six months later, eight months later, a year later, they're back in the same position.

What I've found with these lies of money within us is that it's about what we're lying about as our reality, so 'who are you being with money' is the first lie.

Two, what are you being with money? Second lie.

Who are you being?

There's an energy that comes up and we'll get in to it. You're being that energy and probably many different energies.

And with that energy, you create something.

Then, there's a 'what' that comes in.

What are you being with money?

Perceive that energy and all of the people, situations, events that correspond to actualize whatever that is – now you've got a 'who' or 'whom.'

Then, you got a 'what' and all those situations and you're actualizing that.

If you're being a 'who' and you're being a 'what,' what are you not being?

You.

And you call that true.

Right, wrong, good and bad, POD and POC, all nine, shorts, boys and beyonds®.

This energy in here right now, this is a lie. This is the energy of when you're lying. I'm the one that's speaking but I'm speaking to the lies known and unknown, seen and unseen. Certainly, with some of the ways you're looking at me right now, the 'what' and the 'who' have not come in to your awareness in this way.

Right, wrong, good and bad, POD and POC, all nine, shorts, boys and beyonds®.

You're going to be really, really pissed at me when you find out who you have been creating your money flows on and then you're going to be really, really, really thankful.

Right, wrong, good and bad, POD and POC, all nine, shorts, boys and beyonds®.

The third lie is about the judgments that you refuse to receive that block your financial prosperity from ease. I know you all want to run out now like, "Damn! I'm going to listen to this crap now? Who, what, and judgments?"

If I were to define what the lie of money is, it's a who. It's a what. It's a judgment. Put it together and it's a trifecta of poop that you have a multi-entry visa to.

Everything that brings up and lets down, because I do, too, could we destroy and uncreate it?

Participants: Yes.

Dr. Lisa: Right, wrong, good and bad, POD and POC, all nine, shorts, boys and beyonds®.

Your self-worth isn't connected to your net worth.

What I've found over and over again in doing these Tasters is that it really is within us to recognize the lies that we're choosing to believe and actualize. And it takes the uncloaking of those lies, like the fraud patrol, if you will, to uncloak all of that so you can see what's true.

There are so many lies that people are unwilling to lose so that they can actually choose. You guys all know this.

Right, wrong, good and bad, POD and POC, all nine, shorts, boys and beyonds®.

I'll tell you anyway.

Cash gives you freedom, choice, possibility always. So does money.

Why, if we know that – and we are that as infinite beings – how is it that we would put ourselves in constant positions of stress, strife, struggle, not enough-ness, and having to choose vacation or retirement or something like that?

What is that about? It makes no logical sense. It's insane.

Right, wrong, good and bad, POD and POC, all nine, shorts, boys and beyonds®.

What have you made so vital, valuable, and real about the fraud patrols of your financial reality, cash and money, your reality with money, linearity, relationships, families, spiritualty, sex and sexual freedom, ethnicity, law, cultural separation, humanoid embodiment, and healing that keeps you seeking the wrong-ness of you through them and everything they are and making that the lack of money you have as you? Everything that is, will you destroy and uncreate it?

Participants: Yes.

Dr. Lisa: Right, wrong, good and bad, POD and POC, all nine, shorts, boys and beyonds®.

Everybody, just for fun, say with me "fraud patrol."

Participants: Fraud patrol.

Dr. Lisa: Say it again.

Participants: Fraud patrol.

Dr. Lisa: Say it again.

Participants: Fraud patrol.

Dr. Lisa: Right, wrong, good and bad, POD and POC, all nine, shorts, boys and beyonds®.

"Fraud patrol," say it again please.

Participants: Fraud patrol.

Dr. Lisa: Again.

Participants: Fraud patrol.

Dr. Lisa: Thank you. All the fraud patrol, decisions, judgments, conclusions, computations, lies essentially around your money flows, your cash, your finances, in this lifetime, dimension, body, and reality or any other lifetime, dimensions, body or reality, can we destroy and uncreate that?

Participants: Yes.

Dr. Lisa: Right, wrong, good and bad, POD and POC, all nine, shorts, boys and beyonds®.

Dr. Lisa: You know about the one, two, three's; one, two, three, four's; one, two, three, five's, those things? Let's do a couple of one, two, three, five's.

Ready?

Just take the energy and throw it right out there.

One, two, three, four, five. Let's break it up. One, two, three, four, five. Let's break it up. One, two, three, four, five. Keep going with your five. All the algorithmic, computations of all the lies of the fraud patrol around your money, your cash, your financial reality, can we destroy and uncreate it?

Please now, on three, give it to the earth.

One, two, three. One, two, three. One, two, three. On four, open the door to a new possibility just 1° more.

Right, wrong, good and bad, POD and POC, all nine, shorts, boys and beyonds®.

Lighter, heavier, more space, less space?

Participant: Lighter.

Dr. Lisa: Yes. Can you breathe a little bit now?

Participant: Yes.

Dr. Lisa: Because you've been carrying a lot of fraud on you and a lot of lies on you! We just did a booty dance, got them off you!

What have you made so vital, so valuable, and real about the fraud patrols of your financial reality, your monetary reality, your cash reality, money in general, linearity, relationships, families, spiritualty, sex and sexual freedom, ethnicity, law, cultural separation, humanoid embodiment, and healing that keeps you seeking the wrong-ness of you through them and everything you are? Everything that is, will you destroy and uncreate it?

Participants: Yes.

Dr. Lisa: Right, wrong, good and bad, POD and POC, all nine, shorts, boys and beyonds®.

Okay, the lies: who are you being with money, what are you being with money, what are you being with money and judgments, which we'll talk about separately. Your financial reality is based on the who, the what, and the judgments you're refusing to receive. Would you like to change that 1° more?

Participants: Yes.

Dr. Lisa: Just 1°.

Right, wrong, good and bad, POD and POC, all nine, shorts, boys and beyonds®.

Let's go to the who. Let's get them off you.

You didn't know you were going to a weight-release clinic, did you?

Right, wrong, good and bad, POD and POC, all nine, shorts, boys and beyonds®.

Dr. Lisa: Instead of get in my belly, it's going to be get out my belly.

Right, wrong, good and bad, POD and POC, all nine, shorts, boys and beyonds®.

I'll come up with some better jokes. First I'll have to fan myself with my hundred-dollar bills. Gary said laughter has the capacity to heal the planet. Let's laugh at the dissociative fugue of our money flows that we've created.

Right, wrong, good and bad, POD and POC, all nine, shorts, boys and beyonds®.

Okay. The who's are the vibrational, virtual reality, somebody else's vibrational, virtual reality, somebody else's hypnotic trance, somebody else's awarenesses or unconsciousness that they created that you thought was a good idea to adopt, too.

For instance, I remember my father. He used to take a stack of $100 bills, about 2,000 of them, and he'd put it on the counter by the side door in my childhood home for my mother. He'd do this each week on a Monday before he walked out the door.

When I was a kid, I was like, "Damn, yes."

Then, there was my mother…drumroll, please…who was so mad at him, so mad. It seemed nice – $2,000. He'd leave it just to get the hell out of there as quick as he could, feed her with money. She would take that money and she'd make us get things. Did we ever ask for them? Did we want them?

I didn't, because one of those things were 8 or 10 of those stupid, scary Cabbage Patch dolls. They'd have adoption papers or something. It was the big craze in the early 1980's. Then, she'd stick them in my room at the top shelf and I'd walk in my bedroom, "Oh my God! What is that?" Because we needed it.

Then, sneakers and clothes for me and my brother and my sister – just everything – and then it would be gone. We were in all these different activities. Again, never asked, forced to be in.

Cheerleading, I hated it. I still remember the cheer. "S-U-C-C-E-S-S. This is the way we spell success," whatever the team was. I hated every minute of it just like I hated standing up and modeling.

To me, money had many different points of views and meanings to me. It meant abuse. It meant resentment. It meant get out. It meant escape. It meant, "FU." It meant, "I'll get you."

The more she spent the money, the more he had to give the money, and the more he had to leave and work for the money. And the more he left and went to work for the money – well, as it turns out he created another family that he supported which we didn't find out until many years later. That's what he was doing.

Maybe I would, too, given what was going on there.

She got more and more and more and more resentful, more and more angry, more and more expensive, and all that resentment grew between the two of them.

Then they would say, "I love you" to each other.

Here I am, a little kid watching them. This is still on the 'who,' by the way – the first lie of money. There's a lot there.

Now you know why I'm standing up here doing this.

I know a lot about it.

Right, wrong, good and bad, POD and POC, all nine, shorts, boys and beyonds®.

Thank God when you do those 3,000 hours for your internship to become a licensed something, you have to go to therapy yourself.

Right, wrong, good and bad, POD and POC, all nine, shorts, boys and beyonds®.

They come in and say, "Oh, I love you."

"I love you, too."

And I'm looking at them like, "There's something going on there that is a lie, because underneath that is the belly of death and destruction and ice picks and guns and machetes and sickles and, and, and, and, and World War III."

I had to choose what I was going to be.

How do you choose as a child between your mother and father?

Right, wrong, good and bad, POD and POC, all nine, shorts, boys and beyonds®.

I chose the worst of them and the best of them as one does at age 3, 4, 5, 10, 15, or 20.

Right, wrong, good and bad, POD and POC, all nine, shorts, boys and beyonds®.

Dr. Lisa: Mostly, I hated her and everything with money, the way that she was. I blamed her for years. I loved him because I would sit in the basement with him and work and handle the rents on his apartment buildings. He was fun, she was mean. Or so the child in me believed.

Dr. Lisa: Right, wrong, good and bad, POD and POC, all nine, shorts, boys and beyonds®.

He was an accountant with a Masters in Business and Real Estate and, in the early 1980's, the whole big thing was apartment buildings and flipping foreclosures in New York, New Jersey, and all over the Hudson. He'd get 20-family apartment buildings for $10,000 because they were in foreclosure.

He made billions of dollars without putting billions of dollars out.

My job as a kid was to sit there in the basement with him. He had his desk. I had my desk. I felt so professional. And I would be away from her. Seriously.

I was like, "Yes, Dad!"

I was also learning a lot of other things. I would count the money. You remember those green ledger things and pencils? Remember pencils with erasers? Those old adding machines and whatnot?

Literally, it was in cash. It was an all-cash business. My job was to balance all the rents, count the money, and put it in order. That's why I still put my money in order to this day. I attribute this to him. You can tell the love in it. My hundreds stay with the hundreds. Everything is in order. I have no control issues. I'm not OCD. I just like my money ordered. That's what I used to do as a kid.

Stacks and stacks of money…

I licked it. I loved it.

I loved the way it smelled. I loved the way it tasted.

I even worked in a bank in the summers of my college years because I love money. I loved when the Brinks trucks would come by. I would go in there with them and play with all the jewels and the money. I learned that from him.

But it became this polarization about money because of what I thought about my mother, which you'd be hearing until next year if I started. She's been my best resource for my best stand-up comedienne stuff in my facilitation. I've learned so much from her.

I had to align and agree with him while resisting and reacting to her, and it created all these different lies around money. I had to actualize what he was saying to me in one way, but also what she was being for me in another way.

And when you actualize a disparate reality, you get nothing but catastrophe and crisis.

All of the disparate realities, incongruent realities that you are living financially as the 'what' of your reality, can we destroy and uncreate that?

Participants: Yes.

Dr. Lisa: Right, wrong, good and bad, POD and POC, all nine, shorts, boys and beyonds®.

Dr. Lisa: Everything that brings up and lets down and whoever it is that owns those disparate realities that you have aligned and agreed with and resisted and reacted as yours and created your current financial reality actually, can we destroy and uncreate that and revoke, rescind, recant, renounce, denounce, destroy and uncreate the forever commitment to it?

Participants: Yes.

Dr. Lisa: Right, wrong, good and bad, POD and POC, all nine, shorts, boys and beyonds®.

All the vibrational, virtual realities that you created related to them, the 'who's,' those 'who's' of those realities, can we destroy and uncreate those vibrational, virtual realities?

Participants: Yes.

Dr. Lisa: Right, wrong, good and bad, POD and POC, all nine, shorts, boys and beyonds®.

Dr. Lisa: Can we pull you out of them a little bit more, like 1°?

Right, wrong, good and bad, POD and POC, all nine, shorts, boys and beyonds®.

All the secret, hidden, invisible, covert, unseen and unacknowledged, unspoken, undisclosed agendas to the what, your mother, your father, your sister, your brother, your aunt, your uncle, your grandmother, your grandfather, your Italian-Irish heritage or whatever heritage you are that you're carrying, can we destroy and uncreate that?

Participants: Yes.

Dr. Lisa: Right, wrong, good and bad, POD and POC, all nine, shorts, boys and beyonds®.

On five, can we interrupt the algorithmic, mechanical, robotic amalgamation of your financial reality that isn't even yours?

Participants: Yes.

Dr. Lisa: One, two, three, four, five! One, two, three, four, five! One, two, three, four, five! One, two, three, four, five! One, two, three, four, five! One, two, three, four, five! One, two, three, four, five!

Can we return it to sender with consciousness attached and pull off the vibrational, virtual reality of the 'what' that isn't yours or pull back the financial acumen and the intelligence and brilliance that you truly be so you can actualize the 'what' that your financial reality truly is as the infinite being you truly be?

Participants: Yes.

Dr. Lisa: Everything that brings up and lets down, can we destroy and uncreate it?

Participants: Yes.

Dr. Lisa: Right, wrong, good and bad, POD and POC, all nine, shorts, boys and beyonds®.

On four, one, two, three, four. Open the door to a new possibility.

Right, wrong, good and bad, POD and POC, all nine, shorts, boys and beyonds®.

What is, who is your financial reality based on? Truth.

Participant: My mom.

Dr. Lisa: My mom! Who else?

Participant: My dad.

Dr. Lisa: My dad.

Participant: My community.

Dr. Lisa: Your community. All the moms, all the dads, and all the community of people that you thought were smarter than you that you'd like to adopt their financial reality as you, can we return that to sender with consciousness attached?

Participants: Yes.

Dr. Lisa: Get it off your body now and destroy and uncreate it.

Right, wrong, good and bad, POD and POC, all nine, shorts, boys and beyonds®.

For me, the 'what' with my father was, "Damn, I'll be happy to make billions of dollars." The 'what' with my mother was, "Damn, I'd be happy to be resentful and make somebody pay and pay and pay and pay and pay and pay and pay."

Right, wrong, good and bad, POD and POC, all nine, shorts, boys and beyonds®.

You're all laughing at that. All the slave owners that you've been in any lifetime, dimension, body, and reality to make someone pay and pay and pay, can we destroy and uncreate it?

Participants: Yes.

Dr. Lisa: Right, wrong, good and bad, POD and POC, all nine, shorts, boys and beyonds®.

Whose financial reality are you being?

Right, wrong, good and bad, POD and POC, all nine, shorts, boys and beyonds®.

Everywhere your mother's or your father's or your community's or whoever's financial reality that you're being the 'who,' that's the lock and you're the key.

You're the lock and that's the key.

We put the lock in the key and the key in the lock and all the locks and all the keys and all the keys and all the locks and all the locks and the keys and the keys in the locks and the locks and the keys and all the demons and the entities that you employed. If you think it was a good idea to keep employing them in this disparate reality of this lock and key, truth, who are you all?

Truth, and before that and before that and before that and before that and before that and before that and before that and before that and before that and before that and before that and before that.

Who will you be after that and after that and after that and after that and after that and after that and after that and after that? The deal is done. Your services are no longer requested, required, desired, wanted or needed. You get to leave now. Be free.

Take all your electromagnetic imprinting, chemical imprinting, biological imprinting, financial imprinting, chemical imprinting, neurotransmitter imprinting, cellular imprinting, financial imprinting, cash imprinting, money imprinting, and leave now. All pledging allegiance to the forces of darkness around money, can we destroy and uncreate it?

Participants: Yes.

Dr. Lisa: Right, wrong, good and bad, POD and POC, all nine, shorts, boys and beyonds®.

Dr. Lisa: Lock in the key and the key in the lock and the lock in the key and the key in the lock and set this free.

Right, wrong, good and bad, POD and POC, all nine, shorts, boys and beyonds®.

Light or heavy, more space, less space? We haven't got in to the 'what' yet.

All the lies that you're buying into to keep the 'who' here and not you here, could we destroy and uncreate those?

Participants: Yes.

Dr. Lisa: 1% more.

Right, wrong, good and bad, POD and POC, all nine, shorts, boys and beyonds®.

All the projections, separations, expectations, resentments, rejections, regrets to the 'what's' that you've made your financial reality that had nothing to do with you that keep you from existing as you, so that you'll never be financially free like you were born to be, can we destroy and uncreate it?

Participants: Yes.

Dr. Lisa: Right, wrong, good and bad, POD and POC, all nine, shorts, boys and beyonds®.

Participant 1: When you ask whose it is, I get everybody but mine.

I'm sitting here thinking, "I'm buying everybody else's financial reality but mine. What the heck is mine?" My whole brain goes, "I have no idea."

Searching for an answer is just a limitation.

When there's the energy of blank, what do you do with that?

Dr. Lisa: Excellent question. That energy of blank is actually the space and energy and consciousness of opening up to what is your financial reality by becoming aware that nothing has been your financial reality – so it's beyond.

Participant: Totally.

Dr. Lisa: All the beyonds, creating the beyonds, eternally the beyond that keep you in everybody else's financial reality and you call that you, can we revoke, rescind, recant, renounce, denounce, destroy and uncreate that right now?

Participants: Yes.

Dr. Lisa: On three, one, two, three. One, two, three. One, two, three.

Right, wrong, good and bad, POD and POC, all nine, shorts, boys and beyonds®.

Truth, if everybody's reality is your financial reality, what do you love about being the hoarding, storage, container of everybody else's interesting point of view about money and never being you around money?

Participant: All I could hear, instead of hoarding, was whoring.

Dr. Lisa: Very good. What do you love about it?

Right, wrong, good and bad, POD and POC, all nine, shorts, boys and beyonds®.

Listen. The whore gets the money.

Participant: I know. I may be a slut. I'm so wrong for the whore.

Dr. Lisa: A slut receives everything, everywhere.

Whatever makes unconsciousness, give me my body to be the whore and the slut that I truly be in this reality for all of eternity.

Right, wrong, good and bad, POD and POC, all nine, shorts, boys and beyonds®.

And would it be okay if you were the whore and the slut and that was your financial reality, i.e. the whore gets the money and the slut receives everything?

Participant: Yes.

Dr. Lisa: We'll get to the receive everything when I talk about Lie #3 – the judgment part of money – but I want to go with this for a second.

Right, wrong, good and bad, POD and POC, all nine, shorts, boys and beyonds®.

Dr. Lisa: So the whore – right there—that opened something up for you. But you also then judged yourself because, wherever this reality says something like a whore, there's energy there.

What's a whore? A slut.

What's a slut? A whore.

Participant: A cheap whore.

Dr. Lisa: A cheap whore, exactly.

So we can keep going back and forth and back and forth and back and forth on this, but you never get to claim, own, and acknowledge that there's some energy in the whore that is actually your financial reality.

I was telling you about me with my dad in the office. There's money all over the place. I'm like licking it. I'm putting it all over me. I'm sleeping with it – you know what I mean? I'm counting it up. I'm holding it. I know what $1,000 feels like.

I know how much it weighs. I know what $10,000 feels like. I know what $100,000 feels like. I know what it's like to get a $300,000 check. I know the density of it. I know how much it would fill a room to get billions of dollars.

That's a whore. I'm obsessed.

Participant: I'm obsessed with money.

Dr. Lisa: I know, but we make that wrong.

So wherever we make that wrong instead of a strong-ness, we develop another point of view.

It's insanity what we do to ourselves.

And then we lock ourselves out of where we be because this reality says a whore is something wrong. So of course, I wasn't going to be that, because to be that brings all the judgments back, which I will get to in Lie #3.

Right, wrong, good and bad, POD and POC, all nine, shorts, boys and beyonds®.

What is it that makes everybody else's financial reality more real than your financial reality?

Than you?

Everything that brings up and lets down, can we destroy and uncreate it?

Participants: Yes.

Dr. Lisa: Right, wrong, good and bad, POD and POC, all nine, shorts, boys and beyonds®.

Dr. Lisa: You being you is the gift of changing the energy, space, and consciousness of the planet's financial reality, let alone your financial reality and the future of this earth, because you're the one that will sit in these classes and take a look at this stuff.

Even 1° can turn and tilt the earth on its axis.

Right, wrong, good and bad, POD and POC, all nine, shorts, boys and beyonds®.

Lighter, heavier, more space, less space, something else?

Participant: It's lighter. It's great.

It's being willing to be that and then hide it, right?

Dr. Lisa: Exactly.

Participant: Being willing to be it and feel guilt.

I spent a week in California and Vegas and I was like a whore in the sense of money and joy and ease and fun. I was having dinners with the fanciest, coolest freaking people and, then, I'm like, "Oh, wait, but I better be quiet about it. Oh wait, but I better not be as excited and joyful about the reality I just created."

Participant: I feel like, "I'm a single mom. I better not have too much fun."

Dr. Lisa: Disparate reality.

Participant: Right.

Dr. Lisa: So I can be in Vegas because, you know, "What happens in Vegas stays in Vegas, baby," right? And you can do it in California because you know everybody just does whatever they want in California. You know that damn state. But then when you come here to Colorado, it's "I'm a mom. I feel so tight I can't breathe."

Right, wrong, good and bad, POD and POC, all nine, shorts, boys and beyonds®.

So the tightness that you're aware of – whose is it and what is it?

Participant: Not mine.

Dr. Lisa: It's not yours, so it doesn't matter. Stop trying to change it. Stop trying to be it. Be you.

Participant: Oh, the hiding isn't even mine.

Dr. Lisa: The hiding isn't even yours.

Participant: Okay, that changed it.

Dr. Lisa: How many people do you know that hide their money, and how much of you do you hide your money?

Participant: Yes.

Dr. Lisa: Would you have kept this in your wallet (stack of 100's in a gold money clip on table) and not shown that you had it, afraid somebody would have taken it?

Right, wrong, good and bad, POD and POC, all nine, shorts, boys and beyonds®.

Would you not have put this out and shown this because you would have been afraid of the judgments you would receive?

Right, wrong, good and bad, POD and POC, all nine, shorts, boys and beyonds®.

So, would you be willing to give up even 1% more of the 'who' that you've made your financial reality?

Participants: Yes.

Dr. Lisa: Right, wrong, good and bad, POD and POC, all nine, shorts, boys and beyonds®.

Now, the 'what.' What are you being when you're being the community – your mother, your father, the hiding, the not sharing – all the stuff that we've talked about.

What are you being? Truth.

What are you being with money when you're living the 'who's?' You're living in 'whoville' which is 'pooville.'

Participant: Well, I'm definitely not being me, but it's like I'm being everyone else's –

Dr. Lisa: What are you being? You're being everyone else's thoughts and feelings. And when that actualizes, what is that?

Participant: A lie.

Dr. Lisa: It's a lie. It's not true.

Participant: It's not me.

Dr. Lisa: It's not you.

So all the ways that you're being a lie that's not true, that's not you, and calling that your bank account, your net worth, can we destroy and uncreate that?

Participants: Yes.

Dr. Lisa: Right, wrong, good and bad, POD and POC, all nine, shorts, boys and beyonds®.

But, literally, what are you being when you're being a lie? How does it show up for you? What are you being?

Participant: A slave?

Dr. Lisa: A slave. Okay. And what's the posturing, the characteristics, the traits of a slave?

Participant: Working for others.

Dr. Lisa: Working for others. Can't have.

What else?

Participant: Suffers.

Dr. Lisa: Suffers. Oh, the martyr. Love it.

Participant: Tired.

Dr. Lisa: Tired. Constricted. That's the 'what'.

So here you are being the 'who' – your dad, your mom, community, the world, right?

And now you're being the 'what,' which is the slave, the "I can't, I won't."

We had a little bit of lightness and now it's like "Wahhh..." but when I put this wad of money out and waved it, everybody got happy.

This 'what' is a lie. And 'who' is it is not even yours, but you're actualizing it and you're living it. So then you become the slave. The constriction. The diseased one. The chronic, tired one. The "No matter how hard I try…I did so much… everything should have already changed by now. I spent so much money."

Right, wrong, good and bad, POD and POC, all nine, shorts, boys and beyonds®.

You know what happens when you believe?

You leave your body behind.

So all the 'what's' – this constriction energy – that you would risk everything for and leave your body behind for, can we destroy and uncreate it?

Participants: Yes.

Dr. Lisa: Right, wrong, good and bad, POD and POC, all nine, shorts, boys and beyonds®.

All the vibrational realities, the fake artificial realities that you've created underneath that and underneath that and underneath that and underneath that and underneath that and underneath that and underneath that and underneath that and this group – underneath that and underneath that. Underneath that and underneath that and underneath that and underneath that and underneath that – and all the implants and explants, secret and invisible, covert, unseen, unacknowledged, unspoken, undisclosed agendas underneath that and underneath that and underneath that and underneath that and underneath that.

I'm not just doing that for fun. I'm waiting for this energy to shift a little bit.

Underneath and underneath that and underneath that and underneath that. I'm not like a record player that's stuck for no reason. And underneath that and underneath that and underneath that and underneath that – can we destroy and uncreate it?

Participants: Yes.

Dr. Lisa: Right, wrong, good and bad, POD and POC, all nine, shorts, boys and beyonds®.

And can we fire all those people that you've hired to think this was smart to do?

Participant: Yes.

Dr. Lisa: So fire them all – and your severance package is that you actually get to create your financial reality. And who the hell cares what happens to them? Return to sender with consciousness attached.

So what is this energy when I said, "Who the hell cares, return it back to them?" What was that energy?

Participant: You're supposed to care.

Dr. Lisa: You're supposed to care for others, okay.

Everywhere that you thought it was a bad or a wrongness or that we were evoking some demonic death on them, can we destroy and uncreate it?

Participants: Yes.

Dr. Lisa: Right, wrong, good and bad, POD and POC, all nine, shorts, boys and beyonds®.

Dr. Lisa: Basically, you're just saying, "Go take care of your own shit. I've carried it long enough for you. But I'm choosing me. I'm committing to me. I'm collaborating with the universe conspiring to bless me, and I can't be bothered with you on me. I'm creating."

Right, wrong, good and bad, POD and POC, all nine, shorts, boys and beyonds®.

Everywhere that the 'what' of your financial reality told to you by the whomever that if you actually cared for you, you wouldn't be caring for them, can we destroy and uncreate that?

Participants: Yes.

Dr. Lisa: Talk about a disparate reality.

Right, wrong, good and bad, POD and POC, all nine, shorts, boys and beyonds®.

That's where that self-worth and net worth thing comes in.

Right, wrong, good and bad, POD and POC, all nine, shorts, boys and beyonds®.

Because I know for myself that when I'm choosing for me and I'm committing to me and I'm collaborating with the universe, conspiring to bless me and that I'm creating, I care about everyone, including me.

But I'm actually even smarter and I know when someone says something to me that they actually either want to change or they're just lying to me.

Do you know the difference?

What I mean by that is that everywhere you decide to help somebody when they didn't ask you for help, they're going to hate you. And then that is going to stick to you like glue.

So all their hatred, all their projection, all their separation, all their conclusionary realities that you've locked onto your body, creating the 'who' and the 'what' as your financial reality because you're stronger, you're smarter, you're better, you're more psychic, you're more aware, you're more conscious, can we destroy and uncreate that?

Participants: Yes.

Dr. Lisa: Right, wrong, good and bad, POD and POC, all nine, shorts, boys and beyonds®.

Dr. Lisa: And all the oaths, vows, fealties, commealties, commitments, agreements, binding and bonding contracts to that, can we destroy and uncreate it?

Participants: Yes.

Dr. Lisa: Right, wrong, good and bad, POD and POC, all nine, shorts, boys and beyonds®.

What is it going to take for all of us to stop allowing ourselves to use the capacity that we have of awareness to only share what someone can hear and stop helping others who actually don't desire to receive what we can provide?

Right, wrong, good and bad, POD and POC, all nine, shorts, boys and beyonds®.

Have you ever been in situations where you give so much and you give so much and you give so much, and then you keep giving, and you think the person is actually listening?

And you think you're actually helping but they're like talking right through you?

They're not taking anything you're saying in and then they go and do whatever they want to do anyway? That's what I'm talking about here.

So every time you push your information, your help, your awareness at somebody, what it does is bounces off of them and sticks back on you based in all of their judgments, lies, fixed positions, conclusions, computations, configurations, condemnations, incarcerations, incongruities and inconsistencies, incantations, invocations back on you times a godzillion?

So all your causal incarcerations, causal incarnations, causal incantations, causal invocations, causal inculcations, causal incongruities and inconsistencies back on you that you're holding as the 'who' and the 'what' of your financial realities, all because you desired to help and someone said, "Screw you," can we destroy and uncreate it?

Participants: Yes.

Dr. Lisa: Right, wrong, good and bad, POD and POC, all nine, shorts, boys and beyonds®.

Did that help?

Participants: Yes.

Participant: I noticed you seem to make a difference between cash and money. I don't understand that.

Dr. Lisa: Right, wrong, good and bad, POD and POC, all nine, shorts, boys and beyonds®.

There's a lot there. So say I don't understand that, I don't understand that, I don't understand that.

Participants: I don't understand that, I don't understand that, I don't understand that.

Dr. Lisa: Good, because when you try to understand, you're standing under somebody else's point of view and that is not you.

Right, wrong, good and bad, POD and POC, all nine, shorts, boys and beyonds®.

So just perceive the energy of cash right now. Perceive the energy of money right now.

What did you notice there?

Participant: Money felt heavier than cash.

Dr. Lisa: Money, to you, felt heavier than cash.

Participant: Money was bigger. Lighter.

Dr. Lisa: Both of them?

Participant: Yes, cash feels lighter. Money was even more cash.

Dr. Lisa: With money, you can change the world. With cash, you have the freedom to choose.

Can you flip it?

Absolutely.

You could flip it however it works for you, whatever's right and light for you. There's nothing set in stone.

I'm doing a workshop – a telecall series – called Losing the Lack of Cash Flow. I'm actually spending eight weeks just on cash, even though I know cash is money.

There is just something separate, and I don't really have a direct answer for you on that. I can give you my interesting point of view.

I know I have money in the bank and I know I have retirement and I know I have investments and I know I have that. And I know I have cash. But the cash that I'd like to have, I'd like to have in a different way than my money. I like to have it in my wallet, although not all my money is going to fit in my wallet.

When I'm traveling, which I do a lot around the world, I like having cash and lots of cash. I like always knowing that, for example, when you've been in India and your card gets stolen and you can't get back to the states and they don't know that you're you because your cell phone doesn't get the code that they need to send to you to tell them you're you and you've got no money and you can't get anywhere with it – that's energy that I don't want to be in.

And I've been in it one too many times, as well as seeing zero in my bank account one too many times.

So I like to have money and I like to have cash. I like to play with both of them. That's my interesting point of view.

Participant: So this is really good. Thank you for the clarification because it does take it somewhere else.

With cash then, to your point, I'm realizing that money feels more comfortable, safer, because it's almost intangible. Cash is tangible and, maybe because where I grew up, having that amount of cash caught a lot of attention and you can get robbed like that.

Going to the bank and getting a huge amount of cash was so scary.

Dr. Lisa: Where did you grow up?

Participant: Venezuela.

Dr. Lisa: Yes, I know it well. Venezuela, the country of two sets of books. What you show and what nobody knows. Or the Mafia or whatever. Right, wrong, good and bad, POD and POC, all nine, shorts, boys and beyonds®.

Participant: So having said that, I wonder if there is a lie behind it because I'm comfortable with the money, but when it comes to cash –

Dr. Lisa: There is a lie. You just said it, that, "If I put cash out, it would get robbed. I would get stolen from."

So there's the 'who' right there. That's the lie.

Right, wrong, good and bad, POD and POC, all nine, shorts, boys and beyonds®.

Let's say the lie is a hub of a wheel and you believe it.

You have to get the spokes of the wheel to keep that lie in place. And then you've got to put the rim around it to hold that wheel in place and then you've got to put the rubber around it and then you've got to do it again on the other side and on the other side and on this side until you're so locked into your HEPAD (handicapping, entropy, paralysis, atrophy destruction) which is an Access Consciousness™ body process. This is what you do every time you take a fixed point of view and you manufacture a reality based in your own limitation and eventual destruction.

You're so tightly wound up in your fixed point of view that nothing other than being robbed of your cash can come to you. So instead of "Money come, money come, money come," it's like, "Steal from me, steal from me, steal from me, please. Take from me, take from me, take from me."

Right, wrong, good and bad, POD and POC, all nine, shorts, boys and beyonds®.

So all the fixed points of views that you have to keep locking yourself into so that you can believe the lies of the 'who' and 'what' about your money that is you that keeps you actualizing in your reality exactly what you believe coming to you, thereby losing and leaving your body behind so that you never be you, can we destroy and uncreate it?

Right, wrong, good and bad, POD and POC, all nine, shorts, boys and beyonds®.

Would you be willing to give up 1% of that fixed position?

Participant: Yes.

Dr. Lisa: And what would that do to the land of Venezuela?

What would that do to you?

What would that do to everybody from this point forward in your life as you?

Right, wrong, good and bad, POD and POC, all nine, shorts, boys and beyonds®.

It's like, "Ask and you shall receive." The universe conspires to bless you. There isn't any discrimination between what you put out and what it gives you. It gives you exactly what you're asking for.

If you believe someone's going to lie to you, you're going to attract that lie. If you believe someone's going to steal from you, you're going to attract that thief. If you believe you need to help somebody and you can provide better than they can provide for themselves, you're going to get your stuff stolen or copyrighted, whatever.

Right, wrong, good and bad, POD and POC, all nine, shorts, boys and beyonds®.

They're all fixed positions.

Participant: So that limits the receiving as well.

Dr. Lisa: Limits? Yes.

If there's a bigger word for limits, that's true, yes. Limits you times a godzillion and a godzillion and a godzillion. There's no receiving in that. It's just a pile of poo. Your one-way ticket to crap-co.

Right, wrong, good and bad, POD and POC, all nine, shorts, boys and beyonds®.

Good question. Thanks for that.

So, we did the 'who's,' we did the 'what's'. Now we're going to do judgments.

Participant: I have a question that relates exactly to that.

Dr. Lisa: Please.

Participant: I know for me, it goes back to that fraud thing too, where if I put myself out there, then people call me a fraud or not to be able to be seen, because I won't even let them see.

There are a whole bunch of judgments that come back and, if I could do it all in secret, that'd be fine. But being open and vulnerable to all that judgment and the criticism – that's where everything gets heavy again, even though I know it's all a bunch of lies.

At the same time, not keeping and not buying it all the time feels really challenging.

Dr. Lisa: It's all a lie, and you know that, but it feels so true.

Participant: Right.

Dr. Lisa: So everywhere you're buying all the lies and still buying it – it's true because they feel so true that you believe them as true – can we destroy and uncreate that?

Participants: Yes.

Dr. Lisa: Right, wrong, good and bad, POD and POC, all nine, shorts, boys and beyonds®.

Everything around a judgment is a lie.

Every judgment is a lie because when you're judging, you're pointing the finger and you're saying someone or something else is that thing, which then gets it off of you because then you believe that thing.

But you took it from somebody else and wanted to get it off of them, and they made it them, right? And they took it from somebody else and they wanted to get it off them and then they took it from them and they wanted to get it off them, and then they took it from them and wanted to get it off them.

So from 4.2 trillion years ago until now, we get slammed with that. Isn't that great? The big 'kaboom!'

Right, wrong, good and bad, POD and POC, all nine, shorts, boys and beyonds®.

Which means none of you get to make any money or have the cash that you want because you'd rather believe the judgments as true.

Right, wrong, good and bad, POD and POC, all nine, shorts, boys and beyonds®.

Now, do you have a specific example of getting out and un-hiding, for instance, and then getting judged? Because I'll show you something.

Participant: Just simply trying to get people to do bars.

Dr. Lisa: What word did she use?

Trying.

Trying to get someone to do the Bars® is like telling somebody to defend against it, to choose no, or to have them run away and never talk to you again.

So stop trying and start being.

What invitation can you be about the Bars® to attract – if this is the business you would like to do to attract the people that would choose similar to you?

Right, wrong, good and bad, POD and POC, all nine, shorts, boys and beyonds®.

So, when I first did the Bars, for instance, my shoulders were up here off the massage table – control freak, right? After 15 minutes or so, they went here. And then in about 30 minutes, they start to go down and down and eventually they touched the massage table. I could actually experience some sort of relaxation or peace to ease that thing they were talking about.

Using something like that in a personal example will be more than an invitation, but people are still going to have their judgments of you.

So what's the worst judgment that you think you would receive if somebody did the Bars® with you – what would they say about your bars?

First thought, best thought.

Just for fun. Play with this.

Participant: That it's crazy.

Dr. Lisa: It's crazy.

Well, it is. It totally is. It's crazy.

Now, when you say that – imagining yourself offering a Bars® class or a Bars® session to somebody and they get the judgment to you that you're crazy – where does that hit you in your body?

Participant: I'm still in my head. It's hard for me to even notice the hits anywhere else in my body.

Dr. Lisa: Okay, so does it hit your head?

Participant: Yes.

Dr. Lisa: So, in your head, does it feel constricted or expansive when they call you crazy because of the Bars®?

Participant: It makes me shut down.

Dr. Lisa: So you get constricted and shut down.

I'd like everyone do this with me as I facilitate this with her, so pick a situation where you were recently judged.

For example, somebody e-mailed me recently and told me that they were no longer going to listen to me on Voice America. They wanted me to know that my viewership was one less person because I was facilitating somebody who had 'too many mother issues' and let them go on with their story too long. Apparently I'm not doing anything else on this radio show that they could listen to, so they wanted to let me know that they were not going to be listening to me.

When you get a judgment towards you like that, it's crazy, it's stupid.

When I first started doing energy work – before Access Consciousness™ when I cured myself of a life-threatening disease with energy healing and Theta Healing™ – I was so afraid of the licensing boards were going to call me up and take my license away because I put my hands on people. That's a pretty big judgment. Have you ever gone through a review like that? I've been through a couple of them. It ain't fun. So find judgments like that.

Everybody got one?

Take that energy, wherever you experienced it about whatever situation is in your life, and perceive where you feel it in your body. Now, for just a moment, expand your energy of space 500 million miles, up, down, left, right, front and back, still perceiving where that judgment hit you in your head or your body.

Whatever it is – your greatest fear, your biggest worry – and wherever it is – breathe energy in through the front of you, through the back of you, to the right, to the left, up through your feet, down through your head.

Now get as big as the earth.

And bigger and bigger, still perceiving that judgment.

Now, pull that judgment – "I'm crazy, you're crazy, you're an a-hole, you shouldn't be doing what you're doing, you don't deserve this license, that license, you're just narcissistic, you just want my money, you're a looney. You should be shot, killed, maimed, tortured, disemboweled (that's another lifetime) – whatever it is, just pull it all the way through you.

Pull it up through you and pull it out through you as big as the universe and say, "Body, what's beyond this? Body, what's beyond this? Body, what's beyond this? Body, what's beyond this?"

Right, wrong, good and bad, POD and POC, all nine, shorts, boys and beyonds®.

Now flip that molecule, wherever you perceive that energy in your body, if it's still there. Return that judgment to sender with consciousness attached and tell me what you notice.

Lighter, more expansive, or denser and constrictive?

Participant: Way more expansive.

Dr. Lisa: One, you didn't get locked into the judgment. Two, you took the judgment and expanded it as space. When judgment and density are hit with space, density releases.

Most of us constrict and defend and do the American thing, which is the litigious society thing. We go to a lawyer. Right? Constrict and defend. I'll get you.

Participant: Take all your money.

Dr. Lisa: Take all your money and go make you pay.

Instead of doing that with judgment, which is the intrinsic thing to do, we blast it out by expanding as space, pulling it through you, asking your body what's beyond it and creating space, which then gives you more options, more choices, more possibilities, and you're no longer stuck in somebody else's tar baby.

Right, wrong, good and bad, POD and POC, all nine, shorts, boys and beyonds®.

So with Bars™ and everything like that, yes, you're going to be seen as crazy. Absolutely. Name it as crazy. Be your own namer of the judgment. People will trust you more.

But do what I said or what I lead you through because that will open up the space to get out of the lie of the 'who' and the 'what' that you're making you that turn what you love to do – the Bars™, for instance – into poo, instead of the financial reality that is true for you.

Right, wrong, good and bad, POD and POC, all nine, shorts, boys and beyonds®.

Because whenever you're in judgments and you believe that, you lose money.

And whenever you receive judgments and perceive it through the universe like I'm speaking to now, you gain money.

When you're in choice and possibility and creation and generation, you're adding. When you're in the judgments, projections, separations, conclusions, expectations, resentments, rejections, regrets, you're like a leaking faucet tar baby, whack-a-mole.

You guys know what whack-a-mole is?

Everybody knows that game. Another leak is going to come up. There's another bill. Paid that one. There's another one. And then you get so much that you can't even pay it.

Right, wrong, good and bad, POD and POC, all nine, shorts, boys and beyonds®.

So all the judgments that you're afraid to receive, would you receive 1% more of them so that you could actually receive the financial prosperity and abundance that is truly yours?

Anything that doesn't allow that, can we destroy and uncreate it?

Participants: Yes.

Dr. Lisa: Right, wrong, good and bad, POD and POC, all nine, shorts, boys and beyonds®.

So as long as you hold onto the judgments, you limit the amount of money you can have and you limit the amount of money that you can receive from people. That's the really weird thing, so that's another lie.

The lie is that if you block the judgments, you'll be free.

But what I'm saying is, if you receive the judgments financially, you'll have more money, more cash and more choices.

Right, wrong, good and bad, POD and POC, all nine, shorts, boys and beyonds®.

So what are you unwilling to choose and what are you unwilling to receive that if you received it, would increase your financial net worth times a hundred godzillion?

Right, wrong, good and bad, POD and POC, all nine, shorts, boys and beyonds®.

And what would it take to create a hundred million dollars every day? Why do I use a hundred million? Because there's so many judgments in it and there's also so many ways that you can't even put in any form, structure, or significance around it.

When density meets space, density dissipates. When space meets density, space prevails. When space prevails, choice, possibility, contribution. Cha-ching, cha-ching, cha-ching. Money come, money come, money come, money come.

Say it with me: "Money come, money come, money come" being the slut and the whore you wish to be, or the john or whatever, of this reality.

Right, wrong, good and bad, POD and POC, all nine, shorts, boys and beyonds®.

Participant: Is it a judgment, or 'who' or 'what,' that tonight I have extreme fatigue listening to this. Actually, any time

I'm working around money, all I want to do is curl up and go to sleep.

Dr. Lisa: Great.

So who curls up and goes to sleep and wants to cry and feels fatigued around money in your life? Truth.

Participant: My mom.

Dr. Lisa: Your mom. And how old did your mom act around money? Truth.

Participant: 12.

Dr. Lisa: So all the ways that you've put your 12-year-old pre-adolescent in charge of your financial reality – the 'who' and the 'what' – all of that energy, can we destroy and uncreate it, and whoever it is and whatever it is for you?

Right, wrong, good and bad, POD and POC, all nine, shorts, boys and beyonds®.

The kid can't even drive and she's in charge of your financial reality.

Right, wrong, good and bad, POD and POC, all nine, shorts, boys and beyonds®.

Let me read the clearing again:

What have you made so vital and valuable and real about the fraud patrols of finance, reality, money, linearity, relationships, families, spirituality, sex and sexual freedom, ethnicity, law, cultural separation, humanoid embodiment, and healing, that keeps you seeking the wrongness of you through those fraud patrol points of views?

And everything they are as you're calling your financial reality and true?

Everything that brings up and lets down, can we destroy and uncreate it?

Participant: Yes.

Dr. Lisa: Right, wrong, good and bad, POD and POC, a nine, shorts, boys and beyonds®.

So what is your financial reality?

The entire time we talked about the lies of money – the 'who' you're being, what you're being, and the judgments you're refusing to receive. Clear all of those, or start to bring at least 1° of clarity to all of that.

Right, wrong, good and bad, POD and POC, all nine, shorts, boys and beyonds®.

Participant: Everything shows up easily. It's always there.

Dr. Lisa: And when you say everything shows up easily, money is always there and more, more, more, is it spacious and effervescent or is it a little dense and a little needy?

Participant: Less space for me.

Dr. Lisa: Great. More. More, more, more. Good. It comes up easily.

You've got to ask, though, if it has a charge on it at all.

If it's heavy or dense, it's a lie.

If it's like bubbly, like really good champagne and you're feeling light and airy and easy and space, space, space, then it's the truth.

Here's your assignment or your 'homeplay':

Ask, "What is my financial reality?" Write it down and stick it on your mirror, or put it on your notepad or speak it to your audio recorder.

Notice if it's a 'who' or a 'what' or 'judgment.' If it's a 'who' or a 'what,' then POD and POC it. If it's a judgment, learn how to receive it and then POD and POC it.

Now ask the question again, "What is my financial reality?" And that's the actual lightness of you.

So then start creating that. "What will this create if I'm that? What will this create if I'm that?"

If you're in a 'who' or a 'what' or refusing to see the judgments, ask yourself, "What will that create?" It's the same question, but two different perspectives.

You want to actualize the energy, space, and consciousness of your financial reality and you want to clear the actualization of the 'who', the 'what,' and the refusal to receive the judgments, so that you can actually receive your financial reality.

"So what can I be or do today to receive my financial reality right away?"

No wonder you guys are asleep. It's like you don't even know what your financial reality is.

Right, wrong, good and bad, POD and POC, all nine, shorts, boys and beyonds®.

Participant: I keep hearing this, "I don't get to have my own reality." It's this energy of 'obliterated.'

I don't get to have my reality.

Dr. Lisa: So when did you obliterate yourself and decide that you don't get to have your own reality? How old were you? Truth.

Participant: Three.

Dr. Lisa: Great. So all the ways that you stopped being you at the age of three and never allowed a financial reality, or anything else of your reality, to truly be, can we destroy and uncreate that?

Dr. Lisa: Right, wrong, good and bad, POD and POC, all nine, shorts, boys and beyonds®.

And revoke, rescind, recant, renounce, denounce, destroy and uncreate the forever commitment to always stay at three and to never move beyond the decisions, judgments, conclusions, and computations that you made then which is now still you?

Right, wrong, good and bad, POD and POC, all nine, shorts, boys and beyonds®.

Who were you at three? What were you at three? And what judgments did you refuse to be that, if you be the 'who' and the 'what' and what you truly be at three, would be the 1% and the 1° of your financial reality now?

Right, wrong, good and bad, POD and POC, all nine, shorts, boys and beyonds®.

So who were you at three? What were you at three? Truth.

Were you carefree? Were you not carefree? First thought, best thought. Don't think about your story.

Or your gory.

Right, wrong, good and bad, POD and POC, all nine, shorts, boys and beyonds®.

And maybe you don't know. What do you get a sense of?

Participant: Just a sense of the heaviness and the density that I went away from.

Dr. Lisa: Great. So how smart is that to go away from heaviness and density? It was a lie.

Were you aware at three? Did you make a good choice for you at three?

Participant: No.

Dr. Lisa: Great. Can you have gratitude for you at three years old right now?

Right, wrong, good and bad, POD and POC, all nine, shorts, boys and beyonds®.

And anywhere that that three-year-old is refusing to show up now and direct you in the awareness and the perception and the strength of knowing that she be, can we invite her to join you eternally?

Look at that smile on her face.

Everything that brings up and lets down, can we destroy and uncreate it?

Right, wrong, good and bad, POD and POC, all nine, shorts, boys and beyonds®.

Now I'm not saying for a three-year-old to be her financial reality, but for the three-year-old to come who can make a good decision for her, who was aware of the trouble, density, heaviness, that sucks.

"I'm out of here," that's pretty damn smart.

And you need to be that with money.

"If I buy this, will you make me money? If I choose this, what will this create?"

That's the energy she had. She had that freedom. She didn't have these HEPADS and fixed positions and choices that we as the adults make now. A-dolt. Adult.

Right, wrong, good and bad, POD and POC, all nine, shorts, boys and beyonds®.

You have to choose to be you. Choose to commit to you. Choose to collaborate with the universe, conspiring to bless you and choose to create.

So, again, the questions are:

What will this create?
Who am I being
What am I being?

If it's part of your financial reality, then receive the judgments and keep choosing for you, creating for you, collaborating with the universe conspiring to bless you, and then committing to what you know is true – like the three-year-old.

Everything that brings up and lets down, can we destroy and uncreate it?

Participants: Yes.

Dr. Lisa: Right, wrong, good and bad, POD and POC, all nine, shorts, boys and beyonds®.

What have you made so vital, valuable and real about the fraud patrols of finance, reality, money linearity, relationships, family, spirituality, sex, and sexual freedom, ethnicity, law, cultural separation, humanoid embodiment and healing that keeps you seeking the wrongness of you through them and everything they are?

Everything that is will you destroy and uncreate it times a godzillion?

Right, wrong, good and bad, POD and POC, all nine, shorts, boys and beyonds®.

I want to leave you with a couple of questions…

How can you create and generate money with the money you have?

Right, wrong, good and bad, POD and POC, all nine, shorts, boys and beyonds®.

And how can you create and generate cash with the cash you have?

Everything that brings up and lets down, can we destroy and uncreate it?

Participants: Yes.

Dr. Lisa: Right, wrong, good and bad, POD and POC, all nine, shorts, boys and beyonds®.

And what are you unwilling to do or be to have everything you desire with total ease?

Everything that brings up and lets down, will you destroy and uncreate it?

Right, wrong, good and bad, POD and POC, all nine, shorts, boys and beyonds®.

And how much money is the greatest amount of money you have decided you can have?

Everything that is, will you revoke, rescind, recant, renounce, denounce, destroy and uncreate the forever commitment where you locked, judged, decided, and concluded that that's the only the amount of money you can have?

Dr. Lisa: Right, wrong, good and bad, POD and POC, all nine, shorts, boys and beyonds®.

Remember, you're an infinite being who can create infinite possibilities with phenomenence and brilliance that this world has yet to see?

Never limit yourself. Never constrict yourself. Never cage yourself. Never destroy yourself.

And get out there and make so much money and share it with me.

Everything that brings up and lets down, can we destroy and uncreate it?

Right, wrong, good and bad, POD and POC, all nine, shorts, boys and beyonds®.

Money come, money come, money come, money come.

Thank you so much for your time. I appreciate your questions and vulnerability and smiles. Thank you for sharing your unconsciousness with me. That was really fun. I totally had a ball!

Never stay stuck in anything – you're amazing.

Be you, beyond anything and create magic…

Now go make some money!

Dallas

Speaker: Dr. Lisa is an amazing facilitator. She's all about excavation and getting down to her root of things. Welcome, Dr. Lisa.

Dr. Lisa: Hello everybody and thank you for coming out tonight.

I want you to take a moment and notice your body and mind – how you're sensing and feeling – because after I start talking and running some clearings, and clear some of this stuff around money, it might feel different in 20 or 30 minutes, more spacious.

In two hours, you won't even notice that there's walls here.

Right, wrong, good and bad, POD and POC, all nine, shorts, boys and beyonds®.

I'm going to tell you what that means in a minute.

I always bring out my wad in the beginning of this class because, well, it's fun. I really do have an obsession with hundred dollar bills. We give so much energy to this piece of paper, right? And it's really cool to have a 14-karat gold money clip to hold this money all together.

I say this because it brings up so many projections, judgments, fears, desires and anger. And this is what I do for a living – talk about all of those things over something like this.

I bring this out first, on purpose.

This is what we're going to talk about, the lies of what this creates. It's literally a piece of paper.

How many of you, including myself, have bended, folded, mutilated, and stapled yourself to try to make a hundred dollars, or even to make a dollar?

Participants: Yes.

Dr. Lisa: Right, wrong, good and bad, POD and POC, all nine, shorts, boys and beyonds®.

Dr. Lisa: Would you be willing to let go of that just 1° right now?

Participants: Yes.

Dr. Lisa: So I'm going to run the clearing statement. Has anybody not heard of the Access Consciousness clearing statement?

If not, you can go to ClearingStatement.com to see that the words I'll be using that sound like Mandarin actually have an explanation. They're acronyms for something.

Dr. Lisa: Right, wrong, good and bad, POD and POC, all nine, shorts, boys and beyonds®.

Think about it this way…

It's like when your computer gets stuck and the hourglass or Mac ball starts to spin and you don't know what's going on. So you're hit Control Alt Delete, or you just press the power button and shut it down. Then you reboot it and, all of the sudden, it works again, but you have no idea what happened.

Is anybody familiar with that?

Participants: Yes.

Dr. Lisa: That's what the clearing statement does.

You don't need to know what happened. You're not really sure exactly what happened, but you feel a little better. You sense things a little better. You get a little clearer.

Whatever the conflict was in your life before – the tension, heaviness, density – it's cleared and then there's space.

My favorite words these days are, "When density meets space density dissipates." So would you be willing to dissipate 1° more of the density that you hold around money?

Participants: Yes.

Dr. Lisa: Around cash?

Participants: Yes.

Dr. Lisa: Around your investments?

Participants: Yes.

Dr. Lisa: That you're carrying for your mother?

Participants: Yes.

Dr. Lisa: That you're carrying for your father?

Participants: Yes.

Dr. Lisa: That you're carrying for your brother and your sister?

Participants: Yes.

Dr. Lisa: Your generations before you, just 1%, it's getting heavier now and for the generations after you, just 1%, would you let go of a little bit more of it?

Participants: Yes.

Dr. Lisa: Right, wrong, good and bad, POD and POC, all nine, shorts, boys and beyonds®.

I just used the Access Consciousness clearing statement to clear that.

I've done a lot of training. I'm licensed as a psychologist, a marriage/family therapist, I have a Master's degree in Theta

Healing™, I'm an Access Consciousness™ certified facilitator, and I'm a body class facilitator. I also have psychodrama/dream drama training.

I don't say this to pat myself on the shoulder or for you to pat me on the shoulder. I say it because I had a life threatening disease that I cured with an energy healing modality called Theta Healing™.

Using these energy modalities, I healed a life threatening disease after the doctor told me that I had three choices: to kill it, take it out, or live on medication for the rest of my life.

I told him there had to be another way, and he said, "There isn't."

That was the first and last time I ever saw him.

And I still have all of my organs and I'm not on the medications.

When I started learning that I could cure life threatening diseases without medications, hospitalizations, anesthetization, or anybody else's help other than me and my choice, I decided that, as a coach, a therapist, and psychologist, my clients needed to know about it.

Of course, I was a little scared at first about getting complaints to the Board of Behavioral Health Services in California because you can't even put your hands on people without a certain separate certification to allow that.

I was nervous about taking this route, but it didn't matter to me because I had a disease. I was on the couch and I couldn't get off it. I was in pain.

I lost my business, my practice, my retirement, my savings, my house – I lost everything, in one respect.

Have any of you ever been to that point with money where you have nothing? Where you actually have zeros in your account?

Participants: Yes.

Dr. Lisa: I don't wish it on anybody, but that's the true story.

There was a time in my life I had nothing but zeros looking at me. There was nobody to turn to, there was nobody I could ask, there was nothing I had left and I had to make a decision that no matter what it took, I was going to change whatever that was that wouldn't let me have money, that couldn't let me have money.

And what I found out was that it had nothing to do with anything outside of myself.

It had everything to do with what was in myself and what my belief systems were.

I don't know if you know this, but whenever you believe something, you leave your body behind.

Everything that brings up and lets down, can we destroy and uncreate it?

Participants: Yes.

Dr. Lisa: Right, wrong, good and bad, POD and POC, all nine, shorts, boys and beyonds®.

How many of you came here because you thought this would finally give you the answer to your money problem?

Participant: At least a little bit.

Dr. Lisa: At least a little bit, okay. A little of bit of honest.

Right, wrong, good and bad, POD and POC, all nine, shorts, boys and beyonds®.

What are these lies about money that say, "There must be something wrong with me that I can't get what everybody else can about this?"

Well the truth is, there's nothing wrong with you.

It's just a choice.

What was it about me that couldn't have money? I mean, I made lots of money. I have a lot of degrees, education, training. I could always work. I started out with a paper route from the time I was 8 and worked at Dunkin' Donuts making donuts at 14.

I always had money, always worked, but never had ease with money.

I've always made every penny that I've ever put out. If I couldn't work, I didn't make money. I learned that very early on from my father, gratefully, although, later, it also caused some problems.

He used to have a joke whenever I needed money. He'd say, "Alright, I'm going to go down to the basement, to the printing press, and it'll show up in your account."

Growing up like that created a little fantasy about money, because I thought everybody should just go down to the basement, print the money, and then it would just show up in my account.

Participant: Oh, lord.

Dr. Lisa: When he died, I was overseas in Australia. I didn't even know he was sick or had left me as the executor of the will.

Everything he'd ever given was completely stripped away from me in the moment he died. It's different now, but in that moment, the entire way that I had lived was over. No backing, no plan.

And this is after the life-threatening illness.

My first moment with zero, standing at a gas station, not knowing how I was going to get gas as a professionally licensed, educated person, was quite the pill to swallow. I literally bawled my eyes out trying to figure out what the fuck I going to do. I'd never had this happen.

What I'm talking about might be kind of extreme to some of you, and you might be wondering, "Why the hell did I come to this person to listen to her talk about this. I don't have that experience."

I get it.

But I always say to the practitioners I work with that you can only teach and facilitate something as far as you've gone yourself.

Participants: Yes.

Dr. Lisa: Have you ever told your story and they don't know squat about what you're saying, but they're telling you they do?

You can feel it.

It's like you can put your hand through them and you think, "Yes, here's $225. You'll never see me again, but I'll pay and learn the lesson to not come back to you."

Money is something I've struggled with – and also something I've been very successful at. And it's something that I'm still growing with because I don't have all the money that I desire in the world.

I'm not 100% set the way that I would like to be set, but I can tell you this: I'm going to get there no matter what – no matter what it takes, no matter what I have to lose, no matter what I have to close down, no matter what I have to shut off, no matter where I have to move, no matter what I have to do, no matter what part of the world calls me.

I'm going to choose what's light and right and what works best for me financially, emotionally, spiritually, and physically.

That's how money comes to thee.

Money comes to the party of fun. Money comes to what's light and right for you. Money comes when you're living true to you. Money comes when you're authentic. Money comes when you're happy. Money comes when you run Bars™.

Participants: Yay!

Dr. Lisa: Do you want to know what the best defragmenter tool is for that computer issue?

Get your Bars™ run.

I've never liked to listen to people facilitating when they say that they have it all together. I don't actually trust it when they have it all together and they know everything, or they've been there and they've done that. I don't trust it. I trust an authentic, genuine story.

We've all got stuff. We all have baggage.

There are all these areas of your life – physical, mental, emotional, spiritual, psychological, psycho-somatic, psycho-energetic, psychic, relational. There are always four or five areas that run really well for you, and then one or two or three that don't.

For me, and for a lot of the clients that I've worked with, the areas that I've had the most difficulty with are money, body, health, and relationships.

Some of you know my story, but I had a very sordid history with money growing up.

As a child, I was forced to model in New York –and was prostituted during that time. When I told a family member what was going on behind the scenes of the modeling agency, they told me I was lying, and I left it at that.

As a result of how I looked, I know what I hated about money.

I know what I hated about receiving.

I know what I hated about my body.

I know my skeletons and I know what's in my closet – the abuses that I suffered – and I speak every day to 205,000 listeners a week on my Voice of America show about moving beyond the abuse, financial abuse, sexual abuse, limitations, and constrictions to what I've termed radical aliveness, which means choosing for you, committing to you, collaborating with the universe conspiring to bless you and then creating.

Today, there's nothing hiding anywhere under any carpet. I'm not afraid of anything. I can face anything. I have lost it all. I have gained it all. I have moved. I've let go of my practice. I've let go of a business. I've created it again. I've closed it down. I've created it again.

I've written books. I've put books out. I haven't put books out.

I just keep choosing what's light and right for me, no matter what trauma, no matter what tragedy, and no matter what story I have.

Would you be willing to give up 1% of your tragedy, trauma, and story that actually actualizes not having all you desire with money and while you may not have all you desire with your body, while you may not have all you desire with your relationships, while you may not have all you desire with your business?

1%.

Would you be willing?

Participants: Yes.

Dr. Lisa: Right, wrong, good and bad, POD and POC, all nine, shorts, boys and beyonds®.

And all the decisions, judgments, conclusions, and computations, that you made at an age, time, place, situation or person or with any person, known or unknown to lock you into those vibrational, virtual, realities of not enough: "I'll never have enough. I'll never be able to do enough. No matter how hard I work, I'll never get there. It's easier for everybody else, not for me. Sure she can do it because she has that or he can do it because he has that, but I don't have that."

Would you be willing to give up those decisions, judgments, conclusions, computations, and configurations that actually prevent you from choosing for you, committing to you, collaborating with the universe, conspiring to bless you and then creating for you? 1%?

Participants: Yes.

Dr. Lisa: Anything that doesn't allow that.

Right, wrong, good and bad, POD and POC, all nine, shorts, boys and beyonds®.

Participant: Why are you letting us give up 1%? Is that a lie? I'm thinking all of it.

Dr. Lisa: I'm doing a telecall series called *Losing the Lack of Cash Flow* and the co-facilitator on the call with me asked the same question, "Lisa, why are you always saying 1%?"

I say 1% because who can't give up 1%?

I also say 1% because I know how humanoids work. Humanoid is a term in Access Consciousness™ that puts you in a different energetic class.

Participant: Exactly.

Dr. Lisa: So 1% because I know what it takes for all of us. We get motivated when we hear we can only do a certain amount. I don't know why that is, but anybody can do 1% realistically. In Access they say humanoids are motivated by what you tell them they cannot do.

I figure that if I say 1%, then I know you're all going to go for 99%. That's the manipulation, right?

Right, wrong, good and bad, POD and POC, all nine, shorts, boys and beyonds®.

However, there's different limitations and constrictions with abuse, so in my other classes that are not Access Consciousness™ classes, when I'm dealing with the intricacies of trauma – post traumatic stress disorder and flashbacks and a 3-year-old, let's say, being raped, I'm not going to ask them to be a humanoid in that moment.

I'm going to guide them to the choice – and all I'm asking them to give up is 1%.

And when you give somebody who's been disempowered and forced to do something they did not want to, although maybe they had some part in choosing loosely, when you give that empowerment back to them, that 1% is a 100%.

I know from that moment – suddenly, molecularly, genetically, circuitry, neurotransmitter, the brain chemistry – they will never ever, ever, ever, ever, not have that route again.

Just from that 1%, and that's why I say it.

One of the things I do in my *Art of Fantastical Facilitation* series is work with practitioners and show them how to use the clearing statement and all these beautiful tools that I'm going to show you throughout the evening.

We still have the rest of the world to talk with and, if you want to have a practice and have people come to you, you can't alienate them with a language that they don't understand, right?

Participants: Yes.

Dr. Lisa: So sometimes I use Access language and sometimes I don't.

1% is my way so I cover everyone – humanoids and the rest of the world.

Participant: Oh that's fun.

Dr. Lisa: It's fun, right? Because we're all here to choose more consciousness.

No matter what you do, I don't know all of you, I believe you are healers of some sort – practitioners, educated, consciousness seekers.

I get the real deep sense that each of you have your own ROAR – the physical actualization of your own tsunami, volcano, earthquake – that lives within you, and that, by you being you, you change the world.

At Safeway, at Whole Foods, on your horse, with your children, with your partner, with yourself, in your money flows, and in your business, would you be willing to step 1% more into your own ROAR, whether it's the first time you've heard of it or not, or it's the eighth millionth time you sensed the energy of what I'm saying or not?

Yes?

Participants: Yes.

Dr. Lisa: Everything that doesn't allow that will you destroy and uncreate it?

Right, wrong, good and bad, POD and POC, all nine, shorts, boys and beyonds®.

And all the ways that you're disbelieving that you even have a ROAR, can we destroy and uncreate that?

Participants: Yes.

Dr. Lisa: Right, wrong, good and bad, POD and POC, all nine, shorts, boys and beyonds®.

So what does this all have to do with money?

It has to do with this: Truth, light or heavy?

Light is kind of bubbly and expansive like really good champagne. You know the bubbles are good at top.

Participant: I can taste it now.

Dr. Lisa: There you go. I was speaking to the right woman.

The density, the heaviness, is like crawling up in a ball. Maybe you feel it in your gut. It's constricted. It's limitation. You might get a little tired or a big yawn.

So here's my question to you:

Are you living your financial reality? Truth? Light or heavy?

A lot of you.

If you didn't raise your hand and are living your financial reality, here's what I'm going to ask you:

Do you have everything that you desire? Truth? Light or heavy? No right or wrongness.

Participant: Heavy.

Dr. Lisa: Exactly.

Here's the first of three questions you can use all the time when it comes to money. Write them down:

1. *Who are you being?*
2. *What are you being?*
3. *What lie are you buying into?*

So "Who are you being, what are you being, and what lie are you buying into?"

Very simple...

Now, that may not seem related to money or cash or anything like that, but I can tell you that, tonight, you'll start seeing something – that what you thought was your financial reality isn't, and the energy that you put into your financial reality that isn't.

And you'll expose the lie that you've made true, but isn't.

You'll actually start to take off the blinders, the cloak, the costume that you've been wearing in your bank account, in your business, in your sexual relations, in your relationship, in your parenting, in your relationship with your animals, in your relationship with your cars, in relationship with the Earth.

And when you start unveiling the cloak, then you start to unveil you.

That's when you ROAR, that physical actualization of the rumble, the earthquake, the tsunami, the volcano – uniquely and solely you – starts to come forth.

That's when providence moves, too, and things start to come your way.

It's not the parking angels that give you the parking spaces, my friends.

It's you stepping up to be up to be more of you.

For instance, after a 90-day notice, I terminated all my staff. Every single person.

Participant: Are you hiring?

Dr. Lisa: Not in these 10 seconds.

It was the largest risk I have ever done to choose for me in terms of my business – because I was being something that, in the business, wasn't working. Trying to get people to work for me wasn't working.

There was an energy that I was being – it was like the telephone game. I'd say, "Get task A done," and it became something in Mandarin and Russian and Spanish, and when it came back to me they'd say, "Here, I did it," I'd say, "But that isn't what I asked for exactly."

It's sort of an extreme example, but the best that I can explain it.

And then there was this other energy around the lie of the way that I had to make money, which is to work myself to the bone. Notice what I said about my father from the beginning: work really hard and not have any ease.

Doing that in 90 days wasn't a binge and a purge kind of thing. It was very pragmatic in timing. I'd say, "We're getting close to 30 days, here's what we have to hit. Here's the target. Let's do this, ba da da da da." It was very clear all along, but I have to tell you, I am scared shitless.

Absolutely, totally vulnerable.

I have to thank Gary Douglas, because he asked me, "What is it costing you to keep them? How much is it costing you to keep your staff?"

"My health, my grey hair. I'm getting some more."

Then I said, "I really want to go with this other marketing firm that I think can take me where I really want to go and what I really want to be doing with the books, certification program, and all of that to transition trauma off this planet.

"Get to work, you. How much is costing you not to do it?"

That's Gary Douglas for you.

And it was so light for me when he said that, but it was also scary because, I don't know about you, but I don't like doing paperwork. I don't like looking at my InfusionSoft system for a contact. I don't even know how to get into my InfusionSoft system.

I'm sharing this with you because I'm actually living what I'm talking to you about tonight. I refuse to live by the lie of money and I refuse to be a slave to money anymore. I've refused to be a slave to abuse anymore, just like I refuse to be a slave to anything other than what's light and right and part of my ROAR (Radically Orgasmically Alive Reality).

So would you all like to join me in that?

Participant: Yes.

Dr. Lisa: And let go of anything that doesn't allow you 1% more to live, know, be, receive, and perceive who you truly be beyond this reality and bring it into this reality. Yes?

Participant: Yes.

Dr. Lisa: Everything that doesn't allow that.

Right, wrong, good and bad, POD and POC, all nine, shorts, boys and beyonds®.

So notice…is it getting heavier and denser in here or lighter and freer?

Participants: Lighter.

Dr. Lisa: Do you have anything you'd like to ask?

Participant: Gosh, so many things.

Let's start with my job. I'm making an hourly wage and I'd like a big-girl salary job and, ultimately, my own company. I just feel really, really pissed off that I'm here when I know that I can be here.

Dr. Lisa: So who are you being when you're here?

Participant: My mom.

Dr. Lisa: And what do you love about being your mom in your job? What do you love about schlepping it to work with you every day? Taking your breaks at work with your mom.

Participant: It sucks.

Dr. Lisa: Eating for her.

Right, wrong, good and bad, POD and POC, all nine, shorts, boys and beyonds®.

And how many of you are doing the same thing with your moms? So who are you being your mom? What do you love about being your mom?

Participant: It's safe.

Dr. Lisa: Okay. So tell me what's actually safe about carrying your mom around eating for her, thinking with her, making your choices about your business with her when you want to be over here, but you're staying here.

Truth.

What's the lie that you're living by?

Participant: I'm not good enough until you have that.

Dr. Lisa: You're not good enough to have what it is she wants. You're not good enough to have what you want. Truth?

Right, wrong, good and bad, POD and POC, all nine, shorts, boys and beyonds®.

Anybody else want to give up 1% of "I'm not good enough to have what I want?"

Participants: Yes.

Dr. Lisa: Right, wrong, good and bad, POD and POC, all nine, shorts, boys and beyonds®.

So what do you love about not being good enough to have what you want?

Participant: I don't have to put myself out there.

Dr. Lisa: If you don't have to put yourself out there, what's the best part of that?

Participant: You can hide.

Dr. Lisa: And if you get to hide and you don't put yourself out there, what's the best part of that while you and mom stay behind your desk and your salary, hourly, wage? And you never get to be where you want to be?

Participant: It hurts so much.

Dr. Lisa: I know.

All I'm doing is connecting with her energy and the words are coming from that. I can feel the constriction in her chest and she's kind of caving in as she's getting her bars run.

Right, wrong, good and bad, POD and POC, all nine, shorts, boys and beyonds®.

But this is what we do.

She's making a decision about not having what she wants by choosing to stay connected to what her mother is. Do you think that's going to affect your money flows?

Participant: Yes.

Dr. Lisa: Energetically? Did your mom like money?

Participant: No.

Dr. Lisa: Did your mom like her work?

Participant: No.

Dr. Lisa: Did she stay at her work when she didn't want to be at her work?

Participant: She can retire right now, but she's not.

Dr. Lisa: So did she stay at her work when she didn't want to stay at her work?

Participant: Yes.

Dr. Lisa: Exactly.

Are you staying at your work when you don't want to stay at your work?

Participant: Yes.

Dr. Lisa: Right, wrong, good and bad, POD and POC, all nine, shorts, boys and beyonds®.

Now, please, unless it's light and light for you, don't leave here and quit your job if you don't have something else in place, because I think there's also a way to be pragmatic.

Your job is giving you money, but your business and your ROAR is where you really want to be – and that will give you everything, including money. Most of us choose to stay because of the money and we neglect our being-ness by choosing what you're choosing.

Right, wrong, good and bad, POD and POC, all nine, shorts, boys and beyonds®.

So everywhere your mom is the lock and you are the key and you are the lock and your mom is the key. Can we put the lock and the key and the key and the lock and the lock and the key and the key and the lock and all the locks and all of the keys for all of you together and begin to set this free?

Participant: Yes.

Dr. Lisa: Right, wrong, good and bad, POD and POC, all nine, shorts, boys and beyonds®.

You know what a lock and a key is? It opens things, so we put them all together and we unlock things. We can start to unlock this.

Right, wrong, good and bad, POD and POC, all nine, shorts, boys and beyonds®.

Some of you don't want to leave your mamas. There was a movie called Throw Mama from the Train. You might want to watch it.

It's a really funny movie, but can you perceive the energy of this in the room, and you're being a great example, so thank you for allowing me to put you on the spot and choosing to go with it because this is the energy that most of us have around money.

I did a workshop in California for 15 years called LEAP – my own creation that stood for the *Life Empowerment Action Program*. One day, we got a big white piece of paper and one of my assistants drew money on it. I had everybody take a black pen and I said, "Write down all your projections on money – all your hatreds, all your whatever."

I thought there would be maybe three.

Oh my god, I couldn't even see the money anymore.

There were the most horrific phrases I've ever seen written out – and I grew up living in a very loud spoken caustic environment.

I was so amazed at all the judgments and all the hatreds, prejudices, condemnations, enslavements, obligations, oaths, vows, fealties, comealties, and curses that everybody felt about money.

For instance, what did your mother believe about money?

Participant: You got to sell your soul to the devil to get ahead.

Dr. Lisa: Oh god, yes. Sign me up, sell my soul to the devil. Rub it on me, right?

So that's going to make you go away from money.

Right, wrong, good and bad, POD and POC, all nine, shorts, boys and beyonds®.

And you're carrying her in your heart, so every time you make money, this is what you're hearing, "Sell your soul to the devil."

Right, wrong, good and bad, POD and POC, all nine, shorts, boys and beyonds®.

But we choose this all the time covertly. You didn't know you were carrying your mom like this, did you?

Participant: No.

Dr. Lisa: Well, would you like to make more money?

Participant: Yes.

Dr. Lisa: Because if you keep unlocking this with that key and lock thing, you'll actually allow more receiving, because you're telling me that she believed money was the devil, essentially.

Devil is just lived spelled backwards, you guys. Desserts is stressed spelled backwards. It's like a trick of this reality.

Everything is the opposite of what it appears to be. Nothing is the opposite of what it appears to be.

Right, wrong, good and bad, POD and POC, all nine, shorts, boys and beyonds®.

But as long as we go through life somnambulantly, numb and anesthetized through life, we don't ever have to change our jobs. We don't ever have to change our money flows and you never have to go for what you want.

You want something big, don't you?

Participant: Hell, yes.

Dr. Lisa: Anybody else want something bigger than what you got?

Participants: Yes.

Dr. Lisa: You've got to get mama and daddy and all the culture and the Vatican and whatever other church you believe in out of your body so that you can hear you.

That's the "Who am I being?" question.

Now 'what' are you being?

When you're being your mom, money is the root of the devil incarnate times a godzillion, 'what' are you being?

Participant: A pussy.

Dr. Lisa: Okay, when you say the word pussy as the energy of 'what' your being, what are your thoughts? What do you guys hear?

Participant: Scared. Thin.

Dr. Lisa: What else?

Participant: Wimp.

Dr. Lisa: What else?

Participant: Paralyzed.

Participant: Shrinking.

Participant: It's also like a held down by the man.

Dr. Lisa: Okay, so all of that energy, how much can you receive when you're being in that energy?

Participant: Not like that.

Dr. Lisa: Like not.

Okay, so that's 'what' are you being. You're being a held down, scared, paralyzed, constricted pussy held down by the man.

I didn't say that, though – she said it.

Participant: Yes.

Dr. Lisa: Right, wrong, good and bad, POD and POC, all nine, shorts, boys and beyonds®.

Check in with your chest. Is it lighter or heavier?

I know mama is still there, but...

Participant: A little more space, but I see cage bars.

Dr. Lisa: So focus on that space because when space meets density, density dissipates. When your body feels a little bit more space, even though there's density there, focus on the space.

Most of us focus on the density and the density is the lie.

You cannot change a lie. You can only change the space and the truth.

The space, the truth, is the lightness within you, so focus on the molecules of space inside of you and ask them to keep turning and turning and turning and turning and turning and turning and turning and turning and turning and turning and turning and turning and turning and turning and turning and turning until more of you steps inside of you. And less of your mom stays in you.

Just see how you do 1°. That's a 1° shift right there to get space like that. That's a success, right?

Right, wrong, good and bad, POD and POC, all nine, shorts, boys and beyonds®.

So in whatever walk of life that you do facilitation that says, "Unless I get it all, I haven't succeeded or nothing changed," can we destroy and uncreate that?

Participants: Yes.

My dad was Italian type. You know, "You have to work really hard." He didn't say that, but I saw him leaving the house every morning. So sometimes I ask myself, "Am I really working hard for my money?"

Dr. Lisa: Oh, that sounds fun. "Let me limit myself with you. Let me bend, fold, mutilate, and staple myself into your limitation."

Everywhere all of you have done that a little, a lot, or a megaton of mocha choco-latte, can we destroy and uncreate that 1°?

Participants: Yes.

Dr. Lisa: Right, wrong, good and bad, POD and POC, all nine, shorts, boys and beyonds®.

And all of the people's realities, financial realities that you've embodied consciously or unconsciously, known or unknown, creating the artificial reality that you're calling you, can we revoke, rescind, recant, renounce, denounce, destroy and uncreate just 1° of that.

Participant: Yes.

Dr. Lisa: Right, wrong, good and bad, POD and POC, all nine, shorts, boys and beyonds®.

And can we return the energy to them with consciousness attached?

Participants Yes.

Dr. Lisa: So this is something we do in Access.

Everybody, take your hands and pretend like you're grabbing something. Just grab some of the energy and throw it right out in front of us on the count of three. Return the energy of whoever you're carrying back to them with consciousness attached.

Ready, one, two, three. And do it again, one, two, three, one, two, three, one, two, three.

And on four, right out in front of you again, let's open the door to a new possibility. One, two, three, four, expand your energy as space.

Just think it, perceive, 500 million miles up, down, right, left, front, and back.

Breathe energy in through the front of you, in through the back of you, in through the sides of you, up through your feet and down through your head.

Just think it, perceive it, know it, be it, say hi to your body.

Yes, that is your body right underneath you.

Hi, body, hi, body, hi, body.

I like to tell everybody in my classes that I have hammocks out there for them, with heat lamps and coconuts brought by their favorite gender, male or female in skimpy whatever, and they'll be fed coconuts right off the tree all day long – and I only request one thing of them: That their heads roll out on the hammocks and they never bring their head into my class.

I only want their body.

Why do I do that? It's because our mind is 10% of our body and our body is 90%, but we live in our head and make all of our decisions here, yet everything that can change anything is stored in the body.

You're perceiving knowing, being, receiving, being. It's here in your body and that should inform your mind.

Then, together, bam!

But when we just come from our mind, leave our body behind, we limit our choices.

I don't know about you, but I like to have a plethora of choices:

> *What will this create?*
> *What will that create?*
> *What will this create?*
> *What will that create?*

When you're in your head and you have a fixed position, you can only create the fixed position.

You can't create the possibility.

So everywhere all your fixed positions about money are actually limiting tens of thousands of dollars coming to you right now, would you be willing to give up 1% more of your fixed positions?

Participants: Yes.

Dr. Lisa: Right, wrong, good and bad, POD and POC, all nine, shorts, boys and beyonds®.

Do you know what a fixed position is?

Everything that you know, that you're right about and everybody else sucks and is wrong. That's a fixed position.

Participants: Yes.

Dr. Lisa: Right, wrong, good and bad, POD and POC, all nine, shorts, boys and beyonds®.

Dr. Lisa: As a facilitator, if I came in with that energy that everything you're saying is wrong and I have the right answer, I couldn't ever facilitate anyone or change anything in a group like this.

As a facilitator, I have no position. I'm just sharing and then I'm listening, sharing and listening, and I'm still working with her. That was just the first level.

Participant: Yes.

Dr. Lisa: Can I ask you a question?

Is your dad with you right now? Yes, or no?

Participant: Yes.

Dr. Lisa: Say no.

Participant: No.

Dr. Lisa: Light or heavy, which one's lighter?

You're thinking too much, your head's not on the hammock.

Dr. Lisa: So he's with you.

Participant: His heaviness. I think so.

Dr. Lisa: Absolutely, he's absolutely with you. He was not wanting to be seen, but I see him. He's right with you.

She's not so abnormal, okay? She carries around her dad, and all of us carry around our parents. But get rid of anybody that you're carrying around and it's the best weight loss thing – if you want to release some things – and some chronic diseases, as well.

So truth, what do you want to do with it? What do you want to do with him now that you know that? Want to keep him in you?

Participant: No.

It's lighter than heaviness.

Dr. Lisa: Yes, and if you're being your dad, how are you being your dad with money? Truth?

Participant: I work harder for things.

Dr. Lisa: There you go.

What's your dad's ethnic background?

Participant: Italian and Argentinian.

Everything is so hard to get. That's why I'm here.

Dr. Lisa: There you go. "Everything is so hard to get. I have to work hard for my money."

Say, "I have to work really hard."

Participant: I have to work really hard.

Dr. Lisa: "I have to work so hard." Say it again.

Participant: Ugh, I have to work really hard.

Dr. Lisa: And say it again.

Participant: I have to work really hard.

Dr. Lisa: And say it again.

Participant: I have to work really hard for my money.

Dr. Lisa: And again.

Participant: I have to work really hard for my money.

Dr. Lisa: Is that light or heavy?

Participant: Heavy, heavy.

Dr. Lisa: Right, wrong, good and bad, POD and POC, all nine, shorts, boys and beyonds®.

When you say it, is it light for you or is it heavy for you? Truth?

Participant: It's light.

Dr. Lisa: It is very light because that's the truth of him.

Participant: Yes.

Dr. Lisa: So tell me this, what do you love about mimicking your father's working hard mentality? What are three things you love about it? Truth?

Most people only do what they're doing because they're getting something from it, which means they love it. And that's why I used this question always ad infinitum.

Participant: Wow…

Dr. Lisa: Exactly for that reason – because you're going to find out what you're really doing.

There's a phrase, "Everything is the opposite of what it appears to be. Nothing is the opposite of it appears to be™," that applies right now.

Have you heard that phrase before? It's the crazy phrase.

Participants: Yes.

Dr. Lisa: I learned a long time ago that nothing that comes out of anybody's mouth makes any sense, including when I'm being facilitated. It's just what's light or heavy.

It's what we mimicked. It's what we embodied.

It's what we configured and how we've oriented ourselves as men and women in our lives. When we come to classes like this or run Bars™, it comes clearly in our face. Then we have the choice whether to keep choosing it, even though it's insane or not.

And I have to tell you, I still have chosen insanity more often than I've chosen not. I'm just in a place and space in my life that I choose less insanity than I've ever chosen. I choose more for me and committing to me and creating for me, even though it scares the crap out of me – like letting go of the 12 people I work with.

And, you know, I've really enjoyed not having to pay them this week for the moment. Not that I didn't like paying them – it was more just the energy of, "Oh, that's nice to not have to do that."

But it's still freaking me out.

It's like, "Oh, but when you don't do that, this doesn't get done and then it's not so nice."

So it's nice and then it's not so nice – that's the insanity.

I have to step out of that and ask, "Okay, what will this create if I'm no longer being somebody else? If I'm no longer lying to myself, what is this going to create?"

And I don't exactly know.

I have glimpses of it. I know what will be included. I don't know how it's going to form or show up in existence, but it's light when I look five years from now, or next month, or three weeks from now, even 10 seconds from now.

As long as it's light, and it feels better in my body and not constricted, and I'm not lying to myself, I will choose that over and over and over and over and over again.

Because when I have, the universe has always blessed me.

And when I have not, the universe has blessed me with my destruction because I asked for it.

So would you be willing to give up 1% more of your suffering, destruction, and trauma and drama of what no longer serves you.

Participants: Yes.

Dr. Lisa: On five, one, two, three, four, five, all the algorithmic, computations and configurations, one, two, three, four, five. One, two, three, four, five. One, two, three, four, five. One, two, three, four, five.

Right, wrong, good and bad, POD and POC, all nine, shorts, boys and beyonds®.

And on four, open the door and to yet another possibility. One, two, three, four.

Participant: I just got that I sold myself when I was four or five. My dad used to take me when he was working in construction. I was having fun working with my dad.

And now what I get is, "Wow! Haven't I already made so many different choices?" I invest, so I'm thinking, "I'm going to work really work hard for my money? No!"

Dr. Lisa: So good. That's her 1%. That's her 1° right there.

She never saw it that way before.

That's the space of "When density meets space, density dissipates."

So can I ask you a question?

Participant: Yes.

Dr. Lisa: At age four, did you decide that, no matter what, in order to make money and no matter how much money you made, somewhere it had to be hard. Truth?

Participant: Yes, it kept me connected with my dad.

Dr. Lisa: So where is that four-year-old inside of you right now who made that decision? Truth?

Where in your body?

Participant: It's here.

Dr. Lisa: In your heart, your solar plexus, in your head, where?

Participant: It's in my heart.

Dr. Lisa: Okay, so hold that energy there.

Now imagine her, at four, looking at your portfolios. Imagine her looking at your estate planning and looking at the choice to make an investment.

How big is the four-year-old?

Participant: Tiny.

Dr. Lisa: Tiny, right?

How does she like that decision as you sense into her now? What's the energy in the room? Light or heavy?

Total heaviness. Can you sense that?

Participant: Yes.

Dr. Lisa: Would you be willing to energetically say to her, "I'm now going to revoke, rescind, recant, renounce, denounce, destroy and uncreate the obligation, oath, vow, fealty, commitment, agreement, binding and bonding contract, covert, secret, hidden, invisible, obligation, vow, oath, and marriage to working hard?"

Participant: Yes.

Dr. Lisa: Everything that doesn't allow that and, for all of you, whatever age you all made your younger selves your CFOs, Chief Financial Officers, can we destroy and uncreate that?

Participants: Yes.

Dr. Lisa: Right, wrong, good and bad, POD and POC, all nine, shorts, boys and beyonds®.

Dr. Lisa: And let them go freaking play.

Participants: Yes.

Dr. Lisa: Get them a swing, go down to the basement and print money? Right?

Revoke, rescind, recant, renounce, denounce, destroy, and uncreate the forever commitment.

Right, wrong, good and bad, POD and POC, all nine, shorts, boys and beyonds®.

Thank you for every decision, judgment, conclusion, computation, and configuration you made since age 4, or whatever age, up until your current moment that has prevented and blocked and armored and defended a tank of money coming to you, ease coming to you, joy coming to you, kindness coming to you, receiving coming to you. Can we revoke, rescind, recant, renounce, denounce, destroy, and uncreate the forever commitment to that?

Participants: Yes.

Dr. Lisa: Right, wrong, good and bad, POD and POC, all nine, shorts, boys and beyonds®.

And all the artificial, virtual realities and configurations that you've embodied making those decisions at 4, 5, 6, 7, all the way up to 20 to 30 to 40 to 50, whatever decade you are now, can we destroy and uncreate those?

Participants: Yes.

Dr. Lisa: Right, wrong, good and bad, POD and POC, all nine, shorts, boys and beyonds®.

And all of the demons or entities or any other energies that you've employed to keep those decisions, judgments, conclusions, computations, and artificial, vibrational, virtual realities in place in your bank accounts as your CFO's that are denying you more than a million, ten billion, whatever.

Can we destroy and uncreate that?

Participants: Yes.

Dr. Lisa: Right, wrong, good and bad, POD and POC, all nine, shorts, boys and beyonds®.

Dr. Lisa: Truth who are you all, truth who were you before that, and before that and before that and before that and before that and before that and before that and before that and before that and before that and before and before that, and who will you be after that and after and after that and after that and after that and after that and after that and after that.

The deal is done, your services are no longer requested required, desired, wanted or needed. You get to leave now and be free. Take all your electromagnetic imprinting, chemical imprinting, biological imprinting, hormonal imprinting, genetic imprinting, ancestral imprinting, psychological imprinting, psychosomatic imprinting, genetic imprinting, neurotransmitter imprinting, hormonal imprinting, financial imprinting, and leave now. Go back from whence you came, never return to this dimension, reality, body again. Go back from when you came, never return to this dimension, reality, body, again.

Right, wrong, good and bad, POD and POC, all nine, shorts, boys and beyonds®.

And all of you who've pledged allegiance from those ages to the forces of poverty, struggle, bankruptcy, disease, dis-ease, chronic pain, no ease, work to the bone, work your body to the bone, don't work at it, hide it under the covers, and just numb yourself with psychotropic medications.

Right, wrong, good and bad, POD and POC, all nine, shorts, boys and beyonds®.

Can we revoke, rescind, recant, renounce, denounce, destroy, and uncreate the forever commitment to that?

Right, wrong, good and bad, POD and POC, all nine, shorts, boys and beyonds®.

Participant: I feel like I just had my house cleaned.

Dr. Lisa: It's like Roto Rooter, baby!

You should come over. I like a clean house.

Right, wrong, good and bad, POD and POC, all nine, shorts, boys and beyonds®.

And will you all give your children a big, big gratitude of thanks for what they carried on their shoulders for you? Let them know that their job is done.

Collaborating with the universe conspiring to bless you is actually knowing that the universe has your back, but you can't know that the universe has your back until you have your back.

How many people have tried to tell you that they have your back and you're like, "Fuck you. Get away."

It's because you don't know what it is to have your own back.

None of us really do until we start choosing for us, committing to us.

The only way I knew how to exist in the world was if somebody was screwing me, literally and figuratively. It took a lot of work to undo and rewire that, and to disseminate that there are actually good people in the world who aren't out to screw me.

The harder part was disseminating that there are actually people in the world who don't give a crap about me and would like to walk all over me.

You have to be aware of everything.

I don't know why, but there are just some people that don't like me. Don't you know that there's some people that don't like you? And aren't there people that you don't like at first meeting and you have no idea why?

Participants: Yes.

Dr. Lisa: Right, wrong, good and bad, POD and POC, all nine, shorts, boys and beyonds®.

Dr. Lisa: It's like my little nephew said when my mom tried to get him on the elephant in the circus when he was four years old, "Not for me, mommy. Not for me."

I had to learn how to have my own back and change that. Gary Douglas always says to me, "With everything that you've gone through, and the abuses that you've lived through –

en and lived through – how is it that you're so kind and actually care about people, and you're invested in their nge and growth and transformation as well as your own?"

I said, "I have no idea. Isn't everybody like that?"

That's when I started to look at the fact that there's a difference in me. Now, I'm not saying that isn't a difference in each of you. I actually wrote a dissertation on this terminology called *Soul Printing.*

A soul print is our own unique fingerprint, the unique character and contour of our soul, our ROAR. If we had to have a job, target, or whatever you want to call it, that intention is to unleash that ROAR, your soul print on the lips of this reality.

My ROAR is what I do it with my classes, practice, writing, the radio show, and transitioning trauma off the planet, moving beyond the cage of abuse, limitation, and constriction to radical aliveness. That's what I'm all about. I talk about it every day. I write about it every day. I don't know how the hell I've had over a 100 shows on Voice of America about this very topic, because I would think I would be bored right now, but shows keep being created.

So many people call up on the radio show to be facilitated. I recently had one lady who called in from Saudi Arabia, and she had to talk under in a desk on Skype because if she was found out asking questions about this, she would be killed. I'm keeping that show on the air for another person like that who may never get the chance to speak what's true for her except for that one moment of space in Saudi Arabia. That's my soul print.

I don't know what you're all going to do, but something's going to shift. The people and things you're invested and involved in – your children, your family, your money flows – are going to change because you're going to look at it differently.

When you see that account go down and you get that familiar feeling in your body, maybe you'll say, "Who am I being right now?"

I don't care if you don't use the Access Consciousness™ clearing statement. Whatever it is that changes the energy and wakes you up and then says, "Okay, if I'm being this right now, how does that feel?"

"Well that feels pretty horrible, anxious. What can I choose that's lighter and righter for me?"

Pick up the phone and call somebody, get a session, or whatever. Sell a condominium or a house. Whatever – there you go, you got money.

"What am I being when that familiar feeling and the bank account goes down?"

"What am I being right now?"

Usually, it's pathetic. You're usually scared, overwhelmed, shutdown, dense.

"Okay, how is that serving what I'm creating? Is that destroying my creations or creating my creations?"

If it's not creating your creations, then make a different choice and do whatever it takes: get out of the house, go for a walk, climb on the Earth, climb on a horse, climb something else.

Right, wrong, good and bad, POD and POC, all nine, shorts, boys and beyonds®.

Whatever you've got to do. It's about doing, not about thinking. It's about doing from a space of perceiving and receiving. Then, the best question you could ask is, "Okay, that's going on. What lie am I buying into right now that I've assumed is true?"

And when you get the answer, if it's heavy, don't believe it. It's a lie because you can't change a lie. You can't change the heaviness. You can only change by doing what's light and right for you.

Every time, follow what's light for you. Light breeds light.

Somebody give me an insane thing that they know that they're doing, and I'll walk you through it.

Participant: Does it have to do with money?

Dr. Lisa: Whatever you want.

Participant: Sitting around, hoping that I don't have to run a business or do anything. I just want to relax.

Dr. Lisa: Okay, great. So do you have money?

Participant: No.

Dr. Lisa: That's a great example of the insanity thing.

Participant: I don't have an income. I don't have a job, and I don't have a car.

I drove somebody else's car. I don't have a house.

Dr. Lisa: It's working for you, right?

So here she is saying, "I don't have a job. I don't have a house. I don't have a car and I drove somebody else's car. I have no income and I don't want to have a business."

What do you love about that? What do you love about everything you just shared?

And, for the rest of you, when she was sharing that, was it light or was it heavy in the room? You have to get out of your own stuff about, "Man, that would freak me out," because I heard some of your heads. Some of you were like, "What?"

Participant: The room seems lighter.

Dr. Lisa: It did because it was her truth.

There's something about that that's really true for her, something light about it. You don't want to have a business. You don't want to have an income.

Participant: I'd like to have an income.

Dr. Lisa: Ah. Okay.

Participant: I don't know.

Dr. Lisa: And can you only have an income if you have a business? Truth?

Participant: No.

Dr. Lisa: Okay, say, "Yes."

Participant: Yes.

Dr. Lisa: What's lighter?

Participant: The no.

Dr. Lisa: Okay.

Participant: The yes.

Participant: The yes?

Dr. Lisa: Let me help you here.

Have you ever gotten food poisoning?

Participant: Yes.

Dr. Lisa: What did you get sick on?

Participant: Kettle corn popcorn.

Dr. Lisa: And can you feel it in your body right now?

Participant: Yes.

Dr. Lisa: Light or heavy?

Participant: Heavy.

Dr. Lisa: Very good. That's your heavy.

Participant: Okay.

Dr. Lisa: So whenever you want to know what your heavy is, it feels like kettle corn food poisoning.

Very simple. Don't spend $25,000 of the money you don't have looking for light or heavy.

Participant: Right.

Dr. Lisa: Right, wrong, good and bad, POD and POC, all nine, shorts, boys and beyonds®.

So now, truth, what's your favorite food?

Participant: Pizza.

Dr. Lisa: Like any good New Yorker. I don't know if you're from New York but I love my pizza, too.

Where do you perceive that in your body?

Look how much you smiled – so, right there, with that feeling and a smile, that's your light. Whenever you're eating pizza, you're in your light. Whenever you're vomiting over kettle corn, you're in your heavy, okay?

Now you've got it. At the very least, you've come here and you now understand your light and heavy.

So, for you, particularly, put your head out on the hammock because we all know the answer to this question. The lies of money are not about knowing the answer. The lies of money are what you've embodied as a truth.

That's the lie, and part of it is with our belief systems.

So, truth, can you only have income if you have a business? Light or heavy? kettle corn or pizza?

Participant: It's heavy.

Dr. Lisa: Yes, so for you, it's the truth that you can only have an income with a business.

Participant: I got it.

Dr. Lisa: Okay, now you know that's not true. You can have an income by working for somebody else's business.

Participant: Yes.

Dr. Lisa: But there's something about that as I am talking to her that's heavy. Can you hear it?

For her, there's something joined together about income and business, which somehow is limiting her and constricting her to changing this position of, "I don't have this, I don't have that. I have to do this and I don't have to do that. And I have to do this. And I have to do that. And I should just have it, damn it."

Participant: My sister gave me the fifty bucks for tonight.

Dr. Lisa: My sister! Yes, yes, yes.

Participant: She has money.

Dr. Lisa: Exactly, so what do you love about manipulating people that have money to give you money? Truth.

Participant: I want some of that.

Dr. Lisa: You do.

Participant: I would have some of that.

Dr. Lisa: But you are doing it.

Participant: I know.

Dr. Lisa: The thing is you can't have anything yourself.

Participant: True.

Dr. Lisa: You have to always manipulate somebody else to get what you want. Therefore, who has more power? Them or you?

Participant: Them.

Dr. Lisa: Exactly. So who's the powerless dweeb?

Participant: Me.

Dr. Lisa: What do you love about being the powerless dweeb around money? Truth?

Right, wrong, good and bad, POD and POC, all nine, shorts, boys and beyonds®.

The only answer that you couldn't give right away. Now we're getting somewhere.

What do you love about being a powerless dweeb around money?

Right, wrong, good and bad, POD and POC, all nine, shorts, boys and beyonds®.

This is how I know I'm getting somewhere with somebody – when they can't regurgitate their defense mechanism about what they know to be true. There's actually a 1° shift going on here.

This is what the 'beyonds' and the clearing statement are all about.

When you can't put words to it, it's a beyond. It's so far out of your realm of consciousness that you can't even put a form and a structure or a word on it yet because you've never allow yourself to get here.

This is a one big degree. Do you see that right?

Participant: Yes.

Dr. Lisa: Right, wrong, good and bad, POD and POC, all nine, shorts, boys and beyonds®.

So, if you're a practitioner, practice listening. You have two ears and one mouth for a reason. The person always gives you the way in, if you listen. But if you're in your head about what you want them to get, you've lost it, you've lost the moment. They'll just keep coming back to you and paying you money to get nowhere.

Right, wrong, good and bad, POD and POC, all nine, shorts, boys and beyonds®.

Dr. Lisa: What do you love about being the powerless dweeb around money?

Participant: I don't know.

Dr. Lisa: Say, "I don't know."

Participant: I don't know.

Dr. Lisa: Again.

Participant: I don't know.

Dr. Lisa: Again.

Participant: I don't know.

Dr. Lisa: Right, wrong, good and bad, POD and POC, all nine, shorts, boys and beyonds®.

So all the 'I don't knows' that are an artificial, virtual reality of secret, hidden, invisible, covert, unseen, unacknowledged, unspoken, and undisclosed agenda to get you only get money from others but you never allow yourself to be the one that has the money, can we revoke, rescind, recant, renounce, denounce, destroy and uncreate that?

Participant: Yes.

Dr. Lisa: Right, wrong, good and bad, POD and POC, all nine, shorts, boys and beyonds®.

At what age did you make that decision? Truth?

Participant: 10.

Dr. Lisa: Right, wrong, good and bad, POD and POC, all nine, shorts, boys and beyonds®.

So what do you love, if you did know beyond the 'I don't know?' What's the best part about getting the money from your sister who has money?

Participant: You don't have to do anything.

Dr. Lisa: Right, you don't have to do anything. And what do you love about doing nothing?

Participant: I love doing nothing.

Dr. Lisa: What do you love about it?

Participant: I love it.

Dr. Lisa: What do you love about it?

Participant: I can wake up in the morning and just have coffee.

Dr. Lisa: You wake up in the morning and just have coffee right? No obligations.

Participant: Yes.

Dr. Lisa: No responsibilities

Participant: That is why.

Dr. Lisa: Right. No obligations, no responsibilities, no one's knocking on your door and no one is calling you.

Participant: Nobody wants you.

Dr. Lisa: Right, wrong, good and bad, POD and POC, all nine, shorts, boys and beyonds®.

Dr. Lisa: In fact, everybody doesn't call you because they know that, in fact, when they call you, you're going ask for money.

Participant: I don't actually ask for money.

Dr. Lisa: What?

Participant: I don't ask for money.

Dr. Lisa: What do you do?

Participant: I don't know.

Dr. Lisa: Do you just exude that you don't have it and people just give?

Participant: Yes.

Dr. Lisa: So, essentially, this is really, in a certain way, a capacity. This is a capacity.

Dr. Lisa: Right, wrong, good and bad, POD and POC, all nine, shorts, boys and beyonds®.

The 1° is you're really good at not doing anything, but getting what you desire when you need it. Right?

Participant: Yes.

Dr. Lisa: That's a capacity. That's a resource.

Participant: Absolutely.

Dr. Lisa: So could you just acknowledge yourself for this capacity that is very different in this reality. It kind of goes against the norm? It's kind of irreverent?

Participant: Yes.

Dr. Lisa: And you like that.

Participant: Yes.

Dr. Lisa: Could you acknowledge that?

Participant: Yes.

Dr. Lisa: A little bit more? And a little bit more?

Participant: Okay.

Dr. Lisa: And a little bit more?

Yes, there you go, breathing would will help. And usually breathing sounds like this because there's an inhale.

Right, wrong, good and bad, POD and POC, all nine, shorts, boys and beyonds®.

Participant: Thank you. Thank you.

Dr. Lisa: I am just giving space for the acknowledgement of it because it's a real capacity. It is a real capacity.

However, there is the 'however.'

Imagine if you turn that capacity the opposite way you've been turning it, which is making everybody else powerful and you powerless, to making you powerful. Not anybody else powerless, but you're powerful, too.

What could your life be then?

Participant: $25 million?

Dr. Lisa: There you go. I double-dog dare you to flip that molecule the other way and see what you could create because you don't like it. Just the other way. It's not enough for you anymore. You want something different.

Participant: Yes.

Dr. Lisa: Yes, but you have to be willing to choose that. And right now, you love not having to do anything way more.

Dr. Lisa: Right, wrong, good and bad, POD and POC, all nine, shorts, boys and beyonds®.

Participant: Because I don't want it to be hard.

What significance does it have? Why is 'hard' so significant in our world? People think that when you work hard for money, it's better than getting for nothing, like it's admirable.

Dr. Lisa: So, here's what maybe you were skipping that I'm going to shine a flashlight on.

Participant: Please.

Dr. Lisa: It's been really easy for you. You don't even have to ask for it and you get the money. They will just give it to you. Right?

So you already know how to create money with ease, so what if, as you flip that molecule the other way, you actually use that to create what you would like equally as easy.

Right, wrong, good and bad, POD and POC, all nine, shorts, boys and beyonds®.

Dr. Lisa: And everywhere you aligned and agreed and resisted and reacted against making money because it's going be hard, and therefore you've locked yourself into it only being hard which has now completely bypassed all these decades the capacity of ease that naturally comes to thee, can you revoke, rescind, recant, renounce, denounce, destroy and uncreate that?

Participant: Yes.

Dr. Lisa: Right, wrong, good and bad, POD and POC, all nine, shorts, boys and beyonds®.

So more space or less space inside?

Participant: I don't know, more I think. I think I can't.

Dr. Lisa: So hold on.

What's your light and heavy?

Remember, is it kettle corn vomit or is it pizza?

Participant: I'm on the pizza side.

Dr. Lisa: So is the dizziness that change showing up in the different way than you expected?

Participant: Yes

Dr. Lisa: Great! Pizza, right?

Participant: Yes!

Dr. Lisa: Great! Now here's what I want to say – your molecules are shifting the other way right now, that's the dizzy.

Participant: Thank you, because that was my question.

Dr. Lisa: Yes, I know, that's why I said I'm actually here to facilitate, I'm actually here to help. So if you just allow it, it will come.

Right, wrong, good and bad, POD and POC, all nine, shorts, boys and beyonds®.

Dr. Lisa: Seriously, can you perceive the ease that she has in getting the money?

Participant: Yes, yes.

Dr. Lisa: Now you just have to choose that you're damn worth it.

Participant: Yes.

Dr. Lisa: And that you can do it easy.

This is the thing that some of you have heard in Access before: What's the thing that you do that is so easy for you, that takes nothing from you, that makes you money right away.

Participant: I feel like there's something that I need to do, like counseling people. I do that a lot and I don't make a dime. I'm really good at it and I've looked at going to school and jumping through all the hoops so, as my sister says, "Now you can put your shingle out."

Dr. Lisa: Yes.

Participant: But, what I really want to do, the reason why I would follow that, is because I want to create something. I love creating something. It just flows out of me. I feel like I'm on some kind of drug. I don't really know what that feels like because I've never had a drug, but I think that's what it would feel like.

Dr. Lisa: The drug of you? You're so open.

I get it completely.

Participant: I just float.

Dr. Lisa: Yes.

Participant: I love it.

Dr. Lisa: When you love that creation, see if you can take a breath and breathe this in.

That creation is you being you. That creation is the physical actualization of your particular ROAR. That is you choosing for you, creating for you, committing to you, collaborating with the universe, conspiring to bless you.

Molecule and molecule, space meets space. ATP is in our body, adenosine triphosphate. It's in every cell of our body.

It's the same molecule, the same energy, that's made of the universe, that's made into this desk and the chairs you're sitting on.

We all have it.

When you're the space of you, you collaborate with the universe that is conspiring to bless you and there is no limitations or cage or constrictions. There is only 'pronoia,' which is an actual word. We've got it wrong, it's not 'paranoia.'

Pronoia is the universe that's conspiring to bless you. That's why you love it.

Participant: I understand the value to me. I'm like you, I like seeing people happy and it matters to me. That's something I get connected with.

I get really frustrated because creativity is unlimited. It's like going to a restaurant – there's so many things to choose from I can't slow down long enough to pick out on the menu what it is that I want do.

And I would really like to make some money doing something that I love and that other people love. How cool could that be?

Dr. Lisa: What if other people don't love it?

Participant: Then I don't get money for it.

Dr. Lisa: Well, hold on a second, I talk about abuse every day. I talk about the things no one wants to talk about.

Participant: Yes.

Dr. Lisa: I talk about rape. I talk about physical violence. I have a license plate that says "Stop child abuse" and people ask me all the time about it. I donate to that. I have a business beyond the radio show, Beyond the Abuse, Beyond Therapy, Beyond Anything.

I certify people in trauma stuff. I've got a manual about moving beyond trauma and how to use the tools of Access Consciousness™ with that.

That's what I talk about every day.

Do you think people love it?

In fact, no. Most people run away from me because they're afraid that I'm going to see something that they don't want to talk about.

Years ago, I decided, "Alright, I'm just going to just do workshops on money." But that wasn't as fun as doing workshops on money and body and relationships – tying it together to moving beyond abuse.

Because I can move somebody out of a trauma. Somebody told me in 6 minutes I helped them clear 10 years of therapy.

That's fun for me.

You can't tell me a story about abuse that I haven't walked through myself. I only told you one portion of my story. There's a couple of decades of abuse that I know very well.

And I've turned and faced all of it. That's why anybody can dump their whole story to me.

It doesn't mean you have to have abuse to work with me.

I've had hundreds of people, even in Access Consciousness™, who've said, "I had no idea this is what you did. When I heard it's about abuse, I just turned and walked the other way because I don't have that in my history."

I tell them, "Give me a chance. Give me 1°. Ask me one question. Tell me your limitation, tell me your constriction, and if you've got abuse, I'm probably the person to walk you through it."

It's fun for me.

Why?

Because people get free. They're no longer in that cage. It's abusive to live with other people in our bodies.

Participant: I understand that.

Dr. Lisa: Right, wrong, good and bad, POD and POC, all nine, shorts, boys and beyonds®.

There is nothing that I want to anesthetize myself from, hide from, or not be aware of. Consciousness includes everything and judges nothing®.

I want to know.

I'm an excavator. I want to know.

And I want to know what makes me happy, and whatever makes me happy brings people. They say, "I don't know why, but I want to talk to you about something because I know you can move me through something."

I'll bet you have that in you, too, if you're willing to.

Participant: To talk to people about their problem?

Dr. Lisa: I don't know, what you said.

Participant: I've been doing that for years.

Dr. Lisa: Right, but you said you aren't making money on it.

Participant: Right.

Dr. Lisa: I get paid every day for it. Why aren't you making any money?

Participant: Because I believe that you've got to have a license in order to.

Dr. Lisa: Okay, so everything is the opposite of what it appears to be, nothing is the opposite of what it appears to be™.

Participant: Don't forget the creating.

I realize that creates peace for people, but I really want to make something with my hands and hang it on wall where people go, or whatever that looks like.

I can't seem to ever get to a place where people like it.

Dr. Lisa: Because you refused money.

Participant: I refuse money.

Dr. Lisa: That's why.

Participant: Nice.

Dr. Lisa: So you counsel people every day and make no money because you believe that you need a license in order to get paid. Can we destroy and uncreate that?

Right, wrong, good and bad, POD and POC, all nine, shorts, boys and beyonds®.

Dr. Lisa: If you do it every day, you're giving your money away.

Participant: Yes.

Dr. Lisa: But, I'll tell you what, when people put their money down and they pay you, they're going to show up.

When you don't charge them and you give your feedback, they don't listen and they don't change. People will pay if you will allow yourself to step into that and then, when you make your bundles, go create your wall hanging thing. And then it's the best of both worlds.

Participant: I don't want to keep it. I want somebody else to want it.

Dr. Lisa: Exactly, sell it.

Every time I say something that gives you what you are saying to choose, you have a deflection away from it.

Right, wrong, good and bad, POD and POC, all nine, shorts, boys and beyonds®.

Dr. Lisa: So all the deflections that we all have that keep us away from actually doing what we really choose to be and do can we destroy and create it?

Participants: Yes.

Dr. Lisa: Right, wrong, good and bad, POD and POC, all nine, shorts, boys and beyonds®.

I'm with you. I guarantee that you have insight and a lot of brilliance to offer to people. And I'm saying charge for it.

Charge for it.

And I guarantee that there's something with your hands that you can create that nobody else can create. And I say, use that money from the brilliance of you to create more brilliance to sell more brilliance of you, so that more brilliance of you shows up in the world.

Every time it flows and creates more.

Because you're stepping up to be your ROAR and you being you does that.

You don't need a license or a certificate. Create a Bars™ class, hang your Bars™ facilitator's license on the wall and say, "Come on in, open house, $50 bucks a pop, no trades, just money. Show me the money and I will help you" is the energy you desire to put out because the people that pay really desire to make a change.

And here's the thing I've learned recently since I started using this 1°, because I can give the world to people, right?

When somebody comes to me and opens the door one degree, I can go all in. I can rescue the best of them. I'm a middle child. I know how to get through things. I survived a lot. I can handle a lot, so present something to me, no problem.

But I had to learn to pull my energy back, expand my space, use my two ears, and when anybody comes in for individual work, I say, "Alright, when you leave here what do you want to have left here, just for today?"

They usually say, "I don't know."

"Well you're paying me. What do you want to do?"

And I make them come forward and say what they would like to do so that we can then go to that space that empowers them to keep choosing more, which is the lightness of you.

The most important thing for you to do is do what you love, do what's easy for you, get paid for it and then keep creating – because that's radical aliveness.

When we're living other than that, we're dead.

And I don't know about you, but dead 'ain't' no fun.

Right, wrong, good and bad, POD and POC, all nine, shorts, boys and beyonds®.

Notice how little we're talking about money in this money taster, because that's the whole thing. The money problem we have really has nothing to do with money. It has to do with the lies that we bought as true.

Participants: Yes.

Dr. Lisa: That third question that we've configured into the costume we're all calling us or you.

Everything that brings up and let's down, can we destroy and uncreate it?

Participant: Yes.

Right, wrong, good and bad, POD and POC, all nine, shorts, boys and beyonds®.

However, when you are specifically talking about money and you get constricted about money or you're trying to create something, who are you being? And then POC and POD it. Run the clearing statement.

"What am I being when I'm choosing my mom and my dad?" POC and POD that.

"What lie am I buying into that I'm calling true that keeps me choosing against me?

Dr. Lisa: Right, wrong, good and bad, POD and POC, all nine, shorts, boys and beyonds®.

Now that I know it's my mom and dad and not me." POC and POD that.

Those are the easiest things that I can tell you to walk yourself through. That will open up the space to choose a different possibility.

The question is would you be willing to do that for you? 1° more?

Participants: Yes.

Dr. Lisa: Everything that doesn't allow that to be, destroy and uncreate it.

Participant: Yes.

Dr. Lisa: Right, wrong, good and bad, POD and POC, all nine, shorts, boys and beyonds®.

Did you have a question?

Participant: Yes, I'm in a place where I'm really stuck.

I'm in some money business, which I love.

What's hard is, I started my financial planning practice in Chicago 5 years ago and, just when I was getting ready to take off, I had a baby and then found out I was pregnant again – plus we moved 1,000 miles away.

My husband is always gone, so it was like being a single parent who's married. I still have the practice in Chicago, which afforded me the ability to be home and still work and make a nice living. My baby is now four years old.

This January has been my first foray into trying to build a business in Texas because I don't have any clients here. And

I feel like a total failure right now. I just can't get anything to close. We bought this house and we're doing remodeling – and I'm just spiraling in my head.

Dr. Lisa: A lot of money going out.

Participant: Yes.

Dr. Lisa: No ROI.

Participant: Yes, and I feel so stuck.

Dr. Lisa: So this taster tonight in Dallas is the 'hard taster.'

Everybody's said, "Hard, hard, hard, hard, hard, hard."

So do me a favor, just say, "I'm stuck, I'm stuck, I'm stuck, I'm stuck."

Participant: I'm stuck, I'm stuck, I'm stuck.

Dr. Lisa: And again.

Participant: I'm stuck, I'm stuck, I'm stuck.

Dr. Lisa: Say, "I'm the best I know at being stuck."

Participant: I'm the best I know at being stuck.

Dr. Lisa: "I'm an expert stucker."

Participant: I'm an expert stucker.

Dr. Lisa: "I can be stuck like the best of them."

Participant: I can be stuck like the best of them.

Dr. Lisa: Right, wrong, good and bad, POD and POC, all nine, shorts, boys and beyonds®.

So say, "I'm stuck, I'm stuck, I'm stuck" again.

Participant: I'm stuck, I'm stuck, I'm stuck.

Dr. Lisa: "I'm the best I know at being stuck."

Participant: I'm the best I know at being stuck.

Dr. Lisa: Nobody can be as good a stucker as you, could they?

Participant: No.

Dr. Lisa: You could stick yourself better than anybody, right?

Right, wrong, good and bad, POD and POC, all nine, shorts, boys and beyonds®.

You're from Chicago, of course.

Dr. Lisa: Right, wrong, good and bad, POD and POC, all nine, shorts, boys and beyonds®.

Participant: Married to an Italian.

Dr. Lisa: Married to an Italian. There you go.

Right, wrong, good and bad, POD and POC, all nine, shorts, boys and beyonds®.

So, truth, when your business was about to take off, right before that second kid, you're in the 'halleluiah.' Everything's working, the business is going well, and you found out you were what?

Participant: Pregnant.

Dr. Lisa: Exactly.

Participant: Yes.

Dr. Lisa: So it was the pregnancy, and then having to move, that changed everything.

Participant: Yes.

Dr. Lisa: Got it.

Participant: Especially considering I'm pregnant.

Dr. Lisa: Right.

Participant: I'm about to be pregnant again.

Dr. Lisa: So how much did you exist in that moment?

Participant: I didn't.

Dr. Lisa: Exactly.

Participant: At all.

Dr. Lisa: And how much did you exist prior to knowing that you were pregnant?

Participant: A lot more.

Dr. Lisa: Yes, so this is nothing about kids.

Participant: Yes.

Dr. Lisa: This is a very sensitive subject I'm dancing around here.

Participant: Yes.

Dr. Lisa: But I just want you to see and get a sense while I'm exploring this with you.

Participant: Right.

Dr. Lisa: So everything seemed to change in that moment.

Participant: Right.

Dr. Lisa: In Access we call that a 'trifold sequencing system.' It's a loop.

It's a loop where people date something that occurred in their life, and that changed in their life back to that moment.

Dr. Lisa: Right, wrong, good and bad, POD and POC, all nine, shorts, boys and beyonds®.

I'll give you an extreme example.

After my father died, for months, and still to this day whenever we talk about him, my mom calls him the same obscene name she called him when he was alive.

At first when he died, I said, "Mom, he's dead. Can it die, too?"

She said, "No, that bastard, da, da, da, da, da."

That's an example of an extreme trifold sequencing system. It just loops to the same thing over and over and over and over and over and over and over and over and over again every which way, no matter how many times you try to interrupt it.

You date it back to that moment.

So can we just interrupt that moment a little bit here? 1°? And everything that died in that moment, back then four years ago, when you were about ready to soar – you and everything around you – your husband, the kid, the business, the move – took over where you didn't exist like you used to exist.

Participant: Right.

Dr. Lisa: Can we destroy and uncreate that?

Participant: I think so.

Dr. Lisa: Right, wrong, good and bad, POD and POC, all nine, shorts, boys and beyonds®.

Dr. Lisa: Why do you say, "I think so?"

Participant: I feel like I haven't recreated how I do my business.

Dr. Lisa: I get it.

But you're still bringing 'back then' in to the present now. That's what I'm asking you to let go of.

Participant: Okay.

Dr. Lisa: What secret, hidden, covert, unseen, unacknowledged, unspoken, and undisclosed agenda, that is still potentially sticking you.

Participant: Yes.

Dr. Lisa: Would you give up 1% of that now?

Participant: Yes.

Dr. Lisa: Right, wrong, good and bad, POD and POC, all nine, shorts, boys and beyonds®.

And all the ways that you were then, that you aren't now, and that you had to change to fit into then, folding, mutilating, stapling yourself into this new reality. Because you're amazing and you can do that, but you still love some of that, and didn't take some of that with you because this is all new.

Participant: Yes.

Dr. Lisa: Can we destroy and uncreate that?

So that some of this can come here with you, instead of staying in the past, stuck without you.

Participant: Yes.

Dr. Lisa: Everything that brings up and let's down can we destroy and uncreate it?

Participant: Yes.

Dr. Lisa: Right, wrong, good and bad, POD and POC, all nine, shorts, boys and beyonds®.

This money stuff is tricky.

You have to really listen to people's insanity and their brilliance, otherwise you're not going to get anywhere. And it's not because I'm watching you.

You're really listening and looking at this, and that's wonderful – because all I'm attempting to facilitate is you being more of you. And if you bring more of you that got left back there, here now, I think you're going to soar.

Participant: It's getting that energy freed up so you can create from today and not the past.

Dr. Lisa: What I'm saying is not to get the connection back.

Participant: Okay.

Dr. Lisa: What I'm saying is to destroy and uncreate the decision that it is actually lost and gone, never to return again.

Participant: Okay.

Dr. Lisa: The you that fully existed back then and don't now.

Participant: Okay.

Dr. Lisa: Right, wrong, good and bad, POD and POC, all nine, shorts, boys and beyonds®.

So everywhere the decision you made in the past is influencing what you can't create in the present and in the future. Can we destroy and uncreate that?

Participant: Yes.

Dr. Lisa: Right, wrong, good and bad, POD and POC, all nine, shorts, boys and beyonds®.

Everything you had in the past that you couldn't bring to Texas, can we ask it to come follow you now? Yes?

Participant: Yes.

Dr. Lisa: Everything that doesn't allow that to be, can we destroy and uncreate for thee?

Participant: Yes.

Dr. Lisa: Right, wrong, good and bad, POD and POC, all nine, shorts, boys and beyonds®.

Because how much can Texas use your brilliance?

Participant: A lot.

Dr. Lisa: Yes, exactly.

Participant: The way I see.

Dr. Lisa: And how much can Chicago use your brilliance?

Participant: A lot.

Dr. Lisa: And is there more of your brilliance in Chicago or more of your brilliance in Texas? Truth.

Participant: I think now in Texas.

Right, wrong, good and bad, POD and POC, all nine, shorts, boys and beyonds®.

So, everywhere you've refused to claim and own, this land as your bitch, can we destroy and uncreate it?

Participant: Yes.

Dr. Lisa: Right, wrong, good and bad, POD and POC, all nine, shorts, boys and beyonds®.

And everywhere you forgot your potency in Chicago and forgot to unleash it in Texas, can we call it forward now?

Participant: Yes.

Dr. Lisa: Right, wrong, good and bad, POD and POC, all nine, shorts, boys and beyonds®.

Dr. Lisa: And on four, open the door, a new possibility. One, two, three, four. And what I like to do is do is ROAR on the four.

Would you do it with me?

Participant: Yes.

Dr. Lisa: One, two, three, four, ROAR. Everybody. One, two, three, four.

Everybody: ROAR!

Dr. Lisa: One, two, three, four.

Everybody: ROAR!

Dr. Lisa: One, two, three, four.

Everybody: ROAR!

Dr. Lisa: One, two, three, four.

Everybody: ROAR!

Dr. Lisa: One, two, three, four.

Everybody: ROAR!

Dr. Lisa: This is the energy you bring with you:

"No matter what it takes, no matter who I have to talk to, no matter what it's going to cost me, as long as it's light and right, then I'm going to choose it."

And what's going to create something for you?

Light and right. Pizza, not kettle corn.

You'll know this forever.

Right, wrong, good and bad, POD and POC, all nine, shorts, boys and beyonds®.

And if it doesn't start to move, who are you being? Are you being the old Chicago you? Or are you being the new Texas you?

What are you being? Are you being the old business you or are you being the new business you?

What lie are you being? I can't have it in Texas because I had it then there.

Right, wrong, good and bad, POD and POC, all nine, shorts, boys and beyonds®.

And just for fun, everything between you and your husband, you and your husband's business, and you and your child. Is it a daughter or a son?

Participant: Daughter.

Dr. Lisa: Daughter, okay, that got configured into this decision, judgment, conclusion, and computation of you not being fully you from back then, can we just revoke, rescind, recant, renounce, denounce, destroy and uncreate all of it?

Participant: Yes.

Dr. Lisa: Right, wrong, good and bad, POD and POC, all nine, shorts, boys and beyonds®.

And all decisions, judgments, conclusions, and computations between all of you, can we destroy and uncreate it? Covert and overt.

Right, wrong, good and bad, POD and POC, all nine, shorts, boys and beyonds®.

And all causal incarceration, causal incarnation, causal incongruity, and inconsistencies creating any of these known or unknown, could we destroy and uncreate that?

Participant: Yes.

Dr. Lisa: Right, wrong, good and bad, POD and POC, all nine, shorts, boys and beyonds®.

Free everybody, on five. One, two, three, four, five. One, two, three, four, five. One, two, three, four, five. One, two, three, four, five. One, two, three, four, five. One, two, three, four, five.

And on three, dissipate and release to the earth. One, two, three. One, two, three. One, two, three.

And on four, open the door, new possibility.

Participant: Yes.

Dr. Lisa: Lighter or heavier?

Participant: Lighter.

Can I ask you another question?

In Texas I'm in a different stage of life. I've got kids. My daughter's got scoliosis, so I'm wrapped up in those. The time is more limited. I don't have 24 hours to go out and build this network in terms of getting a new claim.

Dr. Lisa: That's what I was saying about the old you and the new you.

Participant: Yes.

Dr. Lisa: So everywhere the old you would go out and build the network and the new you has to create a new way of doing business.

Participant: And that's huge, yes.

Dr. Lisa: That's what has to occur. It's a new way and, if anybody can create it, you can create it. You know how to manage time. Right? You can get more done in 30 minutes than anybody can. So I have no doubt that you can create a business regardless of where you are. It's just about doing it and choosing it, and not being Chicago you, being Texas you, the you you are now.

Participant: Okay.

Dr. Lisa: Try it out. And when you get stuck, like you said, ask, "Who am I being, what am I being, and what lie am I buying into?"

And then, "Is this creating what I choose? Or is it just showing what I desire?"

Right, wrong, good and bad, POD and POC, all nine, shorts, boys and beyonds®.

Participant: I have this big – something – coming from inside and it's crushing. I need to get it off.

Dr. Lisa: So who are you being with this big invisible thing that's crushing you? Who are you being? Truth.

And "I don't know" is not the answer. It's not allowed.

Right, wrong, good and bad, POD and POC, all nine, shorts, boys and beyonds®.

Who are you being? First thought, best thought? You already heard it. Who are you being? Truth.

Right, wrong, good and bad, POD and POC, all nine, shorts, boys and beyonds®.

What are you being? Truth.

Right, wrong, good and bad, POD and POC, all nine, shorts, boys and beyonds®.

What lie are you buying into that you're being?

Right, wrong, good and bad, POD and POC, all nine, shorts, boys and beyonds®.

Truth. Who are you being?

Participant: Small.

Dr. Lisa: Right, wrong, good and bad, POD and POC, all nine, shorts, boys and beyonds®.

What do you love being small with this big thing that's crushing you. What do you love about being small? What's the best part of it?

Participant: We can hide.

Dr. Lisa: Right, wrong, good and bad, POD and POC, all nine, shorts, boys and beyonds®.

What do you love about hiding this big thing that's crushing you?

Participant: I can hide behind it.

Dr. Lisa: So you can be small. You can hide behind it and then you can hide it. You really like to hide.

So what are you hiding?

Right, wrong, good and bad, POD and POC, all nine, shorts, boys and beyonds®.

Truth. What are you hiding?

Participant: My greatness.

Dr. Lisa: What are you hiding of your greatness? Truth.

Participant: Being seen.

Dr. Lisa: Great. So, what do you love about hiding yourself from being seen with a big crushing thing that's crushing you? Truth.

What makes it so beneficial to hide all of you and to feel like crap, like you do, to want to vomit?

That's, that's the lie. Right there.

To still do it even though it's making us feel sick, bad, heavy, or like we have this boulder crushing us.

We'd rather experience that than the ease, joy and glory of choosing for us, committing to us, collaborating with the universe conspiring to bless us and creating.

That's the crazy thing about insanity.

Right, wrong, good and bad, POD and POC, all nine, shorts, boys and beyonds®.

And the epidemic about abuse in this reality is that it's the norm of this reality – dis-ease with being us.

The lies of money are really about confronting, "Who am I being, what am I being, what lie am I buying into that I've made as true?" It's not work for the weak. It is work for the wicked ROAR inside of you that's says, "No more. It's not worth hiding behind that anymore."

That's what I said when I turned and faced and looked at all the decades of perpetration and all the shit that I had to face.

No more.

I was not going to be a slave to that.

And if I can help one person by what I'm talking about, I'm going to talk about it. And I'm going to get out there because there are many other people like me who will get out there too, because I'm talking about it. They can see that they're not going to die if they speak what's true for them.

But we hide behind our boulders and our beliefs systems and our point of views and our mother and our father and our jobs and our poverty and our stuck-ness and our failures and our this and our that.

And we keep ourselves pathetic.

If you're sitting here in this class, there's nothing pathetic about you. You are the people that demand to have money because money in your hands will change this world.

Money in your hands will tilt the world on its axis, just not the fault lines. And if it does, it's okay because you'll be ROARing.

Right, wrong, good and bad, POD and POC, all nine, shorts, boys and beyonds®.

Lighter or heavier?

Participant: Heavier.

Dr. Lisa: Is the heavy you more embodying you or you less embodying you? Truth. Say, "More."

Participant: More.

Dr. Lisa: Say "Less."

Participant: Less.

Dr. Lisa: Which is lighter?

Participant: Less.

Dr. Lisa: Great, so you really love not embodying you.

Can you acknowledge yourself as a wonderful creator of not embodying you?

Right, wrong, good and bad, POD and POC, all nine, shorts, boys and beyonds®.

I think full disclosure and transparency is just about choice of possibility.

What do you choose?

Right, wrong, good and bad, POD and POC, all nine, shorts, boys and beyonds®.

So you're a really great creator of hiding you. You're the best you know at hiding you. What do you love about it, because it's knocking everybody out of the room? What do you love about knocking everybody out? Including you. Truth.

Participant: I have to be seen.

Dr. Lisa: But is that true? Because I'm seeing you right now and so is everybody else. So, truth, do you love the attention that it gets? That you can talk about how not seen you are and how much you can hide?

Light or heavy? Attention.

Participant: Heavy.

Dr. Lisa: Say, "Attention."

Participant: Attention.

Dr. Lisa: Say, "It gets me attention."

Participant: It gets me attention.

Dr. Lisa: Say, "It gets me no attention."

Participant: It gets me no attention.

Dr. Lisa: Which one is lighter?

Participant: It gets me no attention.

Dr. Lisa: Okay. So, what is the best part about you hiding? Because here's the thing...

I don't get a sense that you want to change this.

You asked the question, but what do you want to change?

Right, wrong, good and bad, POD and POC, all nine, shorts, boys and beyonds®.

What's your 1° shift here right now – so, when you leave, you know you made a shift?

Participant: I do want to change. Since we sat down tonight, it's just been building and building and building and building and increasing. I want to cast if off.

Dr. Lisa: You want to cast off the boulder that you used to hide behind, so that you keep hiding that you love to do it? Truth? Am I getting you right?

Participant: Yes.

Dr. Lisa: Right, wrong, good and bad, POD and POC, all nine, shorts, boys and beyonds®.

Participant: It's something else.

Dr. Lisa: What is it?

Participant: Some of it is not mine.

Dr. Lisa: What do you love about carrying something that's not yours? That you know is not yours, but you're still carrying it, and you can't cast it off. Truth.

Participant: I can.

Dr. Lisa: Excellent. Cast it off.

Right, wrong, good and bad, POD and POC, all nine, shorts, boys and beyonds®.

Is two hours long enough for you to sit with that? Or do you want to do it for another two? Or 24 decades?

Right, wrong, good and bad, POD and POC, all nine, shorts, boys and beyonds®.

Dissipate and release it to the earth. When space meets density, density dissipates. Did something change?

Participant: It's spread more to my face.

Dr. Lisa: So you didn't cast it off, you increased it? And you kept it.

Participant: Yes.

Dr. Lisa: So again, how can I help you? Because it doesn't seem like I am.

Participant: I don't know. It seems like it's something else.

Dr. Lisa: Great.

Participant: I don't know.

Dr. Lisa: What does "It's something else" mean?

Participant: A boulder.

Dr. Lisa: So what is it? You know you best.

What is this boulder, that isn't you, hiding behind, and not being seen, or wanting not to be seen, that it's something else?

Everybody expand your energy spaces, because I know everyone's getting tired in here. It's dense, but you can help this energy by expanding your energy of space 500 million miles up, down, right, left, front, back. Breathe energy into the front of you, in through the back of you, into the right of you, into the left of you. Up through your feet. Down through your head.

Right, wrong, good and bad, POD and POC, all nine, shorts, boys and beyonds®.

All this is density, heaviness – it's a lie you bought into.

And as long as we all suck into it, we become that. So, the more that you can expand your energy space, the density will dissipate.

If you breathe, it really helps.

Right, wrong, good and bad, POD and POC, all nine, shorts, boys and beyonds®.

So, what is it? What is all that now?

If you put words to it, what would it say?

Participant: Heavy. Hot.

Dr. Lisa: So, say, "I'm heavy and I'm hot."

I really want to ask you if you want facilitation here?

Participant: Yes, I do.

Dr. Lisa: So if I say please say, "I'm heavy and I'm hot," please say it because this is really thick, so stay with me here.

So say, "I'm heavy and I'm hot."

Participant: I'm heavy and I'm hot.

Dr. Lisa: Say it again.

Participant: I'm heavy and I'm hot.

Dr. Lisa: And again.

Participant: I'm heavy and I'm hot.

Dr. Lisa: A little louder so it matches the energy that we all feel in the room.

Participant: I'm heavy and I'm hot.

Dr. Lisa: And you guys back there, tell me when she hits it. Louder.

Participant: I'm heavy and I'm hot.

Dr. Lisa: Louder, baby!

Participant: I'm heavy and I'm hot.

Dr. Lisa: Say it again, Sam!

Participant: I'm heavy and I'm hot.

Dr. Lisa: And again.

Participant: I'm heavy and I'm hot.

Dr. Lisa: Now we're getting somewhere. Again.

Participant: I'm heavy and I'm hot.

Dr. Lisa: Right, wrong, good and bad, POD and POC, all nine, shorts, boys and beyonds®.

And all decisions, judgments, conclusions, and computations to keep yourself heavy, to keep yourself hot, keep yourself constricted, keep yourself hidden, keep yourself bouldered behind you, to never be you, so it's always 'something else,' and never allowing anybody to help you, see through to something else that you built as you, can we revoke, rescind, recant, renounce, denounce, destroy and uncreate to forever commitment through a labyrinth of suffering.

Right, wrong, good and bad, POD and POC, all nine, shorts, boys and beyonds®.

And all the artificial, vibrational, virtual reality that you've created on top of that and underneath that and underneath that and underneath that and underneath that and underneath that and underneath that and underneath that and underneath that and underneath that and underneath that and underneath that and underneath that and underneath that and underneath that and underneath that.

All the demons and entities you've employed to keep that in place that you can never get beyond it, never get facilitation beyond it, and never allow yourself beyond it because you can't even see what's beyond it because it's so far beyond you, truth, who are you, truth, who you were before that and before that and before that and before that and before that and before that and before that, and who'll you be after that and after that and after that and after that and after that and after that and after that.

The deal is done. Your service is no longer requested, required, desired, wanted, or needed. You get to leave now and be free. Take all your electromagnetic imprinting, chemical imprinting, biological imprinting, hormonal imprinting, genetic imprinting, ancestral imprinting, psychological imprinting, psychosomatic imprinting, psychophysiological imprinting, boulder imprinting, and leave now. Go back from whence you came. Never return to this dimension, reality, body again.

Can we please fire this 'something else' from its position?

Participant: Yes.

Dr. Lisa: And could we give it its severance package to get the hell out of here?

Participant: Yes.

Dr. Lisa: And could you then receive your severance package for carrying it?

Participant: Yes.

Dr. Lisa: Right, wrong, good and bad, POD and POC, all nine, shorts, boys and beyonds®.

Now we're getting somewhere.

That's all you need to do – talk money.

Right, wrong, good and bad, POD and POC, all nine, shorts, boys and beyonds®.

Everywhere that is the lock and your body's the key. Your body's the lock that is the key with the lock and the key, and lock and the key, and the key and lock, and the key and the lock, and the key and lock, the key and the lock, and the key and the lock together and set it free?

Participant: Yes.

Dr. Lisa: One, two, three. One, two, three. One, two, three. And all pledging allegiance to the forces of the boulders of this something else.

Right, wrong, good and bad, POD and POC, all nine, shorts, boys and beyonds®.

And everywhere your bodies have been the hoarding storage container for 'something else' that isn't you, would you like to give 1% of that up?

Participant: Yes.

Dr. Lisa: Everybody, on six. One, two, three, four, five, six! One, two, three, four, five, six! One, two, three, four, five, six! One, two, three, four, five, six!

And all the causal incarceration, causal incarnation, causal incongruities, inconsistencies, and inculcations to embodying and being the storage hoarding container of everybody else's crap, to keep you from being you, can we destroy and uncreate that now?

Participant: Yes.

Dr. Lisa: Right, wrong, good and bad, POD and POC, all nine, shorts, boys and beyonds®.

Dr. Lisa: And let's attract all the money to you.

Everybody with me:

Money come. Money come. Money come. Money come. Money come. Money come. Money come. Money come. Money come. Money come. Money come. Money come. Money come. Money come. Money come. Money come. Money come. Money come. Money come. Money come.

What energy, space, and consciousness can me and my body be? Can we and our bodies be to receive unconditionally all financial currencies with total ease? Anything and everything that doesn't allow that can we destroy and uncreate it?

Participant: Yes.

Dr. Lisa: Right, wrong, good and bad, POD and POC, all nine, shorts, boys and beyonds®.

As you breathe more into you, now, and expand down, up, to the right, to the left, front and back, breathe energy in, breathe energy in, breathe energy in, breathe energy up, breathe energy down.

Better, worse, the same?

Participant: Way better.

Dr. Lisa: Alright.

Participant: Yay!

Participants: Yay!

Dr. Lisa: So, remember:

Who are you being?
What are you being?
What lie are you buying into?

Thank you so much for your attention. Thank you for your vulnerability. Thank you for your sharing. Thank you for coming out and gifting me the pleasure and possibility of allowing 1° of shift in your life.

Right, wrong, good and bad, POD and POC, all nine, shorts, boys and beyonds®.

That was good energetically, wasn't it?

Participant: Woohoo!

Participants: Thank you!

Dr. Lisa: Right, wrong, good and bad, POD and POC, all nine, shorts, boys and beyonds®.

Thank you, thank you, thank you.

Money come, money come, money come, money come, money come, money come.

Be you, beyond anything and create magic!

Orlando

Speaker: Welcome to all of you here.

We have the honor and the privilege of hosting Dr. Lisa, who's a beautiful and amazing, incredible Access Consciousness facilitator, #1 best-selling author, and the host of an amazing Voice America show. She's on an international tour and we captured her to come and facilitate with us.

We're so blessed to have you with us, and thank you so much for bringing the Lies of the Money to us tonight, following that with ROAR, and then a three-day body class.

Please give Dr. Lisa a great big round of applause!

Dr. Lisa: Thank you!

Hello everybody, this is the Lies of Money, a 2-hour 'taster.'

I'm going to give you a taste of my version of the Lies of Money using the Access Consciousness™ energy clearing statement and other tools from Access, as well. If you want to learn more about Access Consciousness™ and the clearing statements, specifically, just go to www.theclearingstatement.com.

I'm going to use this statement often throughout this 2 hours, and to many of you it will sound like Mandarin, especially if you're brand new. I do not speak Mandarin, but it's going to sound like Mandarin to you.

You're probably not going to get my sense of humor at first, but I guarantee it's my goal and my target to make you laugh out loud for at least the time that we're spending together.

Money is such a heavy topic for people.

It brings up so much junk and gunk, negativity and destruction, blockages and heaviness and density and fear – everything under the sun, basically.

And, so why do I start my week with this topic?

I'm not really sure.

I was thinking of that when I was walking in here today. And I thought, "Maybe I should talk about sex or something. But that would probably be as heavy as the money topic.

I use the Access Consciousness™ clearing statement because, it's so comprehensive, it wipes the slate clean.

And, believe me, I've used a lot of tools.

As some of you know, I have a fair amount of licenses, education, and training outside of the Access Consciousness™ modality in and of itself, including a couple of master's degrees, a marriage and family therapy license, and a psychology degree.

So have you ever had your computer get stuck?

Remember the AOL days where it used to say, "File Not Found, toot, toot?" There'd be this little hourglass and then, all of a sudden, you restart the computer and whatever that issue was, wherever it was stuck, it's gone?

And you don't know why because your computer can't talk.

That's what the Access Consciousness™ clearing statement does for me, so when I go around the world talking about the stuff that I do like this, I find that using that makes it all so much lighter and easier and 'funnier' – if that's even a word.

And then, people actually get outside of their cage and outside of their limitation and outside of their constriction, more easily, more quickly, more effortlessly.

Theta Healing™ is also a good technique that I've used for a long time, and that I still really love and enjoy. If you're familiar with that, you'll see it in some of the things I talk about, particularly the early days in hypnotherapy, somatics, and trauma training that I have.

I use everything that I've been trained in to move people, myself included, if they're willing to get outside of their own cages and limitations.

And money I find to be the biggest cage.

In over 20 years of private practice, group practice, international practice, people have come to me for three reasons: money, health, and relationship.

I worked on the health part first, and got very successful in my practice in San Francisco helping people to literally let go of their life-threatening illnesses and diseases. I also had a life-threatening illness and disease at one point, which I'll talk about because it was a choice I made that let me experience for the first time what it actually meant to see my bank account at zero.

Has anybody here experienced that?

Participants: Yes.

Dr. Lisa: It's quite an experience, and I see you survived, too.

I'll get into that a little bit more, but I felt really good about doing the health thing, especially when the diseases that people came into my office with were leaving more naturopathically than allopathically, myself included.

It was like, "Okay, that's cool. I got that."

Next it was the relationship issue. People came in, worked through the conflict and all that, and I got really successful at doing that. People were either out of relationship or in relationship, but they were happy.

My clients were succeeding, myself included, and then, this money thing.

No matter what got better in people's lives, including in my own life at one point, money never changed. It was the same lateral movements – looked good, got successes, always had money, my clients were doing better, too, but then it would always kind of like go away and feast or famine. I don't know if any of you have experienced anything like that.

I could always make money, but never could just allow myself to have it. And then I started noticing that there was a pattern in my clients who had the same 'presenting problem,' where they could create money, but they never kept it or had it.

Some felt they couldn't create money – and, therefore, they couldn't create it and they couldn't have it.

I started watching and witnessing these people who I was working with, really great people, succumb under this guru, god thing, and I thought, "Alright, I've got the health thing, got the relationship thing. I'm going to commit to this money thing."

Then, some time ago, something completely shifted for me, financially and energetically, where a lot of the things that I talked about here just went away. I don't even know what happened.

It wasn't like a parting of the seas, Moses and the whole thing.

It just seemed to change.

Now, it doesn't mean that it's perfect or I can't do better because, for me, I'm always growing, right? I'm always doing better.

If you cure yourself of a life-threatening disease without allopathic medicines, you gain something from it. I gained something from that and put everything on the line financially to do that.

It was the best financial decision I ever made, and what I learned from that is, you'll always make more money.

And I did.

As long as you go with what's light and right and what's in front of you, and you follow that energy, money will follow you – because of what's inside of you.

However, as my financial reality energy shifted, I saw that so many people I worked with, and colleagues, were not shifting out of it.

That's when I decided to really put my energy and attention on, "What is this money thing?"

Like, really, what is it?

I don't pretend to stand up here saying that I have all the answers, but, if it's okay with you, I'm going to share what's worked for me and what I've become aware of.

Would that be okay with you?

Participants: Yes.

Dr. Lisa: Some of you are smiling.

Okay, and everywhere you're trying not to smile, just to prove me wrong because there are no control-freaks in this room, can we destroy and uncreate that?

Participants: Yes.

Dr. Lisa: Right, wrong, good and bad, POD and POC, all nine, shorts, boys and beyonds®.

There's that Mandarin statement.

That's the clearing statement from Access Consciousness™, and I'm going to say it a lot, even though it's not going to make sense why I'm saying it. I use it just like I use that example of the computer.

By what we believe, we leave ourselves behind – not only ourselves, but our bodies – so when we use the Access Consciousness™ clearing statement, all the leaving of us behind, all the limitations, all the decisions, all the judgments, all the conclusions, all the computations, all the configurations, all the oaths and the vows, and the fealties and the commitments and the binding bonding contracts and all the secret and hidden and invisible and covert, unseen, unacknowledged, undisclosed agendas to not having ease, joy, glory, money in this case, in your life get cleared and you have more space to choose when your 'yes' is your 'yes' and your 'no' is your 'no.'

So is that cool with you?

Can we do that here?

Participants: Yes.

Dr. Lisa: Right, wrong, good and bad, POD and POC, all nine, shorts, boys and beyonds®.

If you don't understand anything I'm saying, it's okay. I appreciate when people don't understand because, when you do understand, you're just standing under somebody else's point of view.

And I don't want you to stand under somebody else's point of view because there's been so many decades we all have embodied and embraced ourselves under somebody else's point of view – and then called that our reality.

So everywhere you've called your reality physically, psychologically, somatically, energetically, or financially, your reality when it was actually someone else's point of view that you configured your body, your mind, your psyche, your life into, can we destroy and uncreate that?

Dr. Lisa: Right, wrong, good and bad, POD and POC, all nine, shorts, boys and beyonds®.

Just 1%.

Destroy and uncreate just 1%.

It only takes 1° or 1% of a desire to change that can interrupt everything that we've locked ourselves into.

Would you all be willing to make a 1° shift here tonight?

Participants: Yes.

Dr. Lisa: I know some of you competitive freaks are going to say, "But I can do 99.9%."

Go for it, but I'm only looking for one.

Right, wrong, good and bad, POD and POC, all nine, shorts, boys and beyonds®.

What I have learned in doing this money taster is very interesting. It's different every time. I'm learning even more about how the energy of this money thing is so different all over the country with every person, with everybody – and it's just amazing.

Participant: Do you feel the energy different in Orlando than other places that you do the seminar, just because of the flows?

Dr. Lisa: Well, I'll know more of about that as we go further tonight.

It may surprise you that a lot of what I'm going to talk about tonight has nothing to do with actual cash or money, but it has everything to do with what you actually use to create your 'money flow' – or lack thereof – in your bank account, portfolio, investments, checkbook, and in your pocket book right now.

Everything that we're going to talk about is what actualizes as your financial reality.

And my target is to allow each of you, to the best of my ability, to change that 1% or that 1°, so that you step out of this room knowing 1° more what your financial reality is and what it isn't.

Dr. Lisa: One of the reasons why I can stand up in front of you is because of my father. I grew up with a man who was an entrepreneur, and my job as a kid was to sit in the basement with him. That's where his office was at that time.

In the early 80s, he made a lot of money through foreclosures and real estate in New York and the New Jersey area. At one point, he had 16 different multi-family units that he owned, and that's when things started to change in our life.

It was both a curse and a blessing for me because, since I was 23, I was out on my own as an entrepreneur.

I couldn't work for anybody.

But something I'm doing, thanks to him, is right, and I always bring him up and say thank you to him.

If you know some of my story – about the focus I've had on moving beyond abuse and limitation and constriction, which I know very well personally – he was the one major shining light throughout my whole life because, in those moments when I sat in the basement with him, I would count the stack of money.

And it was all in cash back then.

Remember those green ledger pads and the old kind of adding machines? And what was a computer back then? I don't even know. I think it was just before the time of the microwaves.

I would stack the money and order it in the ledger, and he'd say, "Lisa, it's not just a man's world. It's a woman's world. Do what you love. Be your own boss. Never work for anyone. And never give up on your dreams."

I might talk to him about that part, because it presented a little bit of a problem, a little bit of an entitlement in a certain way.

But he also impelled a potency within me when he said it.

He always told me about relationship, as well. He said, "They say opposites attract. That's what I got. And you see how that worked out for us?" He was talking about his marriage.

That was another problem and I went to a lot of therapy for that.

That's why I got a psychology degree, so I can prevent other people from doing that. You get taught what you need to do in life in a certain way.

He told me something to the effect, "Really get with somebody that you can collaborate with, somebody that you can work with, strive toward, and create something together. But don't put all your eggs onto and into someone to make your life."

I took those things he told me in those moments as the best business and financial education I could have.

I wasn't a business major. I was a psychology major. I took economics in college and I wanted to shoot myself in the head. I couldn't do it.

I remember my early days in New York, watching everybody walk to the train station, because I was expected to go work in the city in New York. I was expected to get on the train every day and work somewhere in business. I was expected to wear a suit every day, and put sneakers or trainers on, and my heels in my briefcase, and walk to the subway and get to the city.

That's what I was supposed to do.

I remember looking at the moon out my bedroom window, and saying, "God, whatever you do, whatever you do, do not let me live a soulless life."

Yes, a little bit of a judgment.

Because what I saw – everybody that walked up to the train station, men and women – no one was happy.

No one had a smile on their face. Everybody looked forlorn.

He taught me in those moments in the basement to really be happy and do what I love.

I left New York as soon as I could and went west. When I got to California, everybody was like, "Yes, it's a Friday and a Monday. Let's ride our bikes. And it's a Tuesday and a Wednesday or Thursday...let's ride our bikes. Let's go for a hike."

I thought, "Don't people walk to the train and go to the city and work all day?"

No, they work in jeans and shorts, and they make plenty of money.

Those moments with my dad were really important and that's where I got the love of money.

Do you guys know what money tastes like?

Participants: No.

Dr. Lisa: No? I do. I dare you.

I know it's not that appetizing, but I have to tell you, I would taste the money, even the coins, when I'd stack the money.

Believe me, all my friends know I'll get their wallet and stack their money very nicely together, with $100 bills first, and then $20 bills behind it, then $10s, $5s, and $1 bills – just like my father did.

Everything organized, not crumpled up, like you don't care about it and throw it on the floor, or at the bottom of your purse somewhere.

"Here's a dollar, whatever."

I relished all these things. It's not that he told me to do this, but I just mimicked what he did, and I found myself falling in love with money.

I went to Fairfield University in Connecticut, and in the summers when I'd come back to New York, I worked in a bank. I loved getting into the vault when the Brinks truck would come. They had all the money and jewels there. I just loved it.

When the people placed all their deposits, especially all the lawyers on Friday, they'd come with hundreds and hundreds and hundreds of dollars.

I loved money.

I love the energy of money and I love being gifted with money.

And I love $100 bills – I adore them. I would, if I could, wear them all over my body. I have no idea why and I probably won't do it in the world.

That love from those moments with my father about money changed everything for me.

There was a bit of a struggle during some of those years but now, as I'm remembering these stories and the energy of my love of money, it's actually creating more money, more business, more fun, more joy, more communion with the earth, better sex, and a happier relationship within myself – a healthy relationship within myself and my body.

So there was something about those early moments, about knowing what money feels like, smells like, tastes like, and the love affair that I had with it, really has been the switch that has turned the cash faucet and the money faucet on for me. Otherwise, I never would have known that.

And how did I get here?

I did a lot of clearing of limitations and constrictions in my belief systems that had encapsulated or caged me in a reality that wasn't true for me.

All the realities and points of views that you've impelled on you, that you've embodied as you, that you've created as your life and called you, can we destroy and uncreate that now?

Participants: Yes.

Dr. Lisa: Right, wrong, good and bad, POD and POC, all nine, shorts, boys and beyonds®.

And all the decisions, judgments, conclusions, and computations you made before the age of two about what money meant to you and what you meant to money, what cash meant to you and what you meant to cash, can we destroy and uncreate that?

Right, wrong, good and bad, POD and POC, all nine, shorts, boys and beyonds®.

And everything everybody has told you, as a woman, what money means to you and having money means to you, can we give that up?

Just 1% more?

Participants: Yes.

Dr. Lisa: Right, wrong, good and bad, POD and POC, all nine, shorts, boys and beyonds®.

Why am I asking you to give that up?

Because anything you believe of somebody else that isn't yours, you make as true for you, and then you can never change it or get beyond it because it's not yours. You can't change something that isn't yours.

Dr. Lisa: Right, wrong, good and bad, POD and POC, all nine, shorts, boys and beyonds®.

Anybody have something in your life that isn't changing?

From this day forward, I hope you ask, "Is it mine?"

Because if you don't get that it's light and sparkly and bubbly and expansive when you ask the question "Is it mine?" and, instead, it feels dense and constricted in your gut and heavy, it's a lie that you're buying.

If it feels light, expansive, free, joyous – it's true.

So all the decisions, judgments, conclusions, and computations that everybody told you about what it means to be a man/woman with money, and what it means to have money as the man or as the woman, can we destroy and uncreate that?

Right, wrong, good and bad, POD and POC, all nine, shorts, boys and beyonds®.

See, there's a pattern here.

I'm saying all these things to destroy and uncreate everything that I can possibly can.

To the best of my ability, I want you all just 1% more, to be a little bit more of an open slate than how you came in here. Because we all come in with our points of views, our reality, our desires, our problems, our issues that we need our tissues for – all the things we've felt unable to move beyond.

And what I've found with my clients and for myself is that they're not even ours.

We've adopted them.

It's like when we say, "Oh, I've got my mother's eyes or hair or butt, or my father's cheeks."

It's the same thing with belief systems and points of view.

What did your mothers tell you about money? What did your father tell you about money? What has this reality told you about being a woman with money and what have you adopted and been told as men about money?

Right, wrong, good and bad, POD and POC, all nine, shorts, boys and beyonds®.

None of those things are anything about you.

I'm not just having coffee talk with you, and saying these things for no reason. I'm sharing them so that we can get to whatever that 1% is for you – and that I hope will contribute to your walking out of here and getting a phone call about whoever owes you money, that they're going to put a deposit in your account. Or, if you're looking for a new position, that it comes in the mail somehow, or email or phone call.

Or that maybe tomorrow you open the paper, or you look on the internet, and something that you'd been desiring, without even knowing that you're desiring, shows right up on your screen…something like that.

Would you all be willing to be open right now to that 1% more of the infinite possibilities available to you?

Right, wrong, good and bad, POD and POC, all nine, shorts, boys and beyonds®.

Practice with me.

If you just take a moment to expand your energy space – and what I mean by that is just think it – 500 million miles. Notice it's too big a number for you to wrap your brain around, because in my classes your brains go in the back.

I always tell people to roll their heads back on the beautifully colored hammocks I put back there for you, and leave your head there and keep your body here because your body is the gateway to your possibilities with money, cash and everything changing in your life – not your mind.

That's a little different than in this reality, isn't it?

Right, wrong, good and bad, POD and POC, all nine, shorts, boys and beyonds®.

Your mind is 10% of you your body is 90% of you. Why would our entire embodiment be just the 10% in our head?

Right, wrong, good and bad, POD and POC, all nine, shorts, boys and beyonds®.

So would it be okay with you if you would expect something magical to happen? And would it be okay if it's not tomorrow?

Participants: Yes.

Dr. Lisa: Would it be okay if it happens 10 years from now?

Participants: Yes.

Dr. Lisa: Would it be okay if it happened next month?

Participants: Yes.

Dr. Lisa: Everywhere that you may have said "No" inside, but are saying, "Yes" out here, you're eliminating and constricting the possibilities. It's never going to show up the way you think it is. Trust me. I never even knew where Texas was and I just moved there.

Dr. Lisa: Right, wrong, good and bad, POD and POC, all nine, shorts, boys and beyonds®.

The only thing I knew about Texas was my own judgments about George Bush and I was never coming near it. And I didn't even know I had such a judgment about it.

Then, when I actually got to Texas, and I thought, "Hey, I kind of like it here."

I still do not understand it and I don't need to understand. There's a spaciousness there, and a lot of it is because I'm on a 25-acre horse ranch.

It never shows up the way that you think, like that invitation to that possibility and the life that I've created.

I sold everything, let go of everything, let go of anything and everything that did not want to come with me when I left California. I didn't even sell it all. I sold some of it and gifted most of it. It didn't even matter to me.

I just knew that it was time to leave, and when the invitation came, I went.

What has conspired to bless me through the universe from that choice of following what's light and right made me happy. And it wasn't work and it wasn't money that I made the decision for.

It was the Earth. It was horses. It was my body. It was a choice of a relationship possibility and it worked out. I couldn't even have imagined it.

"Whoa, so this is what happens when it's light and right, and you follow it."

And providence moves too. The universe conspires to bless you. I really got after that because, can I tell you a little secret?

The worst part was I'd gotten a little depressed because, after I moved and everything was going so good, then I had to look at every choice I didn't make that was light and right for me.

And that's part of what I do here in the Lies of Money. I talk about stuff that I've actually gone through. I'm not just taking it from a book, or a premise, or it's just catchy to do a money workshop. "Hey, come to me. I have your answers around the Lies of Money."

This Lies of Money taster is what I've learned and seen through me following exactly what I'm saying here, using it with my clients, and watching my entire life expand and my body changing and my health changing and my happiness changing and my money flows changing and my classes changing and my cash changing.

I have ideas growing, books I've written and participated in, and other things that are getting done that I never thought that I would get done. Things that I thought were going to be 20-30 years from now are actually happening right now – just because I said "Yes" to this one possibility.

How many possibilities have you said "No" to that were actually your "Yes" that would change everything that you call wrong in your life right now?

Everything that brings up and lets down, can we destroy and uncreate it?

Right, wrong, good and bad, POD and POC, all nine, shorts, boys and beyonds®.

So here's the biggest lie of money – and I'm really going to disappoint you and I'm sorry.

The biggest lie of money #1 is it has nothing to do with money.

It has everything to do with your belief systems and assumptions about what money means to you, what cash means to you, and what you were told in your points of view about money.

Most of it, as I've said here tonight, has been about me and my "process" in relation to what this reality, or mother or father or whomever, told me about money.

But it's never about money.

This little piece of paper that actually means nothing. This thing here, this is what you're saying is the ruin, destroyer, problem in your life. All of us have.

We say this gives us happiness.

We say this is the root of all evil.

We say we have to work hard for it.

We say we're only valuable if we have it, that we're only worth something to someone by what we drive, by what we wear, by what we adorn ourselves with, by what vacations we can go on.

Now, I'm not saying all those things are lovely or not lovely, because I like them, too. But how much of you has gotten dependent on money as the cause or be all, end all, of your joy or your happiness or your worth?

Dr. Lisa: Right, wrong, good and bad, POD and POC, all nine, shorts, boys and beyonds®.

I did a workshop I created in California called LEAP, The Life Empowerment Action Program, and one day we had a whole weekend on money. I had my assistants draw big dollar bills, and then everybody got a marker and I said, "Write all your judgments down on money."

I'd never seen anything like this before. I couldn't even the see the dollar bill that we drew. It was black and looked like a spider web. There were things on there I can't repeat in here because it would sound so horrible. But you already know it – the judgments, projections, separations, expectations, resentments, rejections, and regrets about money were out of this world extraordinary.

And I thought to myself in that moment that it was no wonder they didn't have enough, that they had to work hard and no matter how hard they try, they never got out of debt, that they're always in debt.

It was no wonder that they were able to make money, but never able to have it or save it or spend it, that they could never go on vacation, and that they had to have three jobs or marry somebody else to give them money because they couldn't live on their own, or they had to borrow money and continue borrowing money from their family or credit cards or institutions and go into bankruptcy over and over and over again.

You know these stories, right?

All for this one thing.

And it was all because they made it about this.

But it's really about you. It's about me.

So would you be willing to give up just 1% more of your lie that money means anything about you, that money is your god or your guru, or that money has anything to do with your self-worth?

Would you be willing to give that up 1% more?

Right, wrong, good and bad, POD and POC, all nine, shorts, boys and beyonds®.

And, everywhere that you believe that your net worth has anything to do with yourself, can we destroy and uncreate that?

Participants: Yes.

Dr. Lisa: Right, wrong, good and bad, POD and POC, all nine, shorts, boys and beyonds®.

And everywhere you did the carrot thing and said, "If I just have this amount of money, then it will be better. If I just do this, then I'll be happy. If I just get $50,000, then I'll be happy. If I get next month's rent paid, then I'll be joyous." Can we destroy and uncreate all of that?

Right, wrong, good and bad, POD and POC, all nine, shorts, boys and beyonds®.

"If I have this amount in my bank account, I'll give that person a tip."

Right, wrong, good and bad, POD and POC, all nine, shorts, boys and beyonds®.

"I'm not going to give 20% because they stepped on my toe," but it's really because you don't have that extra 20% in your mindset.

Can we destroy and uncreate that?

Participant: Yes.

Dr. Lisa: Right, wrong, good and bad, POD and POC, all nine, shorts, boys and beyonds®.

I'll tell you one of my little tricks.

Every time I feel that constriction or cage around money, I give more.

Sometimes it's really hard to give more, and sometimes it's not even with money that I give. Sometimes it's with food or clothes. I go through a lot of things – when I used to have a lot of things – and say, "Hey, I don't want this anymore. Do you want it?"

My friends loved me. "I don't want this chair. I don't want this couch. Here you go. Have it."

I'd rather sit without something than sit with something that doesn't work for me anymore. It took a while to get there, but I made a decision. I made a demand that everything I'm around – that I sit on, touch, or put on my body has to feel a certain way. It has to make me feel good, or makes me feel beautiful. It's soft, not tight. And if it is, then I'm not wearing it until the next time or whatever.

These are the kind of things that lies get us out of remembering – the comfort, the ease, the happiness.

Right, wrong, good and bad, POD and POC, all nine, shorts, boys and beyonds®.

So, why do we make it about money?

This reality likes to point fingers. As long as it's about the other person in the relationship, or the doctor that didn't diagnose you when you found that you had something, or what's not on your bank account, that gets you off the hook.

But what it doesn't do is change the way you are with money.

Would you willing to change the way you are with money just 1% more?

Participants: Yes.

Dr. Lisa: Right, wrong, good and bad, POD and POC, all nine, shorts, boys and beyonds®.

What do I mean by that? Change the way I am with money?

So let's start with this, another lie, #2. I'll go back to the first one I talked about, but let's not make it about the money.

The second lie is that your net worth equates your self-worth.

So, tell me about that, how come you have to have money in order to be worthy?

Participant: TV.

Dr. Lisa: Well, you know, everything you learn on TV is accurate, right?

Participant: Yes.

Dr. Lisa: Everywhere you've dumbed yourself down to buy what's on TV, which is a lie, and called that the truth and made that your reality, can we destroy and uncreate it?

Participants: Yes.

Dr. Lisa: Right, wrong, good and bad, POD and POC, all nine, shorts, boys and beyonds®.

How come, just by being you, you're not financially okay?

Participant: People you date.

Dr. Lisa: Well, you know all those people you've dated and shared those biological, hormonal ties with, that intimacy with? Do you know you actually share their DNA and their belief systems and their points of view.

Participant: I get that now.

Dr. Lisa: And when they leave you, and you're no longer married to them or with them in a relationship, guess what?

Participant: You stay with them.

Dr. Lisa: They stay with you and you stay with them.

Participant: Yes.

Dr. Lisa: Oh, I've got a bunch of sluts in this room. Alright! When I say slut, that just means you receive everything, okay? The whore gets the money and the slut receives everything. I'll have all of that.

Right, wrong, good and bad, POD and POC, all nine, shorts, boys and beyonds®.

I know that's going to turn some heads. I say it purposely because I know it's a different view point.

Participant: Say it again.

Dr. Lisa: A whore gets the money and a slut receives everything.

Right, wrong, good and bad, POD and POC, all nine, shorts, boys and beyonds®.

So all your decisions, judgments, conclusions, and computations about what you know to be a whore and what you know to be a slut or what you've judged to be a whore and a slut, can we destroy and uncreate that right now?

Participants: Yes.

Dr. Lisa: Right, wrong, good and bad, POD and POC, all nine, shorts, boys and beyonds®.

I'll go back that in a moment, but before that, I want to tell you that I had a very sordid, horrific, couple of first decades in my life living through a number of different abuses, including financial abuse.

And when I first met Gary Douglas, the founder of Access Consciousness, he was doing some facilitation on me in a 7-day workshop in New Zealand and said, "Honey, you're a slut."

I started crying because I believed that it was bad to be a slut, and I didn't know that I believed it at that level, or that I believed that the reason I got abused was because I was a slut. I believed I did something wrong.

And so, he said to me, "Honey, would you like to know what I mean by that?"

I said, "Absolutely."

He goes, "Do you have a judgment about anyone or anything?"

"No, not really."

And he said, "Even through all the abuses that you went through, did you hate the people?"

"No."

He said, "Do you know that that's rare and that's different?"

"I do."

And he said, "You can receive from anyone. And you can receive anything, and that's you. So, would you like to embody the slut that you really be?"

And I said "Hell, yes!"

But it took that switch of my judgment about what it meant to be a slut because, until then, it related to my past abuse.

As somebody who did experience a lot of abuse, it took a long time for me to allow my body to enjoy, head to toe, complete orgasmic embodiment. And I still have some stuff around it, but it's 99.9 % better.

Then I said, "But what is a whore?"

And he said, "Hey, baby, the whore gets the money."

And that's truth, because if he or she isn't going to get it, he or she has somebody to go get it.

That's what I want to be.

I'm not saying that I have to pimp myself out or inauthentic, not be genuine. I'm not saying to screw people over, or kill people. And he wasn't saying that, he was framing something so outrageous to me to get me to think outside my own cage of what I wouldn't receive. It was incredibly freeing and I adore him for it.

I'm saying that everything we think destroys our capacity to create and actualize if we have a fixed judgment attached to it.

And, if it's not creating, if you're not creating what you're willing to actualize, if you've got something going on, then there are some decision and judgments that will be good for you to destroy and uncreate, even the ones that you feel a little superior about, like whores and sluts.

Here's a good one: Donald Trump. Like him or hate him?

Participant: Oh, my god. Slut, whore.

Dr. Lisa: Right, wrong, good and bad, POD and POC, all nine, shorts, boys and beyonds®.

Here's the thing...

Are you going to think I'm weird or judge me because I think there's something brilliant about him with money that I'd like to learn about? I don't want him as my president. But there's something brilliant financially about him that he has created from nothing over and over and over again into billions. He's had bankruptcies and things like that.

"Whoa. I want to learn that."

Can you learn from somebody you hate, that you despise? Some of you know you can. But some of you refuse to open to the level and depth of receiving that is possible, even with those you judge.

Do any of you judge your mother?

Participants: Yes.

Dr. Lisa: How much can you receive from her if you judge her?

Participants: Nothing.

Dr. Lisa: Not very much.

Dr. Lisa: Right, wrong, good and bad, POD and POC, all nine, shorts, boys and beyonds®.

You'll notice when you're judging someone, it's like your heart constricts or your body constricts, or you feel kind of dense, or you want to back away.

How much can you receive from them?

It's the same thing with money.

The more judgments you can receive and the more judgments you can let go of, the more money flows and the more cash will come into your life, that you'll receive.

Dr. Lisa: Right, wrong, good and bad, POD and POC, all nine, shorts, boys and beyonds®.

I kind of jumped ahead to lie #3 – it's about receiving.

So the first lie is that it's about money.

The second lie is that your net worth has anything to do with your self-worth.

And the third lie is about receiving and judgments in your life.

The more judgments you receive – you can actually increase your salary $5,000 a month. Would you like that?

Participants: Yes.

Dr. Lisa: I'm not saying to go stand up in front of the room and say, "Everybody, can you judge me? Throw your darts at me."

I just sat with a teenager the other night yelling at their mother, and I went to them and said, "How much more can one person take? Are you done? Do you want me to go hang her up by the fire and let her burn? Like what? Like knock it off already."

Right? Teenagers.

Right, wrong, good and bad, POD and POC, all nine, shorts, boys and beyonds®.

Let's go back to this:

So, all the relationships you're no longer in that left an imprint on you sexually – the sexual relationships that you're no longer in, including the marriages that left an imprint on you, about their points of view about money, about their points of view about you, about their points of view about cash, about their judgments about you that are still swimming around in your cellular consciousness, would you like to be energetically divorced from that?

Participants: Yes.

Dr. Lisa: Would you like to dissipate and release that to the earth?

Participants: Yes.

Dr. Lisa: Would you like to return anything that is theirs to them with consciousness attached?

Participants: Yes.

Dr. Lisa: Right, wrong, good and bad, POD and POC, all nine, shorts, boys and beyonds®.

Would you like to free your whole sexual system from their reality?

Participants: Yes.

Dr. Lisa: And let your sexual-ness flourish, blossom? With new possibility?

Right, wrong, good and bad, POD and POC, all nine, shorts, boys and beyonds®.

Everywhere they're the lock and you are the key, and you are the lock and they are the key, can we put the locks and the key and the key and the lock and all of the locks and all of the keys and all the keys and locks together and set you free?

Participants: Yes.

Dr. Lisa: Right, wrong, good and bad, POD and POC, all nine, shorts, boys and beyonds®.

And everything you thought was your financial reality from them, that you're learning is no longer your financial reality and was them, can we destroy and uncreate that?

Participants: Yes.

Dr. Lisa: Right, wrong, good and bad, POD and POC, all nine, shorts, boys and beyonds®.

And everything they judged, concluded, and decided about you, which they left inside of you, and you made that you, can we destroy and uncreate that?

Participants: Yes.

Dr. Lisa: Right, wrong, good and bad, POD and POC, all nine, shorts, boys and beyonds®.

Notice how the room and the energy in the room "felt" you know, an hour ago, and how it feels now?

What do you notice?

Dr. Lisa: Lighter, more space, heavier, denser?

Participant: Lighter.

Dr. Lisa: You feel heavier, you feel lighter, there's no right or wrong.

Participant: Yes, that's good. There's a different mix of the energy, the light and the heavy.

Dr. Lisa: Yes.

Participant: Right now.

Dr. Lisa: Yes.

Participant: Because I'm feeling disconnected with what you're saying.

Dr. Lisa: Right, so some of you are going to feel light. Some of you are going to be feeling a little bit heavier right now, but here's what I can say.

In the beginning, I usually can't see to a certain point in the room, and then when I start facilitating, the room kind of opens up and I can see more of the faces. As we do more clearings, some of you that are in the back just start popping up a little bit more.

Participant: I remember all the judgements throughout the past 30 years of Jackie Onassis. I would always say that I would never be like her, that I would go with somebody because I love him and not because of the money. She's actually now my hero.

She was a slut and whore.

She actually made a deal with Onassis and said, "Okay, I'll fuck you once a month and you give me everything." She had a yacht, a plane and everything – and she'd fuck him once a month.

Participant: Only once a month?

Participant: Yes, once a month.

Dr. Lisa: Would like to have a billion dollars for fucking somebody once a month?

Participant: Yes.

Dr. Lisa: Right, wrong, good and bad, POD and POC, all nine, shorts, boys and beyonds®.

Everywhere you're unwilling to know, be, receive, and perceive that, can we destroy and uncreate it?

Participant: Yes.

Dr. Lisa: Right, wrong, good and bad, POD and POC, all nine, shorts, boys and beyonds®.

Everywhere an arrangement is not a relationship, can we destroy and uncreate that?

Participant: Yes.

Dr. Lisa: Right, wrong, good and bad, POD and POC, all nine, shorts, boys and beyonds®.

Everywhere an arrangement is not a marriage, can we destroy and uncreate that?

Participant: Yes.

Dr. Lisa: Right, wrong, good and bad, POD and POC, all nine, shorts, boys and beyonds®.

My daddy always told me, "Do what you love, be happy. It doesn't matter how it shows up. This is never going to show up the way that you think it will."

What if you're just happy? What if she was just happy choosing what she did?

Participant: I bet she was.

Dr. Lisa: She has a relationship with someone that she only has to sleep with, or loves to sleep with, once a month and she gets to live the rest of her life being free, not just because she was next to somebody that got shot. But, hey, why not?

Everywhere that is a wrongness and not a strong-ness, can we destroy and uncreate it?

Participants: Yes.

Dr. Lisa: Right, wrong, good and bad, POD and POC, all nine, shorts, boys and beyonds®.

And everywhere it might be wrong in your mind, or in this reality, or in somebody else's point of view that you've made your point of view to be a whore or be a slut and choose something that looks a little different than you know, the black tuxedo and the white gown on top of a cake, can we destroy and uncreate it?

Participants: Yes.

Dr. Lisa: Right, wrong, good and bad, POD and POC, all nine, shorts, boys and beyonds®.

Anybody know what the divorce rate is in this country? I'll have a job for the rest of my life.

So what if we all just made arrangements that worked for both of us.

Participant: That'll work.

Dr. Lisa: Right, is that going to deter your net worth?

Participant: Maybe.

Dr. Lisa: All the net worth that it will deter if you make an arrangement, can we destroy and uncreate it?

Participants: Yes.

Dr. Lisa: Right, wrong, good and bad, POD and POC, all nine, shorts, boys and beyonds®.

So this goes back to lie #1, that it has nothing to do with the money.

Here's something that I love to do because my original background was marriage and family therapy: Money and you go to couples therapy, okay?

The therapist asks money, "Why did you come here today? What would you like to tell your partner? What would you like to tell your beloved, your enjoyable other, your husband, your wife, the one you hate, I mean love? What would you like to tell them?"

So, if your money could talk to you in therapy, what would it say to you?

Participant: If you looked at my purse, it would be spilled out all over the place and totally disorganized, so that mine would say, "She doesn't organize me and keep me in her wallet nice and neat."

I don't respect it.

Dr. Lisa: So money would say to you, "You don't respect me."

Participant: Yes.

Dr. Lisa: "You throw me around, you keep me in the bottom of your wallet, you crumple me up. I can't even go to the dry cleaners and get ironed out because you made me crinkly."

Right, wrong, good and bad, POD and POC, all nine, shorts, boys and beyonds®.

So all the disrespect of money, all the ways that you gave it away, all the ways you never allowed yourself to have it, all the ways you've let it own you and you've never been the owner of it, can we destroy and uncreate that?

Right, wrong, good and bad, POD and POC, all nine, shorts, boys and beyonds®.

Who else? If money took you to therapy, what would it say to you?

Participant: I hear, "You don't love me enough."

But I do everything – I have my $1,000 in my bag. I sleep with it, I kiss it.

Dr. Lisa: So here's what I heard: Her money said, "You don't love me enough," and then she went into all the defenses about what she's doing and she's doing so much.

It's just like a relationship with your spouses, right?

Participants: Yes.

Dr. Lisa: This is what we do.

Your spouse says, "You don't love me enough." You listen for half a second and, before they say 'enough,' you're like, "But I do everything. I do everything, oh my god. I do this and I do this and I do this and you never listen to me at all. No appreciation, blah, blah, blah, blah. What are you going to do to fix it? You're the problem, not me, you're the problem, not me, you're the problem, not me."

Dr. Lisa: Right, wrong, good and bad, POD and POC, all nine, shorts, boys and beyonds®.

Thank you for giving me a great example about my #1 lie of money.

We make it about money, but it's not about money, so here's my question to you: You don't have any demand in your world or control in your world, do you?

Right, wrong, good and bad, POD and POC, all nine, shorts, boys and beyonds®.

So "I do everything" – is that coming from your head or your body when you say you're doing everything?

Participant: My head.

Dr. Lisa: So everywhere you've tried to figure out in your relationship, not just with money, but in relationship with money, what else you can do to make the change instead of asking, "What am I refusing to be to allow the change that I'm looking for," can we destroy and uncreate?

Participant: Yes.

Dr. Lisa: Right, wrong, good and bad, POD and POC, all nine, shorts, boys and beyonds®.

Because I'll tell you what, if someone demands you to be something different, do you go toward it or do you run the other way?

Participant: Run the other way.

Dr. Lisa: I know I would, if someone tells me I need to do something.

In the back of my head, I'm thinking, "Let's see, I was tortured and abused for about two or three decades, I need to do something else."

Right, wrong, good and bad, POD and POC, all nine, shorts, boys and beyonds®.

What are you refusing to be when you put the money in your wallet and ask it what would it like to say, and it says, "You don't love me."

What are you refusing to be that, if you would be it, would change that energy right away?

Dr. Lisa: Right, wrong, good and bad, POD and POC, all nine, shorts, boys and beyonds®.

What are you all refusing to be with money that, if you would just be it – if you would love it, if you would rub it, if you would honor it, if you would respect it, if you would kiss it – I don't care what you do with it – but if you love it, create it from the joy of possibility of who you be and what you would like as your reality, it will come.

Dr. Lisa: Right, wrong, good and bad, POD and POC, all nine, shorts, boys and beyonds®.

The universe will conspire to bless you, but you have to choose you and you have to commit to you.

Commit to you – not just because I tell you to.

Otherwise, you're not using your money as a possibility. And you're not using your money as possibility because you're not willing to be the possibility.

What if you were the possibility walking and that is your financial reality?

Participant: That sounds like a Western.

Dr. Lisa: Totally. Possibility walking.

Right, wrong, good and bad, POD and POC, all nine, shorts, boys and beyonds®.

Participant: Money was always used as a punishment in my family.

My parents got divorced and my dad punished my mom by taking all the money away because he loved her. He wanted to stay with her and she didn't, so we ended up with her living in Paris, but in a tiny apartment being poor. This was after being the daughter of an ambassador living in a huge house in the best place in Paris.

Dr. Lisa: So let me ask you a question…

What did you decide about money right then and there, from what you saw with your mother and father? Truth?

First thought, best thought, no thought.

Participant: That money was mean.

Dr. Lisa: Right, wrong, good and bad, POD and POC, all nine, shorts, boys and beyonds®.

Dr. Lisa: Exactly. Now can I share something with you?

The way that you just talked to your money there, "But I do everything," – that's mean.

Participant: That's mean, yes.

Dr. Lisa: And that's why whatever you want to change with money isn't changing, and it has nothing to do with money.

It has to do with you being mean and choosing to be mean just like your mother and father were with each other.

Everywhere your mother and father's relationship is in the energy of your money, can we revoke, rescind, recant, renounce, denounce, destroy, and uncreate the forever commitment to that?

Participant: Yes.

Dr. Lisa: Right, wrong, good and bad, POD and POC, all nine, shorts, boys and beyonds®.

Dr. Lisa: And all the vibrational, virtual, realities, the persona that you create, the way that you configured your life as your parents' relationship in this.

Participant: Yes.

Dr. Lisa: Right, wrong, good and bad, POD and POC, all nine, shorts, boys and beyonds®.

Dr. Lisa: And I would dare to say in all your relationships – your relationship with yourself and your relationship with others – but we'll just say money for right now, can we destroy and uncreate that?

Participant: Yes.

Dr. Lisa: Right, wrong, good and bad, POD and POC, all nine, shorts, boys and beyonds®.

Dr. Lisa: And all the secret, hidden, invisible, covert, unseen, unacknowledged, unspoken, undisclosed agendas to reliving your parents' divorce, and your money flows, and then your relationship many decades later and calling that saneness, can we destroy and uncreate that?

Participant: Yes.

Dr. Lisa: Right, wrong, good and bad, POD and POC, all nine, shorts, boys and beyonds®.

And all the insanity of your parents' financial reality that you've made your reality and called yourself the CFO (chief financial officer), can we destroy and uncreate that?

Participant: Yes.

Dr. Lisa: Right, wrong, good and bad, POD and POC, all nine, shorts, boys and beyonds®.

How much insanity are you willing to give up tonight about your parents, not blaming them?

Dr. Lisa: Right, wrong, good and bad, POD and POC, all nine, shorts, boys and beyonds®.

How much insanity? Because you can hear when you start telling the story, it was like, "Damn Paris, money, divorce. Get me out of here, save me, save me."

But the reality is we all have that insanity around money.

That's why the lie #2 is that our net worth has something to do with our self-worth. That's why we make it about money and we go to all these money workshops where we think somebody's going to give us the answer to our flow.

Well, the answer is not a configuration or a computation, the answer is you being you.

Are you mean?

Participant: Yes, I am obviously.

Dr. Lisa: Intrinsically, though, are you mean? When you were a kid watching what your parents did, did you like it?

Participant: No, I was going to say I was so mean, but, yes.

Dr. Lisa: Hold on a second…this is good.

Participant: Yes.

Dr. Lisa: So say, "I'm mean."

Participant: I'm mean.

Dr. Lisa: Say, "I'm mean."

Participant: I'm mean.

Dr. Lisa: "I'm really fucking mean."

Participant: I'm really fucking mean.

Dr. Lisa: I definitely know that I wouldn't want to be on your other side, on that mean side, because you could slice me right in half, couldn't you?

Participant: Oh, yes.

Dr. Lisa: Everything that is, can we destroy and uncreate it?

Participant: Yes.

Dr. Lisa: Right, wrong, good and bad, POD and POC, all nine, shorts, boys and beyonds®.

Money comes to the party of fun. It doesn't come to meanness and being sliced apart, everybody will run.

Are you done with people running from you?

Participant: Yes.

Dr. Lisa: And are you done running from you?

Participant: Yes.

Dr. Lisa: Are you done running from you?

Participant: No, I have one more thing.

Dr. Lisa: Of course you do.

Right, wrong, good and bad, POD and POC, all nine, shorts, boys and beyonds®.

Participant: Since my dad wasn't giving enough money to my mother, in vengeance, my mother put me in the most expensive schools in the world so he would have to pay the schools and spend the money.

Dr. Lisa: So the other lie that I was going to talk about tonight is that money is your enemy – money as your perpetrator, not your ally and that's what she's talking about here.

Participant: Yes.

Dr. Lisa: Would you like to give that up 1% more?

Participant: Yes.

Dr. Lisa: Everywhere you projected that if your money went to couples' therapy with you would say, "You hate me. You want to destroy me. You think I'm going to kill you," can we destroy and uncreate that?

Participant: Yes.

Dr. Lisa: Right, wrong, good and bad, POD and POC, all nine, shorts, boys and beyonds®.

My father was brilliant in some ways. He wasn't the best at certain things, like relationship. In fact, he actually had a whole other relationship that we learned about at some point.

So, yes, my mother did have some rightful anger, but there were other things.

He used to leave a stack of money on the counter, $100 bills for my mother at the beginning of the week on the counter out the side door, and it was her contract to stay silent.

It's a little embarrassing, but my mom never asked us what we wanted. She only spent my father's money so that she could ask him for more, because that was all she could get from him.

Money was a punishment, money was control, money was manipulation, and I had to undo all of that – to untwist the insanity.

It would keep her quiet, so to speak.

I remember one day, she got me 8 Cabbage Patch dolls. Do you guys remember Cabbage Patch dolls?

Participants: Yes.

Dr. Lisa: I was a bit of a tomboy and didn't really want cabbage patch dolls, but it was the 80s and it was a big thing back. I'll never forget it. One day I walked in to my bedroom and they were all up on the shelf. My mom told my father about it and said, "I need more money for this. Lisa, tell your father about da, da, da, da."

And I said, "I didn't even, like what? Yes, I got Cabbage Patch Dolls, thanks dad."

I left and went somewhere. "Oh my god, these people are crazy. What is this reality?"

It's insane how people use money.

Did she know any better? No, that was their dynamic, resentment, rejection, regret around money.

So all the resentments, all the rejections, all the regrets around money that you embody as your financial reality, keeping money as your enemy and not your ally, would you like to destroy and uncreate it?

Dr. Lisa: Right, wrong, good and bad, POD and POC, all nine, shorts, boys and beyonds®.

Would you like to pull yourself out of your mother's reality and your father's reality or the police officer's or the IRS' or your ex's?

Participant: Yes.

Right, wrong, good and bad, POD and POC, all nine, shorts, boys and beyonds®.

And would you be willing to drop the meanness that you chose as your costume, your persona, based on what you witnessed.

Participant: Yes.

Dr. Lisa: And step out and be you?

Dr. Lisa: Right, wrong, good and bad, POD and POC, all nine, shorts, boys and beyonds®.

Just 1% more because there's a beauty and softness inside of you that is the real you. I can see that, but it's underneath all of this armoring of that meanness. And there's nothing more painful than living as not you with that armor.

I know because I lived that too.

Once it's gone, once you unzip yourself out of it and step into you, providence will move too.

Right, wrong, good and bad, POD and POC, all nine, shorts, boys and beyonds®.

So you're at couples' therapy with your money. What would you say to it or it to you?

Participant: "You never let me have you," or something like that.

Dr. Lisa: How many of you have heard that from somebody that supposedly loves you? Or that you love?

Or how many of you have said that to somebody?

So what's the best part about not having money?

Participant: I can do what I want.

Nobody bothers me.

Dr. Lisa: Everywhere all of you keep money away from you so that you can do what you want – have control and keep everything away from you including money, can we destroy and uncreate it?

Right, wrong, good and bad, POD and POC, all nine, shorts, boys and beyonds®.

It's like saying, "In order for me to have control, I can't have that."

Participant: Yes.

Dr. Lisa: "So I have to block you and withdraw from you, so that I can have control and do what I wish to do."

But you're pushing away something that in this reality can give you more choice, right?

Participants: Yes.

Dr. Lisa: Money gives you more freedom, right?

Participants: Yes.

Dr. Lisa: This reality pulses on it, right?

Participants: Yes.

Dr. Lisa: You can fight it all you want and create all the stuff you want, but guess what?

If you keep doing that you're going to lose because this reality vibrates differently.

What if you spent all of your energy actually receiving it instead of pushing it away? Who would you be then? What plane would you own? How would the world be different? What presidential race might you join? What might you create that would change something, cure a disease, allow you to be happy?

Instead, you're going to fight the very thing that gives you freedom.

So it's a choice.

Right, wrong, good and bad, POD and POC, all nine, shorts, boys and beyonds®.

I'm saying all these things because I know them.

Believe me, when you have a stack of money on the counter every week and you watch what happens, you develop some limitations. You develop an incarceration and then you create an incarnation every day.

It's the same insanity over and over and over again until you actually forget that you have a different choice, and that what you're creating is not who you be until you wake up that moment and say, "I refuse to do that anymore. I'm being me."

Right, wrong, good and bad, POD and POC, all nine, shorts, boys and beyonds®.

Participant: I'm really good at creating money when I require it, like really fast. And I'm very good at borrowing from people. Then, when it comes time to pay everybody back, I think, "This sucks!"

It's not fun to pay people back or pay my debts back, and I want to know how can I make it fun?

Dr. Lisa: So what do you love about hating paying back?

Participant: It's like once I pay them back, then they can go away.

Dr. Lisa: Does it have anything to do with money?

Participant: No.

Dr. Lisa: No. Lie #1 in action.

Right, wrong, good and bad, POD and POC, all nine, shorts, boys and beyonds®.

Say it again, "So when I pay them back…"

Participant: When I pay them back, then they can go away.

Dr. Lisa: Right, and if they go away, what happens then?

Participant: Then I lose them.

Dr. Lisa: And if you lose them, what does that mean about you?

Participant: That nobody likes me.

Dr. Lisa: And if nobody likes you, what does that mean about you?

Participant: I'm blank.

Dr. Lisa: Good, because now we're getting somewhere that you don't know. That's the look of what she doesn't know and a little bit of pain.

Right, wrong, good and bad, POD and POC, all nine, shorts, boys and beyonds®.

What do you love about not having people around and you get to be alone and be nothing.

Participant: Then I can do what I want.

Dr. Lisa: Oh, here we are again.

So does this have anything to do with money?

No, she's projected it on money, so her whole motto is to be alone and do whatever she wants. She has to project all this crap onto money, this whole dynamic of making it to the last moment with the whole big catastrophe and drama and getting money and borrowing and having people give it to her, and then having to pay them back. She puts the brakes on so that she can stay in control and nobody needs to be with her.

Maybe choose to do it with clothes instead of money.

Right, wrong, good and bad, POD and POC, all nine, shorts, boys and beyonds®.

It's like saying, "Let me take the very thing this reality focuses and functions on and create such a struggle and drama and trauma about it so that I can never actually get beyond it, and never get in relationship with it, and never be an ally with it, so that I can always be in struggle with the very thing that this reality pulses on. Cheers."

Right, wrong, good and bad, POD and POC, all nine, shorts, boys and beyonds®.

How many of you do that, too? What else?

Participant: My story is a little bit different.

I'm able to generate the money for the class, or whatever it is, and then it's like I cut off my receiving.

Dr. Lisa: Everything we're talking about is a cutting off of receiving here.

So what's the problem? What would you like contribution on?

Participant: Not creating enough. I'm creating just enough to get there and then I stop. But I need more to be able to take care of all the everyday stuff that keeps happening.

Dr. Lisa: So what's she's saying is that she creates really well, but she creates for what's right in front of her and not for future.

So, truth, what's your judgment about future?

Participant: I'm judging it from my past.

Dr. Lisa: That's your head talking right now, but, truth, what's your judgment of futures?

First thought, best thought, no thought.

Participant: It's scary for me.

Dr. Lisa: Thank you.

Right, wrong, good and bad, POD and POC, all nine, shorts, boys and beyonds®.

What's your judgment of futures? How can you create for something that you're afraid of?

Right, wrong, good and bad, POD and POC, all nine, shorts, boys and beyonds®.

What's your judgment of futures?

Participant: Still scary.

Dr. Lisa: Right, wrong, good and bad, POD and POC, all nine, shorts, boys and beyonds®.

What's your judgment of futures, truth?

Participant: It's not enough.

Dr. Lisa: Right, wrong, good and bad, POD and POC, all nine, shorts, boys and beyonds®.

For those of you who aren't familiar with Access, every time I run the clearing statement it clears another level.

We're not at the hub yet – that's what I'm looking for right now – we're on some of the spokes.

What's your judgment of futures? What does future mean to you?

This is really good that she actually can't get something, because now I know I'm onto something that she hasn't been onto and that hasn't come out yet.

And, when it comes out, it's going to change her reality, as well as all of you.

Right, wrong, good and bad, POD and POC, all nine, shorts, boys and beyonds®.

What does future mean to you? Truth?

Participant: It is poverty.

Dr. Lisa: Poverty?

Participant: Yes.

Dr. Lisa: Wow.

Right, wrong, good and bad, POD and POC, all nine, shorts, boys and beyonds®.

"Here, let me try to create something for the future when I believe that it's fear, fear, fear, and poverty. Sounds fun. Let's go."

Participant: Welcome aboard.

Dr. Lisa: Right, wrong, good and bad, POD and POC, all nine, shorts, boys and beyonds®.

What's your judgment of futures?

Participant: Wow!

Dr. Lisa: Exactly.

Right, wrong, good and bad, POD and POC, all nine, shorts, boys and beyonds®.

What's your judgment of futures?

Participant: It's not as scary.

Dr. Lisa: Can you guys perceive all the somatic release that's going on here? She's tapping her feet and wriggling in her body.

Participant: I'm scared.

Dr. Lisa: She can't even stand it. She's got tears in her eyes.

I don't know if you're trying to get the right answer, but you're also not sure of something, too, and that's the opening for a different possibility.

Participant: It's both.

Dr. Lisa: I don't expect you to know this, and I expect you to be exactly what you be.

There's something else here.

Participant: Yes.

Dr. Lisa: It's like she's going out of her skin right now.

This is the gold, right?

The entire room is going to shift when she gets to this.

What does future mean to you? Truth? Fear, poverty, fear, poverty, fear, poverty, what's the right answer?

Is there anything light or airy or expansive that's coming off of her body?

Participant: No.

Dr. Lisa: Or about why she would want to create the future? Are you guys getting why she has the issue she's talking about – that she's great at generating 10 seconds ahead or the next day or the next class, but nothing beyond that? She's showing you it right here.

There's a wall, like "boom," right?

Participant: Yes.

Dr. Lisa: Right, wrong, good and bad, POD and POC, all nine, shorts, boys and beyonds®.

Participant: It's like made of oak and 100 light years thick or something.

Dr. Lisa: So help me out here.

Participant: Okay.

Dr. Lisa: It's something that we do in Access Consciousness™. We're going to grab the energy and then throw out in front of you. I'm going to count to 5 and on 5, we're going to just throw the energy out. Just pretend like you're picking energy up and throwing it with your hands.

Okay, 1, 2, 3, 4, 5...1, 2, 3, 4, 5...1, 2, 3, 4, 5...1, 2, 3, 4, 5.

You guys keep going.

All the algorithmic computations and configurations of the future that keeps you in fear and in poverty and in stuck – 1, 2, 3, 4, 5.

1, 2, 3, 4, 5...1, 2, 3, 4, 5...1, 2, 3, 4, 5...1, 2, 3, 4, 5.

And on 3, throw it down to the Earth. 1, 2, 3...1, 2, 3.

What are we throwing down?

I have no idea other than I know it's blockage.

1, 2, 3...1, 2, 3...1, 2, 3.

And on 4, right out in front of you. 1, 2, 3, 4...open the door to a new possibility. What is your fear of the future?

Participant: Success.

Dr. Lisa: There you go.

Right, wrong, good and bad, POD and POC, all nine, shorts, boys and beyonds®.

Clear the energy, move it around a little bit, and she gets what she was looking for instead of wriggling in her seat.

Right, wrong, good and bad, POD and POC, all nine, shorts, boys and beyonds®.

Everything that success means to you, everything that you mean to success, and every decision, judgment, conclusion, computation, and configuration that you embodied to create the limitation, the incarceration and the incarnation of never creating for the future financially, physically, physiologically, somatically, energetically, can we destroy and uncreate it?

Participant: Hell, yes.

Dr. Lisa: Right, wrong, good and bad, POD and POC, all nine, shorts, boys and beyonds®.

What energy, space, and consciousness can you and your body be to embody a future beyond this reality that you are capable of choosing, but only refusing.

Right, wrong, good and bad, POD and POC, all nine, shorts, boys and beyonds®.

That was a big one.

So somebody else…if you took your money to couples' therapy?

Participant: I'll save it for a rainy day.

Dr. Lisa: What does that actually mean? When it rains, that's the only day you can spend?

Right, wrong, good and bad, POD and POC, all nine, shorts, boys and beyonds®.

I know what it means, but I'm just presenting something.

It's like the catastrophe will come.

You don't know when it's going to come but, this reality is so unsafe that you better have every penny saved so that, when disaster strikes and the tsunami volcano, earthquake, World War V, and a car accident and a disease come, you'll have just enough to pay the first day of what you'll need to actually survive that.

Participant: Yes.

Dr. Lisa: Right, wrong, good and bad, POD and POC, all nine, shorts, boys and beyonds®.

What does it mean about you if you don't save for a rainy day?

Participant: Careless.

Dr. Lisa: And if you're careless, what are you? If you're careless with money, what are you?

Participant: Free.

Dr. Lisa: Right, wrong, good and bad, POD and POC, all nine, shorts, boys and beyonds®.

Dr. Lisa: If you don't save, what are you?

Participant: I am shit out of luck.

Dr. Lisa: Right, wrong, good and bad, POD and POC, all nine, shorts, boys and beyonds®.

Dr. Lisa: That's what you are from your head, but what are you?

Participant: That's what I was told I was.

Dr. Lisa: I know, but what did that make you?

When someone says to you, "You're shit out of luck," what does that intimate about you?

Participant: I'm not responsible.

Dr. Lisa: Right, wrong, good and bad, POD and POC, all nine, shorts, boys and beyonds®.

Dr. Lisa: And if you're not responsible, what does that intimate about you?

Participant: I'm not worthy.

Dr. Lisa: Right, wrong, good and bad, POD and POC, all nine, shorts, boys and beyonds®.

Dr. Lisa: And if you're not worthy, what does that mean about you?

Participant: I'm not valuable.

Dr. Lisa: Right, wrong, good and bad, POD and POC, all nine, shorts, boys and beyonds®.

Dr. Lisa: So you're not worthy, you're not valuable, all because you don't save money for a rainy day?

Dr. Lisa: Right, wrong, good and bad, POD and POC, all nine, shorts, boys and beyonds®.

Participant: Yes.

Dr. Lisa: All of you are nodding.

Everywhere we've all been somnambulantly hypnotized to believe that is true and create a reality that isn't about you based on that, can we destroy and uncreate it?

Participant: Yes.

Dr. Lisa: Right, wrong, good and bad, POD and POC, all nine, shorts, boys and beyonds®.

Again, your net worth has nothing to do with your self-worth, and what you don't have has nothing to do with who you be, what you be, what you do, what you know, what you perceive, and what you receive.

But, in this reality how we were reared, it does.

Is that the truth or is that a lie?

It's a lie, so everywhere you've been molding yourself into lies and calling that your reality, your truth, and allowing yourself to be that chief financial officer of a lie reality, can we destroy and uncreate that?

Dr. Lisa: Right, wrong, good and bad, POD and POC, all nine, shorts, boys and beyonds®.

Participant: Yes.

Dr. Lisa: What else?

Participant: I was going to say, is this financial abuse? Is this what this would be called? I'm financially abusing myself?

Dr. Lisa: It could.

Financial abuse is really when somebody using finances, or holding it over you in some way where you have no power. Anything with abuse is a power dynamic.

This is probably more energetic and psychological inferencing.

Participant: Like a judgment?

Dr. Lisa: Yes, that somehow you're less than or worthless because you're not saving.

Participant: Yes, not enough.

Dr. Lisa: Right, wrong, good and bad, POD and POC, all nine, shorts, boys and beyonds®.

Dr. Lisa: Absolutely.

When my father died, he left a mess for me to clean up – a mess beyond messes – and I'm still cleaning up. Thank god it's almost done.

However, he said very clearly when he was alive, "I want you all to have it and to use it, and I'd love to see you all use it and have it, and how I can support you?"

He made the plan. We just didn't listen.

But he had an issue – he couldn't have anything.

He had to give it to everyone. He gave it to my mom, he gave it to me, and my brother and my sister. He paid for a lot of my cousins' weddings. He paid for other people's weddings.

He was just such a giver, overly generous, but it was because he couldn't believe he was worth having any of it. So any and all of that which could be true for you will you destroy and uncreate it?

Dr. Lisa: Right, wrong, good and bad, POD and POC, all nine, shorts, boys and beyonds®.

Participant: My mom does that a lot.

Dr. Lisa: What is having it mean to this reality?

If you have money, you're safe. Well, I know a lot of people that have money and terrible things still happen to them.

How about if you don't have money, you're not safe? Well, I know a lot of people who don't have a whole lot of money and there's nothing wrong with their life. They're just happy.

So these things that people project, are all intimations and judgments and points of view that are designed to control and configure you into somebody else's view.

When you're configuring into somebody else's view, where do you fit in?

You don't.

How much have you abdicated you from your financial reality to fit into this financial reality?

Right, wrong, good and bad, POD and POC, all nine, shorts, boys and beyonds®.

Where are you? Do you want to save for a rainy day?

Participant: Yes.

Dr. Lisa: Okay, did anybody believe her?

Participant: What's the right answer?

Dr. Lisa: What's the right answer? Oh, my god, is this a thing in Florida? Everybody's looking for the right answer?

Participant: Yes.

Dr. Lisa: Because I'll tell you, I'm probably the worst facilitator ever to come here if you're looking for the right answer.

I'll drive you nuts – there is no right answer.

It's what 's true and light and right for you.

That's like the school system in this country that says, "You get this answer, fit it in the box, you get an A. You get so many wrong, you get a B, so many wrong you get a C, so many wrong you get a D."

Or, if you're in geometry like me, you fail it over and over again and get a tutor until you pass, right?

That's this reality. You have to have the right answer to move forward.

It's no different than you need to have money to have your self-worth, be something better than whatever, like I was saying before. It's all backwards.

You said, "Yes, I want to save for a rainy day." Is that true? Does that make you feel good?

Participant: No.

Dr. Lisa: Who told you that?

Participant: My father.

Dr. Lisa: So it makes sense that we embody our mother and father's reality, right?

Participant: Yes.

Dr. Lisa: Right, wrong, good and bad, POD and POC, all nine, shorts, boys and beyonds®.

Dr. Lisa: Well, we're not three or four or seven years old any longer, and what we forget is that we get to actually choose what's light and right for us.

When I'm asking her if she wants to do that, she says, "No," but then, here's the trick: "If I don't do what my mom and dad said, even if I'm 40 or 30 or 20 or 60, what does that mean about me?

"And what does it mean about them? And what does it mean about me in relation to them and them in relationship to me? Does it mean I'm a bad daughter? Does it mean I'm a good son or not a good son? Does it mean I'm a good mother or not a good mother?"

So all those judgments, conclusions, secret, hidden, invisible, covert, unseen, unacknowledged, unspoken, and undisclosed agendas that keep you thinking it's better to save for a rainy day when your body says, "I don't want to do it," can we destroy and uncreate it?

Right, wrong, good and bad, POD and POC, all nine, shorts, boys and beyonds®.

What ROAR is, that we're going to do tomorrow, is being your radical ally – your orgasmic ally – for the creation of an alive reality that is in and of you, committing to you, creating for you, collaborating with the universe conspiring to bless you, and then choosing for you.

Those Cabbage Patch Dolls… did I ever get asked about them?

No, I wanted GI Joe, damn it!

I loved Superman, I loved playing soccer, I loved going into the city.

I did do child modeling in the city, but I didn't want to do the modeling. I liked the helicopter ride over, but the modeling sucked because you had to stand there and put on whatever they wanted you to put on.

There's was no choice.

My mother wanted it, they wanted it. You stand up, you do it.

That's how many people get sick with life-threatening diseases, and so many relationships end horrifically, and people have money flows issues – because we're all choosing to create our life based on something or someone's point of view that's a lie for us.

Dr. Lisa: Right, wrong, good and bad, POD and POC, all nine, shorts, boys and beyonds®.

And I say, "ROAR. No more."

Be the rumble.

Be the tsunami, the earthquake.

Be the flow that you alter physical reality just by your presence. Say "Yes" when you mean yes, "No" when you mean no.

Stop believing that money is the root of all your problems.

Stop believing anything that you were told about money.

Just say, "Damn it, if this is my financial reality, what would I choose? If I was living my financial reality today, what would I choose?"

Dr. Lisa: Right, wrong, good and bad, POD and POC, all nine, shorts, boys and beyonds®.

Because, then, at least you know you're in the present.

Am I saying not to save?

No.

I'm saying not to embody, configure, align, agree, resist or react to anything that isn't your "Yes" – that's light and right and fun for you.

Dr. Lisa: Right, wrong, good and bad, POD and POC, all nine, shorts, boys and beyonds®.

That is being your radical orgasmic ally of an alive reality.

Do that and the universe will conspire to bless you.

That's what that is.

Participant: Amen, sister.

Participant: Amen to that.

Participant: "Hallelujah!"

Dr. Lisa: Was that helpful?

Participant: Yes, thank you.

Dr. Lisa: Okay, was that helpful to you all?

Participants: Yes!

Dr. Lisa: I always like to end with a big thank you for coming out. Thank you for laughing with me. Thank you for your vulnerability and your courage. Thank you for just showing up.

I really appreciate it and I always say, *"Be you, beyond anything and create magic."*

San Francisco

Dr. Lisa: Thank you everybody. Thank you for being with us.

I've done this 'Taster' before – it's my eighth one over the last six months and, every single time, it's changed. How many of you are not familiar with Access Consciousness?

How many of you have never heard the clearing statement?

Even better.

How many of you actually remember the clearing statement?

Oh, good!

How many of you have ever had Bars™ class?

Okay, excellent, so we can go to many different places. How does it get any better?

I'm going to give my interesting perspective, if you will, on money and the Lies of Money, and then I'm going to use the Access Consciousness™ tools to undo the tangled web and money madness that we choose to create upon ourselves, our bank accounts, our business, and in our life, as well as in our families. We'll unwind some of that. I only ask one thing of you. Are you ready?

Participants: Yes.

Dr. Lisa: All you need to do is ask a question – that's it. This will let me get a gauge for the room and what you're really here for. In a smaller, intimate group like this, you get to play and get something that you may not even know you came here for.

I'm like a dog with a bone when it comes to facilitation. I like to take it apart, rip it left and right and get rid of it – and get you out of there as soon as possible and into something new. How does that sound?

Participants: Yes!

Dr. Lisa: Yes, and how many of you are really, really happy with the way your money situation is right now? At least one in the room.

Participant: Yes.

Dr. Lisa: That's great. Thank you for being here because I don't know what would happen if nobody raised their hand.

How many of you would like to increase your awareness and your bank accounts – literally and figuratively? Okay now we've got everybody, so you're in the right place.

How many of you would like to have more cash? Alright.

How many of you would like to have less money?

Right, wrong, good and bad, POD and POC, all nine, shorts, boys and beyonds®.

How many of you came from very wealthy families? Cool.

How many of you came from really struggling, conflictual families with regards to money? Okay, so that's interesting. Everybody raised their hand on coming from some sort of conflict or struggle or problematic situation with regards to money. That is most of this reality's experience, definition, perspective, and understanding with regards to money.

So, first and foremost, would you be willing to give up 1°? Just 1° is all I'm asking for. You can choose your percentage, but would you be willing to give up 1° of whatever it is that you have decided, judged, concluded, and computed about what money is?

Participants: Yes.

Dr. Lisa: Would you be willing to give up 1° of that? Right here and right now?

Right, wrong, good and bad, POD and POC, all nine, shorts, boys and beyonds®.

Would you be willing to give up 1° of what you've already decided that cash is?

Participants: Yes.

Dr. Lisa: Right, wrong, good and bad, POD and POC, all nine, shorts, boys and beyonds®.

Dr. Lisa: I swear, when I walked in here, I felt like I was in a rabbit hole underneath the Earth, hidden, where I can't breathe. There's no air and I'm going to die. It's like being in a coffin.

Everywhere anybody believes that money has something to do with death and a coffin and dying in any lifetime, dimension, body, and reality, can we revoke, rescind, recant, renounce, denounce, destroy, and uncreate this?

Participants: Yes.

Dr. Lisa: Whatever it is.

Right, wrong, good and bad, POD and POC, all nine, shorts, boys and beyonds®.

Okay, you all said you're familiar with the clearing statement and with Access, and everybody's had Bars™ class.

Have you heard about the energy movements of 1, 2, 3 to clear the energy?

This dissipates and releases the energy to the Earth, and it dissipates anything connected to the past regarding it. It opens the door to a new possibility. It also grabs the future and brings it back. So, just for fun – to help me breathe and to help you guys breathe a little better and have a more fun experience tonight – can we do some 1, 2, 3s to open up whatever it is that's in here about money?

Whatever it is that made it a certain way – this room to go from expansive, light, airy, and full of possibilities to dense, constricted, and very heavy – would you help with me that?

Participants: Yes.

Dr. Lisa: Okay, on three, just take the energy, pretend like you're grabbing something. We're going to throw it down to Earth, ready?

1, 2, 3. 1, 2, 3. 1, 2, 3. 1, 2, 3.

Remember I said just 1° release, right? That's all I'm asking for. This is going to be new for some of you. When you dissipate and release it, try opening your mouth and kind of like spit it out.

1, 2, 3. Yes, there you go. Now we're having fun. 1, 2, 3. 1, 2, 3. Move your body. Move your body. 1, 2, 3. 1, 2, 3. 1, 2, 3. 1, 2, 3. 1, 2, 3. 1, 2, 3.

Participant: Cool.

Dr. Lisa: How does it get any better than that?

Right, wrong, good and bad, POD and POC, all nine, shorts, boys and beyonds®.

We're going to do it together on four, right out in front of us, and open the door to a new possibility. Let's do it a couple of times and remember that breathing thing with your lips.

1, 2, 3, 4. 1, 2, 3, 4. 1, 2, 3, 4. 1, 2, 3, 4. 1, 2, 3, 4. 1, 2, 3, 4. 1, 2, 3, 4.

Open the door to a new possibility. Expand your energy of space for a minute, up, down, right, left, front, and back. Breathe energy in through the front of you, in through the back of you, in through the sides of you, up through your feet, down through your head.

Hi, body. Hi, body. Hi, body. Hi, body. Hi, body. Hi, body. Hi, body.

Do you notice anything different in your body right now?

Participant: More space.

Dr. Lisa: More space? Anything noticeable? It's okay if not.

Participant: Vibrant and a little more alive.

Dr. Lisa: A little more vibrant, a little more alive.

Thank you. I can actually see you all now. Before we did the 1, 2, 3s and 1, 2, 3, 4s, you all had this grey haze around you. I don't know what it is about money, or talking about money and cash, that creates that density, but I do know that's one of the reasons this taster class has been quite successful and people keep asking for it.

It's a haze that comes over all of us when we perceive money, or balance our checkbooks, our budgets, our business around money, around cash, around investments. Do you know what I'm talking about?

Participants: Yes.

Dr. Lisa: Right, wrong, good and bad, POD and POC, all nine, shorts, boys and beyonds®.

Dr. Lisa: You came to a topic that has a lot of projections, judgments, separations, expectations, resentments, rejections, and regrets attached to it. Those energies around money color what the energy of money is really about.

Dr. Lisa: Right, wrong, good and bad, POD and POC, all nine, shorts, boys and beyonds®.

In my personal interesting point of view, the energy of money is about freedom, expansion, consciousness. It's about the light, fullness, and freeness of the unique gift and capacity that you be in the world, and to be that in the world and do whatever it is you do, whatever it is that you love to do that's easy and fun for you. And, most importantly, that you're out in the world where the people that are uniquely qualified to work with you, and come to you, get to receive you, and you get to receive that.

Dr. Dain Heer, co-founder of Access Consciousness™, says, "Essentially, what the real energy of money is in this reality is for you to be you and change the world."

Having money is the freedom and expansive possibility of changing this reality according to what's light, right, and fun and expansive for you. What would you like to be and do if you had all of the money that you desired, and you had 10 seconds to live the rest of your life?

What would you choose?

Right, wrong, good and bad, POD and POC, all nine, shorts, boys and beyonds®.

What I have found out in my life is that it's easy for me to generate and create money. It has been really difficult, until the last couple of years, to have money and allow myself to have it consistently and continuously with investments, with travel, with fun, with the pleasure, with going all over the world.

Right, wrong, good and bad, POD and POC, all nine, shorts, boys and beyonds®.

You know you're from San Francisco when you don't mind paying the prices here. I've had my partner here for the last couple of days and she just left yesterday. She was like, "This is ridiculous." She's used to Texas prices, which is like a pancake for 25 cents.

Right, wrong, good and bad, POD and POC, all nine, shorts, boys and beyonds®.

So generating and creating was easy for me, but the having was something I had to cultivate. This is where my first lie of money came to me – that I could only generate and create and not have. Now did I create that myself?

No. I was mimicking my father's reality.

My father was this poor guy raised by an alcoholic and was a self-made multi-millionaire, but squandered everything away because he always told me, "I was a poor boy from Brooklyn. I never expected to make anything. I never deserved it. I had nobody. I had no one that ever showed me anything of kindness, and all I want is for you guys (meaning my brother, sister, mother, and I) to have whatever you want while you're alive. I want it all spent by the time I'm dead because I don't deserve it."

He couldn't have anything for himself but he could give anything of himself to anyone. That made him happy to see other people shine at what they thought they would never have. We'd go to Yankee stadium or Madison Square Garden, or the Super Bowl or World Series, whatever sports season it was, it didn't matter, and we'd have these seats right up front. They were great and he would give the better seats to us kids and he would get a bleacher seat and come visit us up front. My friends loved him. He'd say, "Get your friends, whoever you want to come." He was so generous, but he couldn't have anything for himself.

How many of you here are like that? So generous, but it's hard to have something for yourself?

Right, wrong, good and bad, POD and POC, all nine, shorts, boys and beyonds®.

After I'm tell you a little of my history to bring up the energy, please ask your questions about anything that comes up for you that you may want to change in here. Someone is going to ask a question that's related to this having thing, and that's going to clear the whole room. You're going to be able to feel all of that. Is this making sense?

Participants: Yes.

Dr. Lisa: Okay, so back to the story.

I'd say, "Dad, come sit with us. Come be here."

"No, you kids have a good time. I'm having a great time. I like your faces happy," he'd say. He would take pictures and do all of that kind of stuff. There was just this sadness that it was great to have him there and to do all of that but, as a kid, I really desired to have him there, to enjoy it other than just the 'high fives' of a goal or touch down or, "Hey, we need a beer," or "Hey, we need a hot dog."

Right, wrong, good and bad, POD and POC, all nine, shorts, boys and beyonds®.

Whatever that energy is of choosing to not have, but knowing you can create and generate, that's a double bind. The middle of the double bind is money. One side is "I can't have. I don't deserve to have. I'm not good enough to have" or some version of that. The other side is "I desire you have."

Participants: Yes.

Dr. Lisa: "What else can I give you? Let me do this. Let me do that."

All the double binds from the middle and either side. All of the double binds from either side of the middle. Can we revoke, rescind, recant, renounce, denounce, destroy, and uncreate all of the double binds creating the double binds, eternally double binded between you and your father, you and your mother, you and your family, you and your children, you and your ancestors, you and your grandparents, you and your genetics from here or Russia or wherever you be.

Can we revoke, rescind, recant, renounce, denounce, destroy, and uncreate that?

Participants: Yes.

Dr. Lisa: Right, wrong, good and bad, POD and POC, all nine, shorts, boys and beyonds®.

All the trifold sequencing systems – if you've never taken a body class or foundation class or something, you may not have heard this – but all of the trifold sequencing systems locking those double binds in place to ensure that you never have money or, if you do, it's like feast or famine. Binge and purge. But you always know what the result is to you. You're going to have to get out there and work so that you can go back and have more fun and there's this work fun, fun, work, work, fun, fun, work, but there's never this broad banded harmony with money.

Can we destroy and uncreate that?

Participants: Yes.

Dr. Lisa: Right, wrong, good and bad, POD and POC, all nine, shorts, boys and beyonds®.

All the automatic response matrices system, the systems, the circuitry, the biochemical reaction through your muscles, ligaments, cells, tendons, organs, systems, fascia, of your body locking that into place so that you always live a double bind and you never get to harmony with money, cash in this reality, can we destroy and uncreate this?

Participants: Yes.

Dr. Lisa: Right, wrong, good and bad, POD and POC, all nine, shorts, boys and beyonds®.

Notice, is it lightening up in your world or densifying? Truth?

Participant: It's gotten lighter.

Dr. Lisa: Lighter, yes. It's gotten lighter. There's still density, right?

However, as I'm speaking what I'm speaking, there's something of truth – not the truth, but the energy of truth that is light – hits the density in the room and then boom!

Participants: Yes.

Dr. Lisa: One of my favorite phrases from facilitating in these classes is, "When density meets space, density dissipates."

Would it be okay if your density dissipates at least 1° in these couple of hours in regards to the lies of money?

Participants: Yes.

Dr. Lisa: Cash?

Participants: Yes.

Dr. Lisa: Right, wrong, good and bad, POD and POC, all nine, shorts, boys and beyonds®.

Would it be okay if the decisions, judgments, decisions, and conclusions, and computations, known and unknown, dissipates regarding the money and cash investments, too?

Right, wrong, good and bad, POD and POC, all nine, shorts, boys and beyonds®.

Would it be okay if at least 1° of the oaths, vows, fealties, commitments, agreements, binding and bonding contracts in this lifetime, dimension, body, or reality or any other lifetime, dimension, body, and reality that you've embodied, known or unknown, dissipates with regards to money, cash, portfolios, investments, and energy flows around money?

Could we destroy and uncreate it now?

Participants: Yes.

Dr. Lisa: Just 1°.

Participants: Yes.

Right, wrong, good and bad, POD and POC, all nine, shorts, boys and beyonds®.

Dr. Lisa: Anybody getting a little cooler? Anybody feeling a little bit more air?

Participants: Yes.

Dr. Lisa: That's because we're moving the density out and off of you. That's the best thing about Access, truthfully, when you run the clearing statement over and over and use some of the terminology of trifold sequencing systems or oaths, vows, fealty, or decisions, judgments, conclusion, and computation. It's like an energy vacuum that just goes, "Shroooo!"

We're getting rid of the 'dust bunnies' – the confusion. Access Consciousness™ might call them distractor implants, those things that you aligned and agreed with around money, or resisted and reacted to around money, that actually popped into your body and changed the physical structure of you around money.

Right, wrong, good and bad, POD and POC, all nine, shorts, boys and beyonds®.

Does this make sense?

Participants: Yes.

Dr. Lisa: Intrigued?

Participants: Yes.

Dr. Lisa: Alright, now we're getting somewhere.

Right, wrong, good and bad, POD and POC, all nine, shorts, boys and beyonds®.

We're going to talk about having and refusing to help. We're also going to be talking about receiving.

Gary Douglas, founder of Access Consciousness, has a workbook called, *Money Isn't the Problem, You Are.* When I first saw that I thought, "I'm not the problem, money is."

But, truth, if money was your lover, does it sleep on the couch? Or is it in bed with you?

Right, wrong, good and bad, POD and POC, all nine, shorts, boys and beyonds®.

You know, I used to lick money as a kid. I had a little affair with it. I loved money, I didn't know how to have it.

I grew up in New York and went to school in Connecticut. My friends would come over to my house and we'd drive back to college together. Their dads would be like, "Here's your $20," and my dad would be like, "Here's a few hundred."

I was so embarrassed about it and frankly had no idea how to keep it or use it. It was the most random experience. It's really a beautiful story. I love talking about him because right down the road is where I spread his ashes. It's why I love coming back to San Francisco.

I lived here for 20+ years. I had a clinic and a practice here until about 11 or 12 months ago. It's a very meaningful place for me, and this is the first time I've been this close to where I let his ashes go. That's where he wanted it. It's been very beautiful to be here.

Anyway, I definitely squandered a lot of money. I was the queen of the lies of money.

Right, wrong, good and bad, POD and POC, all nine, shorts, boys and beyonds®.

I thought it was 'go big or go home.' That's one of the things he taught me to my detriment.

Another thing was that, whenever I would ask him for money, or how to create it, he'd say, "Alright, Lisa. Remember what I told you. It's not just a man's world. It's a woman's world. Do what you love. Never settle for anybody or anything. Whatever you do, don't work for anybody. Be your own boss. It's not just a man's world. And, while I'm talking to you, don't get married either. But if you do, don't do the opposites attract thing because it doesn't work."

I was like, "Thanks dad."

There's a reason why I have a doctorate in psychology – because of everything I needed to go through to undo.

Participants: Yes.

Right, wrong, good and bad, POD and POC, all nine, shorts, boys and beyonds®.

The point is that when I would ask him about money, he'd say, "Alright, I'll go down to the printing press and see what I can come up with." Literally. And the next thing I knew, I would see 'x' amount of money in my bank account, thousands of dollars or whatever he chose to gift. My very own ATM.

For years, I never learned how to have money myself, or generate and create it, even though he was telling me over and over and over again it's not just a man's world, be your own boss. He loved what I did. He even came out here and would do these breathwork workshops I facilitated with me. He was so supportive and open.

He had such an influence on my life, and when he left it was kind of a bummer. He did do this other weird thing with money, which was a double bind. You can create anything that you desire, but I'm the source of it. He didn't say that, but that's what I interpreted and intimated and modeled and generated. It took a really long time for me have my own back like that financially.

Everything that brings up and lets down for you, for all of you in here that may not know what it feels like, smells like, and tastes like to have your own back or to be the source for the creation and generation of not only with money, not only cash, but also to know your 'yes' when you mean yes, your 'no' when you mean no. Let's take a step toward the infinite possibilities, the multiplicity of possibilities that come your way that are light and right, and also to say 'no' when something comes your way that you know is a lie.

Right, wrong, good and bad, POD and POC, all nine, shorts, boys and beyonds®.

Because I'm sure none of you in here have ever said 'yes' when you meant no and 'no' when you meant yes. I'm sure I'm the only one that's ever done that. Right?

Right, wrong, good and bad, POD and POC, all nine, shorts, boys and beyonds®.

So let's pretend you bring your money to couple's therapy, what would it say to you? Go ahead.

Participant: Oh, maybe "Ugh," like Charlie Brown.

Participant: What the fuck are you doing?

Dr. Lisa: What the fuck are you doing? Oh, yes, money comes to the party of fun, not judgment.

Right, wrong, good and bad, POD and POC, all nine, shorts, boys and beyonds®.

Participant: Why don't you like me?

Dr. Lisa: Why don't you like me?

Right, wrong, good and bad, POD and POC, all nine, shorts, boys and beyonds®.

What else?

Participant: You don't really love me.

Dr. Lisa: You don't really love me, my favorite one. You don't really love me. What else would it say?

Dr. Lisa: Right, wrong, good and bad, POD and POC, all nine, shorts, boys and beyonds®.

Participant: Where are you?

Dr. Lisa: Where are you? Where did you go? Oh, gone again?

Right, wrong, good and bad, POD and POC, all nine, shorts, boys and beyonds®.

Participant: You only like when I'm here.

Dr. Lisa: You only like when I'm here.

Right, wrong, good and bad, POD and POC, all nine, shorts, boys and beyonds®.

Dr. Lisa: How many times do all of you only feel safe or secure in this world when you actually have money in the account and, when it's in your account, you look at it and you're like, "Ugh." Then you start paying bills and you think you have more than you have. The next time you look at it, you have a dollar in the account and you think, "Whoa!"

Participant: Bastard, you always leave me.

Dr. Lisa: Right, wrong, good and bad, POD and POC, all nine, shorts, boys and beyonds®.

Okay, the third lie of money: What lie am I buying into that actually isn't true? The lie is anything that is heavy, dense, constrictive.

Participant: I only feel safe when I have no money and I'm sitting on the ground under a tree. That's what came up. That's when I feel safe.

Dr. Lisa: Okay. Well, the insanity part of the money class is tomorrow.

Right, wrong, good and bad, POD and POC, all nine, shorts, boys and beyonds®.

All the insanity of money, which is the lie that you're buying into, that you've bought from someone or that you sold to buy as well, can we destroy and uncreate that?

Participants: Yes.

Dr. Lisa: Right, wrong, good and bad, POD and POC, all nine, shorts, boys and beyonds®.

What else would you tell your money in couple's therapy?

Participant: You're dirty.

Dr. Lisa: If you start to yawn when you're in class, that's a lie, un unconscious lie coming up. Those are what's called the SHICUUUU implants and explants in Access Consciousness™. SHICUUUU means secret, hidden, invisible, covert, unseen, unacknowledged, unspoken, undisclosed agendas™.

All the unspoken lies around money and cash, known and unknown, can we destroy and uncreate those right now?

Participants: Yes.

Dr. Lisa: 1° of them.

Right, wrong, good and bad, POD and POC, all nine, shorts, boys and beyonds™.

And anything and everything that doesn't allow you to be, know, and receive, and perceive that that density is not yours, because you can't change something that isn't yours, so you might as well let it go – unless you like torture, which you could in San Francisco, right? There's a whole underground world. You're all laughing because you know about it. I knew I attracted the right people here.

Right, wrong, good and bad, POD and POC, all nine, shorts, boys and beyonds®.

You've got to remember I lived here for 20 years and I've heard every story under the sun. I know about everything here – the above ground, the underground, and the in between.

Right, wrong, good and bad, POD and POC, all nine, shorts, boys and beyonds®.

I'm bound by confidentiality and I love it. Unless you're going to commit a crime or kill yourself at home, mum's the word, go have fun. Look, you're all so happy now. I should have called this the lies of sex. Right?

Right, wrong, good and bad, POD and POC, all nine, shorts, boys and beyonds®.

Any other lies of money? What else does your money say to you in couple's therapy? Anything else want to pop up for now? We can just leave it there and it will come back. You know, therapy can go on and on for decades.

Participant: You never invite me home.

Dr. Lisa: You never invite me home.

Right, wrong, good and bad, POD and POC, all nine, shorts, boys and beyonds®.

What's the first word that everybody said in couple's therapy?

Participants: You.

Dr. Lisa: You (points finger).

Participant: Yes.

Dr. Lisa: You know that when you point the finger, you are devaluing and disowning what's true within you. That actually creates that judgment your projecting outside of you.

Participant: Aha.

Dr. Lisa: If anybody's not happy in relationship, you may want to listen to this part of the recording again.

Right, wrong, good and bad, POD and POC, all nine, shorts, boys and beyonds®.

When you point, you are judging. And, when you judge, you are really taking what is yours and not keeping it as your truth and doing something with it to change it. You're putting it on the money, the person, the relationship, the job, the business, whatever.

Right, wrong, good and bad, POD and POC, all nine, shorts, boys and beyonds®.

What's the purpose of accusing somebody else of what you, yourself, are doing so that you never have to look at you and what you, yourself, are doing? You never have to change what you, yourself, are doing, so everything can stay the same with what you and yourself are doing. You can always have the same

Point = Judge

story of "No matter how hard I try, nothing ever works for me. I've tried."

You have a secret agenda or lie to keep that's locked in as true, the trifold sequencing system, and we never get to the mirror which is you.

Right, wrong, good and bad, POD and POC, all nine, shorts, boys and beyonds®.

Which is what I love about Access Consciousness™. It works fast. It brings stuff up. You get insight after insight after insight. Sometimes really quickly, to where you want to get outside and take a break and smoke, or do whatever it is that you do.

Participants: Right.

Dr. Lisa: It also has so many tools that you can use at any moment to change what it is you're doing to you, i.e. what you're creating and generating with you.

Right, wrong, good and bad, POD and POC, all nine, shorts, boys and beyonds®.

How many lies are you buying into that you're calling creation and generation, which are actually the destruction of you? A little, a lot, or a megaton mocha choco-latte?

Participant: A megaton of mocha choco-latte.

Dr. Lisa: All the megaton of mocha choco-latte of lies that you've bought into and you're creating and generating and instituting as the chief financial officer of your reality, can we revoke, rescind, recant, renounce, denounce, destroy, uncreate that?

Right, wrong, good and bad, POD and POC, all nine, shorts, boys and beyonds®.

When I'm talking about something that we've been doing a lot, in Access we call it 'fraud patrol.' A lot of people think I'm saying 'frog patrol,' like the frog prince, but it's actually fraud, fake, lie, patrol. Basically, it takes the algorithm and the computation, decision, and judgment – the algorithmic computation of how we order things in our reality biochemically, hormonally, genetically, ancestrally, and physically – just by naming and claiming 'fraud patrol' and goes "Rrreeerrr, rrreeerrr."

So what I've been playing with in classes is having you all say 'fraud patrol' a couple of times and me doing the 1, 2, 3, 4, 5s. Do you want to play?

Participants: Yes.

Dr. Lisa: Play with it for a moment. Say, "Fraud patrol. Fraud patrol. Fraud patrol. Fraud patrol. Fraud patrol."

Everyone: Fraud patrol.

Dr. Lisa: 1, 2, 3, 4, 5. 1, 2, 3, 4, 5. 1, 2, 3, 4, 5. 1, 2, 3, 4, 5. 1, 2, 3, 4, 5. 1, 2, 3, 4, 5. 1, 2, 3, 4, 5. 1, 2, 3, 4, 5. 1, 2, 3, 4, 5. 1, 2, 3, 4, 5. 1, 2, 3, 4, 5. 1, 2, 3, 4, 5. 1, 2, 3, 4, 5. 1, 2, 3, 4, 5. 1, 2, 3, 4, 5. 1, 2, 3, 4, 5.

Dr. Lisa: Right, wrong, good and bad, POD and POC, all nine, shorts, boys and beyonds®.

What's the point of doing that?

It's just to name the lies, known or unknown, secret or hidden right now in the room since I've been talking, since you've been responding, and I'm just clearing the energy with the energy movement. 1, 2, 3, 4, 5 does that, and fraud patrol is connected to that.

See if you notice anything different right now. Lighter or heavier, more space, less space?

Participant: Open.

Dr. Lisa: Open. Is that a little different than what it felt like five minutes ago?

It's like you restart the computer, and then you just restart it and everything starts working again about it. That's what fraud patrol is. That's also what the clearing statement is.

Right, wrong, good and bad, POD and POC, all nine, shorts, boys and beyonds®.

Does anybody have any questions?

Participant: I know we were doing what money would say to us, but do we also do what we would say to money?

Dr. Lisa: Absolutely. Go for it.

What would you say to money? Don't scare anybody?

Right, wrong, good and bad, POD and POC, all nine, shorts, boys and beyonds®.

Participant: Why don't you ever come home with me?

Participant: Why aren't you warm and friendly with me?

Dr. Lisa: Come home with me. Be warm and friendly with me.

Right, wrong, good and bad, POD and POC, all nine, shorts, boys and beyonds®.

Now let's say you're on a date, and you think it's getting ready to be done. Would you say, "Why don't you come home with me and X, Y, Z?"

Is that heavy? Light for you?

'Why' is the judgment – 'why don't you' is the judgment. There's nothing wrong with what you said. I'm just using it as an example.

'Why don't you be X, Y, Z?'

How many judgments have you put on your money flows?

Participant: Oh, wow!

Dr. Lisa: Right, wrong, good and bad, POD and POC, all nine, shorts, boys and beyonds®.

Dr. Lisa: Let me ask you this…

When you are judged, does that bring you closer to somebody? Or is it like, "I'm getting away from this bitch."

Participants: Yes.

Dr. Lisa: All the judgments that you put on money and that you put on you about the money you have had or not had. Can we destroy and uncreate those?

Participants: Yes.

Dr. Lisa: Right, wrong, good and bad, POD and POC, all nine, shorts, boys and beyonds®.

Because what judgments do is that they hate energy away. They hate people away.

Participants: Yes.

Dr. Lisa: Right, wrong, good and bad, POD and POC, all nine, shorts, boys and beyonds®.

How many of you have hated money away from you? That leads me to the first lie of money, which is, "Who are you being?"

Who are you being when you say, "Why don't you come home with me and treat me warm and lust after me?" Truth.

Participant: My first thought was my mother and then, I'm like, my father.

Dr. Lisa: When you guys are listening, what is lighter? Mother or father? Light or heavy? Mother or father? Truth. Anybody can play.

Participants: Mother.

Dr. Lisa: Okay, mother. How many of you have issues with your mother here?

Participants: Yes.

Right, wrong, good and bad, POD and POC, all nine, shorts, boys and beyonds®.

When you're in couple's therapy with your money and you're saying all these things, and it's saying the same things back to you, are you being your mother in that interaction with your money?

Participant: Yes.

Dr. Lisa: Okay, so we only do things that are a benefit to us. We're getting something from it.

Right, wrong, good and bad, POD and POC, all nine, shorts, boys and beyonds®.

So give me three benefits to being your mother with money? What does it give you? First thought?

Participant: That she has some.

Dr. Lisa: Right, wrong, good and bad, POD and POC, all nine, shorts, boys and beyonds®.

Dr. Lisa: What's another benefit?

Participant: She knew how to manage it.

Dr. Lisa: Right, wrong, good and bad, POD and POC, all nine, shorts, boys and beyonds®.

Dr. Lisa: Good job.

Participant: She would manage it. I don't often.

Dr. Lisa: She knew how to manage it. She had some.

What was another benefit? What else did you receive? What did you think you were getting by mimicking your mother with money?

She knew how to manage it and she had some, so where did that get you?

I just know that whenever we do at least three benefits, there's something that hits the bull's eye and then we can just like pop it out with the Access tools.

Participant: That's what I'm looking for.

Dr. Lisa: That's the 1°. That's the only target I ever have for anybody that's in class. The rest is up to you, but that's what makes it fun for me.

What is it? What is that?

Participant: Being heard.

Dr. Lisa: Okay, being heard. Is that expansive for you?

Participant: Oh, no.

Dr. Lisa: Okay great.

When did you make the decision to be her? What age? First thought, best thought.

Participant: Five.

Dr. Lisa: So, at five, you mimicked that you had some money and you mimicked how you were with money. She knew how to manage that so you bio-mimetically mimicked that, duplicated, replicated that. That's great.

What does that give you in relation to her as a five-year-old? Truth.

Participant: More choices, more options.

Dr. Lisa: Great.

Participant: With family.

Dr. Lisa: More choices, more options, family.

Dr. Lisa: Right, wrong, good and bad, POD and POC, all nine, shorts, boys and beyonds®.

Now I don't know if you guys are seeing or sensing this, but these are five damn good reasons to choose something as a five-year-old, right? That's a pretty smart five-year-old.

Here's the issue, though. I've got plenty of tissues for your issues.

Right, wrong, good and bad, POD and POC, all nine, shorts, boys and beyonds®.

I always have to say that because I worked at a residential treatment center in my early 20s and there was a little boy who got in trouble. He had to write down what he got in trouble for and he wrote, "I got mad at so and so because he threw my i-shoes in my face." This is how he spelled issues: i-shoes.

Participant: I-shoes.

Dr. Lisa: I thought that was the cutest thing, so whenever I say that in class, I always think of him and wish him well. He's probably about 33 now.

Right, wrong, good and bad, POD and POC, all nine, shorts, boys and beyonds®.

It's funny how you associate and remember things. So, whose financial reality does she live? Her mom's.

So, from five to – are you a little older than five now?

Participant: Yes, just a smidge.

Dr. Lisa: Alright, so we have five decades of locked in, well worn, lies around money.

Right, wrong, good and bad, POD and POC, all nine, shorts, boys and beyonds®.

All the oaths, vows, fealties, commitments, agreements, binding and bonding contracts to obligate your mother's financial reality as your reality can we revoke, rescind, recant, renounce.

Participant: Yes.

Dr. Lisa: Denounce, destroy and uncreate that.

Participant: Yes.

Dr. Lisa: For everybody.

Right, wrong, good and bad, POD and POC, all nine, shorts, boys and beyonds®.

Participant: Yes.

Dr. Lisa: All the decisions, judgments, conclusions, and computations, the five-year-old you made that you're still making as a 57-year-old you now.

Participant: Yes.

Dr. Lisa: Can we destroy and uncreate those?

Participant: Yes, totally.

Dr. Lisa: Right, wrong, good and bad, POD and POC, all nine, shorts, boys and beyonds®.

Dr. Lisa: All the artificial, vibrational, virtual realities that you created over and over and over again for these five decades plus.

Right, wrong, good and bad, POD and POC, all nine, shorts, boys and beyonds®.

All the secret, hidden, invisible, covert, unseen, unacknowledged, unspoken, undisclosed agendas to that – can we destroy and uncreate that?

Participant: Yes.

Dr. Lisa: Right, wrong, good and bad, POD and POC, all nine, shorts, boys and beyonds®.

Are you okay? This is really intense because her mom's in the room.

Participant: Yes.

Dr. Lisa: Right, wrong, good and bad, POD and POC, all nine, shorts, boys and beyonds®.

Who are you being? Truth. If she made the decision at five and she's 57 now, she has spent most of her life literally mimicking her mother's flows with money.

To a 5-year-old, this stuff orders their reality and forms their belief systems. The issue becomes that we are still adhering to that 5 year old mentality when we are 57.

Participant: She had money in that, if I wanted, if desired anything, it would go to her.

Dr. Lisa: Cool.

Participant: Because my father was like, "Don't spend it."

Dr. Lisa: Okay, there you go.

Participant: She was the one where I got new shoes, new dress or school uniform – or field trip, whatever it was.

Dr. Lisa: Is she dead?

Participant: Yes, she's dead.

Dr. Lisa: Did you get some?

Yes or no.

Participant: No.

Dr. Lisa: Okay, so here you are at five still living this, but then she died and you didn't get some, regardless of the story.

Participant: Right.

Dr. Lisa: That's what happens to us when we choose that unconsciously. It helped her then. It makes sense in that moment at five, but then we never change those decisions and we're always creating and generating from them somewhere – usually in the back of our computer, our mind.

Participant: Yes.

Dr. Lisa: We're never actually embodying our true financial reality.

Everything that brings up and lets down.

Right, wrong, good and bad, POD and POC, all nine, shorts, boys and beyonds®.

Everything you learned about your mother, about money, can we destroy and uncreate it?

Participant: Yes.

Dr. Lisa: Right, wrong, good and bad, POD and POC, all nine, shorts, boys and beyonds®.

Everything you misidentified and misapplied about money and cash from your mother, can we destroy and uncreate that?

Participants: Yes.

Dr. Lisa: Right, wrong, good and bad, POD and POC, all nine, shorts, boys and beyonds®.

Everywhere your mother is living on top of your body right now, within your body right now, in your cellular memory from muscles, ligaments, cells, tendons, organs, systems, all the way down to fascia and back up, in the system's circulatory system, you're pumping her blood through you.

Did you know that the research says that 80% of your genes are from your mother, even though they think half and half?

Participants: Wow.

Dr. Lisa: Would you like to give a little bit of that up?

Participant: Yes.

Dr. Lisa: Everything that you're pulsating and vibrating through your body that is your mother and not you, can we say, "Throw mama from the train?" I mean, can we say, "Mama go back to yourself with consciousness attached?"

Participant: Yes.

Dr. Lisa: Everybody on three, 1, 2, 3. 1, 2, 3. 1, 2, 3. Now you're with three because it's your mom. 1, 2, 3. 1, 2, 3. 1, 2, 3. 1, 2, 3. 1, 2, 3. 1, 2, 3. 1, 2, 3. 1, 2, 3.

Everybody: 1, 2, 3. 1, 2, 3. 1, 2, 3. 1, 2, 3. 1, 2, 3. 1, 2, 3. 1, 2, 3. 1, 2, 3. 1, 2, 3. 1, 2, 3. 1, 2, 3. 1, 2, 3. 1, 2, 3.

Dr. Lisa: We're not done yet. 1, 2, 3. 1, 2, 3. 1, 2, 3. 1, 2, 3. 1, 2, 3. On four would you like to open the door to a new possibility with money?

Participant: Yes.

Dr. Lisa: From your embodiment?

Participant: Yes.

Dr. Lisa: Your choice, your financial knowingness. 1, 2, 3, 4.

Right, wrong, good and bad, POD and POC, all nine, shorts, boys and beyonds®.

Lighter, heavier, more space, less lies?

Participant: More space.

Dr. Lisa: Yes, more space.

Okay, so it's like me with my dad, thinking that, when he died, the printing press died for money. He was like my ATM.

I had this whole thing going on, "Oh my God, there's no one to call. My personal banker is gone."

You know what I mean?

Participants: Yes.

Dr. Lisa: Truthfully, there's no right or wrong, no good or bad. It just might have been a little bit more beneficial if I learned that a little earlier.

Participants: Yes.

Dr. Lisa: Right, wrong, good and bad, POD and POC, all nine, shorts, boys and beyonds®.

Or, if I had been aware of a little bit more about what I was creating – and how I could really use that money to really create my business.

My father was an entrepreneur, a self-made millionaire. He was brilliant with numbers. He came from nothing and created everything.

He went to the army and they paid for everything. He did all these different things to get his education, to get his masters degree, and he made his millions by going to auctions in western Newark, New Jersey, in the 80s and buying foreclosed multilevel housing. You can buy them in the auction for $10,000 or more. He bought 16 of them.

My job as a kid was to stack the money, pay the rents and get the rents collected. Lick the money, like we all do, use the adding machine. You guys remember adding machines?

Participants: Yes.

Dr. Lisa: Use the green ledger pad and a pencil.

Participants: Yes.

Dr. Lisa: The money all came in cash. None of it was checks.

We always had them in stacks on the table in the basement. I had my desk and he had his desk and we spent years like that. That was my job. I loved listening to him do business.

I love business. I love money. I used to work at a bank after college because I loved to go sit in the vault and I loved the Brinks trucks that would come in. I loved Fridays. All the lawyers would come in with their envelopes of $100 bills. I am a whore for $100 bills. I don't want the old ones that are crunchy and yucky – I love crisp, right? Of course, I won't send away a non-crunchy $100 bill, you know.

My father taught me to organize your money. I would go in my friends' wallets and think, "Let's see their money." And I'd be like, "No, no, stretch it, organize it!" It was just something that he did and I loved it. I loved when he pulled off this wad of money and a lot of it was singles. It was always in order. There was a energy about it that was affluent, even though he couldn't necessarily receive that energy of generosity of spirit to have. It was just something I picked up and embodied. He was good – just a little wounded and refused to choose to move beyond it.

Participants: Yes.

Dr. Lisa: Right, wrong, good and bad, POD and POC, all nine, shorts, boys and beyonds®.

So, the second lie of money is 'what are you being?' For me it was not having money, kind of binging and purging it, using my father as the source growing up.

I remember when I lived in Arizona and I was getting my master's degree. I was running a residential treatment center where I made $30 an hour. At that time, my way of connecting with money and people was to say, "I'm paying. Come on out."

And I'd put money in the center of the table – not just one $100 bill – and we'd go out until that money was gone.

What was I being?

I was being my father without even knowing it.

Then I started to really get into his psychology, because the only way I had of connecting was through having money. If I didn't have money, no one would want to go out with me, or be friends with me and just be with me without money.

Dr. Lisa: Right, wrong, good and bad, POD and POC, all nine, shorts, boys and beyonds®.

Nobody told me that. I created that because that's what my dad intimated in his own way. He thought he was unlovable. He didn't think he deserved anything. And I made that over and over and over and over and over and over and over and over and over again for years. It went like that until something occurred.

Right, wrong, good and bad, POD and POC, all nine, shorts, boys and beyonds®.

I remember that day well.

I turned on my computer, went into my online banking, and guess what my balance was?

Zero.

I panicked. I was in shock, and I had no one to call because I was too embarrassed to call my father after all the money he gave me. I certainly wasn't going to call my mother because I knew it would end in a litany of Italian curse words and beyond.

What are you being?

I was being my father over and over and over again. Then there was this loneliness that befell me, even when we were out partying or whatever. It became not fun anymore because I wasn't being me. I was being him, and you can only be something a couple of different times before your mind circuitry just kind of shuts off and then it can't be used anymore. It's the same with addictions. You get to a certain level, but then that high goes away and you have to go to the next level. Your tolerance level changes.

Right, wrong, good and bad, POD and POC, all nine, shorts, boys and beyonds®.

You need more, you need more, you need more. What I decided, thankfully, was that what I needed more was to find out who I was and who was I being. I needed to choose to let go of being him. And that came with a whole can of worms. Did I have to let go of his love of business? Was his love of business actually healthy? And, is that really my love of business or what I was mimicking of his?

It's getting cloudy in here again, isn't it? I guess I'm speaking the truth about something.

Right, wrong, good and bad, POD and POC, all nine, shorts, boys and beyonds®.

Was it his love of money or my love of money? Was I in banking and in business school in college because of me or him? Should I be doing psychology or should I work in business in New York like my family, right?

Actually, that was never going to happen. I can remember looking out my bedroom window watching everybody – women and the men walking to the train because I lived right down the road from the train station. They'd walk into the train with their briefcase, and the women would have their high heels in a bag with their trainers or sneakers on to walk to the train. And, guess what? No one smiling on the job. I promised myself that, I would never desire to create a living where I wasn't happy doing my business or wasn't excited about it everyday.

Right, wrong, good and bad, POD and POC, all nine, shorts, boys and beyonds®.

Who were they being?

Right, wrong, good and bad, POD and POC, all nine, shorts, boys and beyonds®.

All the lies that you're buying into right now about who you were being, and all of those beings who actually stepped in here that are saying, "Yes, that's right. I got her. I got him. Don't tell him who they're being. I want to stay here" – all of that energy – can we destroy and uncreate it?

Participants: Yes.

Dr. Lisa: Okay, on three. 1, 2, 3. 1, 2, 3. 1, 2, 3. 1, 2, 3. 1, 2, 3. 1, 2, 3. 1, 2, 3. 1, 2, 3. 1, 2, 3. 1, 2, 3. 1, 2, 3. 1, 2, 3. 1, 2, 3. 1, 2, 3.

Everybody: 1, 2, 3. 1, 2, 3. 1, 2, 3. 1, 2, 3. 1, 2, 3. 1, 2, 3. 1, 2, 3. 1, 2, 3. 1, 2, 3. 1, 2, 3. 1, 2, 3. 1, 2, 3. 1, 2, 3.

Dr. Lisa: On five, say 'fraud patrol' and throw the energy out. 1, 2, 3, 4, 5.

Participant: Fraud Patrol.

Dr. Lisa: 1, 2, 3, 4, 5.

Participant: Fraud patrol.

Dr. Lisa: 1, 2, 3, 4, 5.

Participant: Fraud patrol.

Dr. Lisa: 1, 2, 3, 4, 5.

Participant: Fraud patrol.

Dr. Lisa: 1, 2, 3, 4, 5.

Participant: Fraud patrol.

Dr. Lisa: 1, 2, 3, 4, 5.

Participant: Fraud patrol.

Dr. Lisa: 1, 2, 3, 4, 5.

Participant: Fraud patrol.

Dr. Lisa: 1, 2, 3, 4, 5.

Participant: Fraud patrol.

Dr. Lisa: 1, 2, 3, 4, 5.

Participant: Fraud patrol.

Dr. Lisa: 1, 2, 3, 4, 5.

Participant: Fraud patrol.

Dr. Lisa: 1, 2, 3, 4, 5.

Participant: Fraud patrol.

Dr. Lisa: 1, 2, 3, 4, 5.

Participant: Fraud patrol.

Dr. Lisa: Right, wrong, good and bad, POD and POC, all nine, shorts, boys and beyonds®.

Dr. Lisa: Who are you being right now? Known or unknown?

Participant: Stability and the predictability.

Dr. Lisa: Right, wrong, good and bad, POD and POC, all nine, shorts, boys and beyonds®.

Dr. Lisa: Great. Let's talk about that for a second. Thanks for putting that in the room. Stability and predictability. Truth. Who taught you that?

Participant: My dad and my mom.

Dr. Lisa: Great. Truth, which one is lighter? Mom or dad?

Participant: Mom.

Dr. Lisa: So what's the best part about having stability and predictability around money from your mom's perspective?

Participant: It's known.

Dr. Lisa: Yes.

Participant: The budget is fixed.

Dr. Lisa: Alright.

Who doesn't like to know that it's fixed? Who likes the budget in here? Who's the budget person? No one.

Dr. Lisa: Right, wrong, good and bad, POD and POC, all nine, shorts, boys and beyonds®.

Participant: I am learning.

Dr. Lisa: You're learning. That sounds so fun from the way you said it.

Participant: Oh, yes.

Dr. Lisa: I'm learning.

Right, wrong, good and bad, POD and POC, all nine, shorts, boys and beyonds®.

Dr. Lisa: We talk a lot about the constrictions, the abuses, and traumas and things like that, and I've learned to cultivate a sense of humor and lighten up the load, so to speak. I'm used to dense and heavy topics that people like to run from and keep under the carpets like dust bunnies.

Right, wrong, good and bad, POD and POC, all nine, shorts, boys and beyonds®.

It's fixed, it's known, it's stable, we've got the budget. You know what's coming in. You know what's going out. What's the best part of that?

Participant: It's safe.

Dr. Lisa: Ah, safe. How old were you when you made that decision? Truth. Known or unknown.

Participant: Eight.

Dr. Lisa: Right, wrong, good and bad, POD and POC, all nine, shorts, boys and beyonds®.

Dr. Lisa: Eight, excellent.

You're a little older than eight now, right?

Participant: Yes.

Dr. Lisa: Great, does that mean that they have to change any of this stuff, the benefits?

No, the only thing that I'm attempting to elucidate here is that when you're still making those decisions from these ages and you're not those ages anymore – you're still looking for this – then you're obligating your money flows to and from a 5 or 8-year-old perspective. It means you put a 5 or 8-year-old in charge of your financial reality.

Who has kids in this room? How big is a 5-year-old? How tall is an 8-year-old? What grades are they in?

Participants: Kindergarten.

Participant: Second grade.

Participant: Third grade.

Dr. Lisa: Kindergarten and second and third. Does it make sense to put a 5 or 8 year old in charge of your financial reality?

Dr. Lisa: Right, wrong, good and bad, POD and POC, all nine, shorts, boys and beyonds®.

Everywhere you obligated your mother's way of being with money to be your way of being with money, so that you knew safety, and you're still doing that from then until now – can we fire your 8-year-old from that job?

Participants: Yes.

Dr. Lisa: Right, wrong, good and bad, POD and POC, all nine, shorts, boys and beyonds®.

Dr. Lisa: Give him a severance package of fun, freedom?

Participant: Freedom.

Participants: Yes.

Dr. Lisa: Right, wrong, good and bad, POD and POC, all nine, shorts, boys and beyonds®.

Dr. Lisa: Sexy, luxurious, money-making schemes of the highest order of an 8-year-old?

Participants: Yes.

Dr. Lisa: Or you can just play and surf the waves and be free and let the adult handle the budget?

Participants: Yes.

Dr. Lisa: According to how you be that knows, receives and perceives money in this world, which is different than your mother's world?

Right, wrong, good and bad, POD and POC, all nine, shorts, boys and beyonds®.

Did you notice the energy? It just got lighter and lighter and lighter, more free, free, and free.

Participants: Yes.

Dr. Lisa: Right, wrong, good and bad, POD and POC, all nine, shorts, boys and beyonds®.

Here's the thing...

You obligated your mother to be your stability around money, to be your predictability around money, to be your fixed knowing around money, to be the known around money, to be your budget.

Dr. Lisa: Right, wrong, good and bad, POD and POC, all nine, shorts, boys and beyonds®.

But there's a benefit to that, right? So, when I say you release the obligations, you're basically taking the inculcation of sticking you in a blender, your mom in a blender and, if ice was the money, you just crunch it all up and it becomes a part of you.

And you think it's you, but it's a lie.

Participant: Yes.

Dr. Lisa: Because when you look underneath your mother's stability, there is the 'fixed, known, budget, safe.'

Participant: Yes.

Dr. Lisa: Truth. Was she terrified?

Participant: Yes.

Dr. Lisa: Truth. Was she anxious?

Participant: Yes.

Dr. Lisa: So, what you're really inculcating with the ice cubes is the distractor implants of fear and anxiety.

Participant: Yes.

Dr. Lisa: And you're calling that safety, which is not going to have money come to the party of fun.

Participant: Yes.

Dr. Lisa: That's going to reject it and keep you in a cycle of binge and purge, have and have not, doing good then something happens right. It's called an abundance leak or a money leak or something like that. There's a hole somewhere.

Dr. Lisa: Right, wrong, good and bad, POD and POC, all nine, shorts, boys and beyonds®.

It's like coming to this class. You're being something, you're buying into something. It's an energy of a 'who' and it's an energy of 'what,' and then it's an energy of a lie.

Participants: Yes.

Dr. Lisa: That's what you've created as your money flows.

None of it is true.

None of that is true, so what if you're not as fucked up as you think you are regarding money?

What if it's not as bad as you think you are?

Dr. Lisa: Right, wrong, good and bad, POD and POC, all nine, shorts, boys and beyonds®.

What if you walk out of here with nothing else, but you and the space of being you that actually starts opening you to question possibility and contribution, to what you would choose to create every moment and in every 10 seconds with money?

If you had a magic wand – and you were being you, what would you choose right now?

Dr. Lisa: Right, wrong, good and bad, POD and POC, all nine, shorts, boys and beyonds®.

Would you do your budget or would you have somebody come in to collaborate with you and show you something that's fun for them?

Dr. Lisa: Right, wrong, good and bad, POD and POC, all nine, shorts, boys and beyonds®.

I found this woman who loves numbers and she speaks to me in numbers. She makes everything so clear to me about all of my accounts, about everything, and got me on this whole QuickBooks online thing. It's awesome. That constriction just opened up.

And, I'm starting to feel so expansively generative just knowing that she's handling everything for me, and that I get to talk to her about it. So, when she asks for something, there's an excitement of, "Yes. Here it is," or when she says, "Check this out," I go, "Yes, let's do that."

There's this excitement about it, whereas, after my father died and I didn't have him as the source anymore, I was totally terrified. I didn't know what to do. I had to create my own financial reality and it hasn't been pretty or easy. It's a lot easier now.

Now I'm the "Yes, no, yes, no, yes, no. How much exists? Let's change that. Move this around, here's what I'm looking for. Do this. Don't tell me anymore than I need to know. Get me this. Tell me that. You're telling me too much. Shut up. Just tell me this."

I know what to say. I know what to do. I know what to ask for. I tell her to show me this, show me that.

"This is my projection. This is what I would like. How am I doing? What's the P&L here? How are we doing about this? Where's the P&L for that? What about my expenses? What about this? How much am I spending on that? How much less could a hotel cost than this? What else? How much can I get a ticket for to go overseas?"

Someone does it for me. I just get the information. It's fun. That's great. But my energy is in all of it. I am being the source even though someone else may be organizing it for me.

Dr. Lisa: I know right away when it's a "No, get out of here, I'm not even calling you back."

I know when there's an opening and I'm like, "Yes." I know when that opening now is like, "This is my stuff. I definitely need her or him."

You know what I mean? I know that now. I didn't know that then because I was underneath all of this.

So, if you walk out of here feeling a little bit lighter and expansive and freer, great. If you feel awful and walk out of here thinking, "Oh, shit. I got some things to do," great, because at least then you're acknowledging the lies.

When you acknowledge the lies, 50% of the problem is solved because, when you see something, choice becomes imminent. Choice creates awareness.

Right, wrong, good and bad, POD and POC, all nine, shorts, boys and beyonds®.

Make sense? Are you learning something? Alright?

Right, wrong, good and bad, POD and POC, all nine, shorts, boys and beyonds®.

Who are you being? What are you being? What lie are you buying into? Truth, questions, comments, thoughts?

Participant: What's the difference between lies one and two?

Participant: Who and what.

Dr. Lisa: Who and the what. The who is generally someone, the what is an energy.

How much does this reality order you around money? What you should do? What you should be? What you should have?

From every age – like when you're 20 to 30, 30 to 40, 40 to 50, 50 to 60, whether you're a man or a woman – all the stations in life that this reality order you into with where you should be with money at your particular decade, or your culture, family, genetics, or gender – can we revoke, rescind, recant, renounce, denounce, destroy and uncreate that?

Participants: Yes.

Dr. Lisa: Right, wrong, good and bad, POD and POC, all nine, shorts, boys and beyonds®.

Whatever you're being for safety, for control, for protection, for security, for power, all the ways that you've used those qualities for what, to keep the who within you, which abdicates you from you and separates you from you, and you never get to be the CFO of you and of your living – can we destroy and uncreate that?

Participant: Yes.

Dr. Lisa: Right, wrong, good and bad, POD and POC, all nine, shorts, boys and beyonds®.

Dr. Lisa: Truth. Who are you all? Truth. Who were you before that and before that and before that and before that and before that and before that and before that and before that and before that and before that, and who will you be after that and after that and after that and after that and after that and after that and after that. The deal is done, your services are no longer requested, required, desired, wanted, or needed.

Everybody breathe.

You get to leave now and be free. Take all of your electromagnetic imprinting, chemical imprinting, biological imprinting, hormonal imprinting, genetic imprinting, and ancestral imprinting, psychological imprinting, biochemical imprinting, ancestral imprinting, lifetime imprinting, and leave now. Go back from whence you came never return to this dimension, reality, body again. What's the value of holding on to this body?

This is not your body, what's the value of holding onto this body, this is not your body. What's the value of holding on to this body, this not your body, what's the value of holding on to this body, this is not your body, what's the value of holding on to this body, this is not your body, what's the value of holding on to this body, this body is waking up. It does not want you to hold on to this body anymore. It no longer gives you permission to be in its body and it no longer wishes to be a multilevel marketing hostel for all of you so we're exterminating and fumigating, get out. Go back from whence you came never return to this dimension, reality, body, again.

Everybody, 1, 2, 3. 1, 2, 3. 1, 2, 3. 1, 2, 3. 1, 2, 3.

Everybody: 1, 2, 3. 1, 2, 3. 1, 2, 3. 1, 2, 3.

Dr. Lisa: Go back from whence you came. Never return to this dimension, reality, body again.

Everybody: 1, 2, 3. 1, 2, 3. 1, 2, 3. 1, 2, 3.

Dr. Lisa: Go back from whence you came. Never return to this dimension, reality, body again.

Everybody: 1, 2, 3. 1, 2, 3.1, 2, 3. 1, 2, 3.

Dr. Lisa: Go back from whence you came. Never return to this dimension, reality, body again.

Dr. Lisa: Right, wrong, good and bad, POD and POC, all nine, shorts, boys and beyonds®.

All pledging allegiance to the forces of who you're being, what you're being, and what lie are you buying into with regards to money, your cash flows and your portfolios – can we revoke, rescind, recant, renounce, denounce, destroy, and uncreate it?

Participants: Yes.

Dr. Lisa: Right, wrong, good and bad, POD and POC, all nine, shorts, boys and beyonds®.

Dr. Lisa: Now we're going to this: What does sex with money mean to you?

Participant: Funk.

Participant: Confusion.

Dr. Lisa: Right, wrong, good and bad, POD and POC, all nine, shorts, boys and beyonds®.

Dr. Lisa: And you thought we were done. I just had to throw it in a little.

Participant: Better than before.

Participant: Feelings.

Dr. Lisa: Feelings.

Participant: Better than before.

Dr. Lisa: Right, wrong, good and bad, POD and POC, all nine, shorts, boys and beyonds®.

When I say 'sex,' it brings up a whole other level. We're talking about sex now, but remember that book, *Money Isn't the Problem, You Are?* Gary, the founder and the father of Access Consciousness, always talks about sex being synonymous with receiving. So when we say 'sex,' with regards to something, it hits the place in your brain that mops out the cobwebs of the unconsciousness, known or unknown, and then we get to clear it.

Here you are in couple's therapy. Couples always go to therapy, at least in my office. They come to therapy telling me that they just started getting separate from each other and fighting a lot. It's usually about money and then, once we deal with the money, guess what's underneath that?

Participant: Sex.

Dr. Lisa: It's synonymous.

So, what does sex with money mean to you? Just play here.

Participant: Not enough.

Dr. Lisa: Not enough.

Right, wrong, good and bad, POD and POC, all nine, shorts, boys and beyonds®.

Participant: At first it feels like, "Yes, good," and then it feels like, "No," because it's dirty. Money is dirty.

Dr. Lisa: Good and then dirty.

Right, wrong, good and bad, POD and POC, all nine, shorts, boys and beyonds®.

What is sex with money to you?

Participant: Not enough work.

Dr. Lisa: Not enough?

Participant: Work.

Dr. Lisa: I don't know about you but, if sex is work, I'm out of there, but many of us stay there and are like, "Oh, my God. I'm exhausted."

"Yes, baby, you're having so much fun. Keep it up. Yes, that's what you wanted to do on my stair master tomorrow."

Right, wrong, good and bad, POD and POC, all nine, shorts, boys and beyonds®.

That's no different than leaving your money out on the couch, in your living room.

Participant: Yes.

Participant: It's like sleeping in the car.

Dr. Lisa: Right, or sleeping in the car.

Right, wrong, good and bad, POD and POC, all nine, shorts, boys and beyonds®.

What does sex with money mean to you?

Participant: It does not compute.

Dr. Lisa: Does not compute.

Dr. Lisa: Right, wrong, good and bad, POD and POC, all nine, shorts, boys and beyonds®.

You mean you don't put money out and spread it on the bed and just lie on it like, "Hi, body. Hi, body. Hi, body. Hi, body?"

If you're laughing, your body likes it because bodies love money. Bodies love to play. Bodies love to be lusted after. You can laugh, it's okay. It's just that lusciousness of receiving, and how often do we not let ourselves receive that with money?

I always tell people get a fresh crisp $100 bill, at least one, and put it in your wallet and never spend it. Whenever you're in some sort of money fear or something like that, open your wallet and know that you always have money. You'll always be able to get gas. You'll always be able to get something to eat.

Okay, so you might want to move out of San Francisco. Just kidding.

Right, wrong, good and bad, POD and POC, all nine, shorts, boys and beyonds®.

Seriously, I may have six $100 bills together or more, especially when I'm traveling. Even when I'm home, I usually have $1,000 in $100 bills. On my last trip, when I was going around teaching, I had about $3,000 just in $100 bills.

I was going to put it in my house and it was like, "No, I want it in my wallet so I walk around always knowing I'm wealthy."

I can tell you it was really fun to have that $3,000 in there. I kept looking at it, no matter what was going on, and thanking the contribution of whoever gave it to me. I'm appreciative of it. I fawn over it. I thank it. I love it. I can't wait for somebody else other than Benjamin Franklin to be on there, but I do appreciate that I just like it.

Can you feel the resonant energy?

Participants: Yes.

Dr. Lisa: Happy body.

Participants: Yes.

Dr. Lisa: Now you have that, too.

Participant: Yes, your body likes it a lot.

Dr. Lisa: Yes.

So, what if you allowed money to lust after you and you allowed you to lust after it and be like, "Hi, beautiful, thank you for being whatever energy."

Or, "Hi sexy," – whatever it is you want to tell your money.

Participant: Right.

Dr. Lisa: Right, wrong, good and bad, POD and POC, all nine, shorts, boys and beyonds®.

Dr. Lisa: In Access Consciousness™ we talk about having a 10% account. Some people call it an "Honoring me" account. I do 30% – 10% for my business, 10% for me, 10% for my body.

Participant: Oh, wow!

Participant: Nice.

Dr. Lisa: I can't say I haven't spent any of it. I go up and down with it. They say don't spend it, but I started to do that with the 30%. I started noticing that I could look at it and think, "Huh, this is what it feels like to have."

Participants: Yes.

Dr. Lisa: It wasn't easy for me to do the 30%. I had to start with the 10%, but I really made a focus on this last year when I rearranged my entire business. But start with 10% and yes, do what they say, "Don't spend it. Let it build to an honoring you account."

If you choose to spend it, just go back to honoring you and putting it back in.

It's 10% of everything you make. If you get $1,000, 10% of that. If you get $500, 10% of that. If you get $10, 10% of that. It doesn't matter how small or how large. Gary says he doesn't know why, but it always works. It tells the universe that you are desiring to have.

Ask and it is given and then providence moves, too.

Participant: Right.

Participant: I just don't have that excitement. It's like, "This is nothing."

Dr. Lisa: Right, wrong, good and bad, POD and POC, all nine, shorts, boys and beyonds®.

Dr. Lisa: Great! Whose eyes are you looking through at your money? Truth?

Participant: Russians.

Dr. Lisa: Great. Any particular Russians or the whole country?

Participant: The whole country, maybe.

Dr. Lisa: Okay, so let's pretend it's the whole country.

What is the Russian's view of money? Maybe that's why it's heavy.

Participant: I'm just blanking.

Dr. Lisa: Expansive or constrictive?

Participant: Constrictive.

Dr. Lisa: All of the constrictive color glasses that you view money through that makes you not excited to see what you're actually generating and creating for the brilliant work you do, can we destroy and uncreate it? Yes?

Participant: Yes.

Dr. Lisa: Right, wrong, good and bad, POD and POC, all nine, shorts, boys and beyonds®.

Everywhere you've obligated yourself to this Russian point of view to constrict you and never embody the brilliance of what you actually created...

Participant: It's like it's outside.

Dr. Lisa: It's outside of you?

Is it coming through the source of you or is it coming from outside of you?

Participant: It's outside.

Dr. Lisa: Great, so all of your money has to come to you outside of you, which you can never connect to; therefore, you can never be happy or view it as you – can we destroy and uncreate that?

Participant: Yes.

Dr. Lisa: Right, wrong, good and bad, POD and POC, all nine, shorts, boys and beyonds®.

Participant: Yes.

Dr. Lisa: All oaths, vows, fealties, commitments, agreements, binding, bonding contracts from many lifetime, dimension, body, and reality where you created that, can we revoke, rescind, recant, renounce, denounce, destroy, and uncreate it?

Dr. Lisa: Right, wrong, good and bad, POD and POC, all nine, shorts, boys and beyonds®.

Participant: Yes.

Dr. Lisa: Everywhere outside of you is the lock and seeing your money is the key and seeing your money from within you is the lock and outside of you is the key, can we put the lock in the key and the key in the lock or whatever this is, the lock in the key and key in the lock and the key and the lock and the lock and the key and the lock and the key and the key and the lock together and begin to set this free and unlock this eternally, energetically, bi-coastally, bi-culturally.

Right, wrong, good and bad, POD and POC, all nine, shorts, boys and beyonds®.

Who are you being? What are you being? What lie are you buying into?

Now look at your money. Lighter, heavier, more space, less space?

Participant: More exciting.

Dr. Lisa: More exciting?

Participant: Yes.

Dr. Lisa: How many more barriers of their views can you drop so it gets even more exciting? And how many more 'who's' can you drop so it gets more exciting? And how many more 'what's' can you drop so it gets more exciting? How many more lies can you let go of so it can get more exciting? How much more chaos can you instill so that it gets more exciting?

Right, wrong, good and bad, POD and POC, all nine, shorts, boys and beyonds®.

Participant: It's like it's wrong to have money.

Dr. Lisa: There we go.

"It's wrong to have money." Say that three times.

Participant: It's wrong to have money. It's wrong to have money. It's wrong to have money. It's wrong to have money. It's wrong to have money.

Dr. Lisa: Now say it in Russian out loud.

Participant: It's wrong to have money. It's wrong to have money. It's wrong to have money. It's wrong to have money.

Dr. Lisa: Whatever that is. Whatever that is. Whatever that is, all of the secret, hidden, invisible, covert, unseen, unacknowledged, unspoken, and undisclosed agendas from Russian to English, from English to Russian, can we destroy and uncreate those?

Participant: Yes.

Dr. Lisa: Right, wrong, good and bad, POD and POC, all nine, shorts, boys and beyonds®.

It is getting a little lighter in here.

Participants: Yes.

Dr. Lisa: All the vibrational, virtual realities, damn those Russians take up a lot of space – makes it feel dense in here and all the artificial, vibrational realities. But you're all laughing now. Woo hoo, we got rid of them. All the vibrational, virtual realities, can we destroy and uncreate that?

Participant: Yes.

Dr. Lisa: Right, wrong, good and bad, POD and POC, all nine, shorts, boys and beyonds®.

All the trifold sequencing systems, locking that view in place within you, circuitry-wise, hormonally, genetically, ancestrally, biochemically – can we revoke, rescind, recant, renounce, denounce, destroy, and uncreate that?

Participant: Yes.

Dr. Lisa: Right, wrong, good and bad, POD and POC, all nine, shorts, boys and beyonds®.

All the double binds, creating the double binds eternally double binded, like you can't have it, you want it though, it's not exciting, but you want to be excited. I've made it. I love what I do. I can't have it. All of that. I'm just going to leave it at the store and spend it on somebody else, but me, maybe you. Have a little vodka, fish a little bit, and go in the sauna. You know it's just a normal day in Russia.

Right, wrong, good and bad, POD and POC, all nine, shorts, boys and beyonds®.

Better, worse, or the same. More exciting?

Participant: Better.

Dr. Lisa: Better, good.

Right, wrong, good and bad, POD and POC, all nine, shorts, boys and beyonds®.

Participant: Can I look at something else? When I'm looking at the money, most of dollars, rubles, have a different energy coming.

Dr. Lisa: What does?

Participant: Rubles. Russian currency.

Dr. Lisa: I like it. Say it again.

Participant: What?

Dr. Lisa: Rubles.

Participant: Rubles.

Dr. Lisa: Do it again.

Participant: Rubles.

Dr. Lisa: Again?

Participant: Rubles. Rubles. Rubles. Rubles. It is so much lighter.

Dr. Lisa: It is.

Participant: It is so much lighter.

Participants: Yes.

Dr. Lisa: When you say 'money,' it's heavy, but when you say 'rubles,' it's light. So how about this? See your money in rubles.

Participant: That's what I'm saying. In Russian money, I can't relate to American money.

Dr. Lisa: Right.

How aware are you about American's point of view about money? That makes you go 'frrrrrt' a little, a lot, or a megaton?

Participant: All of it. Lots of it.

Dr. Lisa: Right, wrong, good and bad, POD and POC, all nine, shorts, boys and beyonds®.

Do Americans like money or do they like working for their money?

Participant: Yes.

Dr. Lisa: Yes. Do Russians like money or do they like working for their money?

Participant: I don't know.

Dr. Lisa: Yes, you do.

Right, wrong, good and bad, POD and POC, all nine, shorts, boys and beyonds®.

How much American point of view have you embodied as your view about money when in actuality, the Russian point of view is lighter for you about money. Can we revoke, rescind, recant, renounce, denounce, destroy, and uncreate where you've embodied the vomit of America around money instead of the love of money from your homeland. I'm just seeing the energy. I don't know if there's a right or wrong.

Right, wrong, good and bad, POD and POC, all nine, shorts, boys and beyonds®.

Participant: I've heard a lot of people saying 'money is evil, money is bad' and I'm trying to see things where if you allow it or it's not about money. It's about how you're using it. What if you use it there and there, and still they're like, "It's evil. It's evil. It's evil. It's evil."

Dr. Lisa: Are you saying from over there or here?

Participant: From Russia. My friends, personally.

Dr. Lisa: You know, evil is just 'live' spelled backwards.

Right, wrong, good and bad, POD and POC, all nine, shorts, boys and beyonds®.

What's the benefit of believing or projecting that money is evil?

Participant: Keep evil away.

Dr. Lisa: Right, wrong, good and bad, POD and POC, all nine, shorts, boys and beyonds®.

What keeps you from living? What's the benefit of keeping you from living?

Participant: You don't get to be you.

Dr. Lisa: You don't get to be you.

Participant: Self dying.

Dr. Lisa: Dying.

Participant: It's not fun.

Dr. Lisa: It's not fun.

Participant: Afraid.

Participant: Intuition.

Participant: Cage.

Dr. Lisa: Right, now we're actually naming the energy we started the night with, or getting to it.

Right, wrong, good and bad, POD and POC, all nine, shorts, boys and beyonds®.

What's the benefit of that? You're in a cage, you're not living, you're dead.

Participant: I get to be my mom.

Dr. Lisa: And what's the benefit of that?

Participant: It's better.

Dr. Lisa: What is better about it?

Participant: You justify not living.

Dr. Lisa: That's what you do, exactly.

You're justifying not having money; therefore, you're justifying not living; therefore, you're justifying being alive, but dead; therefore, you have an excuse not to create your own financial reality.

That's the only benefit to believing that money is evil and when you believe, you leave your body behind.

Right, wrong, good and bad, POD and POC, all nine, shorts, boys and beyonds®.

How many of these beliefs have you heard: That money is evil? You can't move beyond your station in life? If you make more than your family, you'll be banished or exiled? Or if you do more than your friends, you won't be loved anymore?

And how much of what you are being is abdicating your financial acumen for something that isn't even you?

Right, wrong, good and bad, POD and POC, all nine, shorts, boys and beyonds®.

Because if I asked you this, beyond your mind and beyond your actual bank accounts, do you know that you are brilliant with money?

Participants: Yes.

Dr. Lisa: Anybody not know that? Truth?

It's okay, you're not going to get into trouble. Say, "I'm brilliant with money."

Participant: I'm brilliant with money.

Dr. Lisa: Light or heavy?

Participant: Heavy.

Dr. Lisa: Heavy. Say, "I used to be brilliant with money."

Participant: I used to be brilliant with money.

Dr. Lisa: Light or heavy?

Participant: Light.

Dr. Lisa: Yes, so when did you stop? Who are you being when you stopped? What are you being? What are you being when you stopped? What lie are you buying into?

Because here's the thing. If she was brilliant with money at one time, she's still brilliant with money at this time. It's just hidden.

Participants: Yes.

Dr. Lisa: Whatever decisions, judgments, conclusion, and computation you have made to keep you locked in a trifold sequencing system so that you never get to live and create your own financial reality and know your financial acumen. Can we destroy and uncreate it?

Right, wrong, good and bad, POD and POC, all nine, shorts, boys and beyonds®.

It sounds a little bit like a conspiracy theory, but it's just a way to order your reality and keep you down. That's what this reality does. It puts you in a box and gets rid of you. It's like the kid toys you played with when you started learning circles and squares, and you would take the circle one and try to slam it into the square. That's like 'money is evil,' and 'I'm not good with money.' And you keep saying it over and over and over and over again, but the circle never goes into the square because you're the circle. The circle goes into the circle because you're brilliant. You're a circle.

Right, wrong, good and bad, POD and POC, all nine, shorts, boys and beyonds®.

I have a history with abuse and trauma and post-traumatic stress. I made a decision at one point that, no matter what was done to my body or what I chose or what somebody else chose to do to me, never ever, could they ever take away me intrinsically. I wrote an entire 420-page dissertation called "Soul Printing," on finding and forming your spiritual identity through a technique called 'cooperative inquiry.'

Your soul print is likened to that of your finger prints, unique to all of us. The only thing we're to do with our soul print is to impress it on the lips of reality with our brilliance, with our phenomenence – with our intrinsic, infinite, nature of the brilliance we be and end the lies that we have bought as us, which are never us.

Never.

Make sense? Are you brilliant with money?

Participant: Yes.

Dr. Lisa: Yes, and would you give up 1° of whatever it was that you chose to not be.

Participant: Yes.

Dr. Lisa: Whatever that emotion is that's giving up, surf it like you're surfing a wave in the ocean. Breathe through your mouth. Emotion, energy in motion. What happens when you try to force and fight a wave in the ocean?

Participant: You lose.

Participant: Trouble.

Dr. Lisa: You lose, right? Surf it because whatever that it is, it's breaking down now and now you can acknowledge whatever it is and open to a new possibility.

Right, wrong, good and bad, POD and POC, all nine, shorts, boys and beyonds.®

I work with this brilliant, stock trader who is making tons and tons and tons and tons and tons of money in Australia. Then something occurred and he made one bad "choice" and, subsequently, every choice after that was bad, to the point where he almost lost everything and had to get out and take six months off and do a whole lot of personal work to get his confidence back.

It was devastating – devastating for him and his wife. They were both traders and, instantly, they couldn't even hear or perceive their brilliance anymore. It was gone.

When something like that happens, for whatever reason because it didn't matter the story, and you start choosing over and over and over again the antithesis of who you be, you begin to actually believe your antithesis of who you be. You forget that you made a million dollars or had been successful. Not just with money, with everything. And to me, that's the greatest abuse of this reality.

It's takes all of our amazingness just for being you and twists it and bastardizes it into something else that doesn't even look like you. Then you look at the mirror and you're like, "Who the fuck are you?" And then you're like, "Oh, yes, it is me. Let me crawl into my hole. I'm going to live in pathetic land."

Right, wrong, good and bad, POD and POC, all nine, shorts, boys and beyonds®.

To me, that's the greatest disempowerment of this reality. It's the thing I despise the most and it's the thing I love the most about all of you coming into a taster like this, or the classes that we're doing, and saying, "I am fucking choosing something different."

Participants: Yes.

Dr. Lisa: Just like that.

Feel different?

Participants: Yes.

Dr. Lisa: It doesn't have to be 20 years in therapy with these tools. Believe me, I know I've gotten rid of some stuff. I know what it is to look at stuff you don't ever want to look at again or feel or taste or smell.

I know that, when I look, I'm empowered because I could totally have a choice. That doesn't mean we don't have choice in every moment, it means we forget, but it's a choice to forget. You come to a class like this, or any of the other classes, and you're choosing to remember.

Participants: Yes.

Dr. Lisa: Is it always going to be fun?

Participants: No.

Dr. Lisa: Is it going to taste like bile sometimes? Yes. Is it only going to taste like bile for a little bit? Yes.

Right, wrong, good and bad, POD and POC, all nine, shorts, boys and beyonds®.

You don't have to spend another 20 years being something you're not and creating the anti-you. You can spend today and every 10 seconds from now being you. Being you, the real you, your soul print, your phenomenence – your brilliance and whatever the Russians are doing over there.

Right, wrong, good and bad, POD and POC, all nine, shorts, boys and beyonds®.

Yes or no?

Participants: Yes.

Participant: I have a question.

I definitely have a lot of my father's stuff about not deserving it. I get confused when I feel like somebody says something about me doing something.

Dr. Lisa: Right, wrong, good and bad, POD and POC, all nine, shorts, boys and beyonds®.

Dr. Lisa: Like because you have money you can do something?

Participant: Yes.

Dr. Lisa: Does it make you want to share what you're doing or hide what you're doing?

Participant: It makes me want to hide.

Dr. Lisa: Yes.

What is it about this reality that if you have money, you have to hide it – because how happy are people for you if you have money? How envious of you? And how much do they project on you because you have money? A little, a lot, or a megaton?

Participant: A megaton.

Dr. Lisa: Right, wrong, good and bad, POD and POC, all nine, shorts, boys and beyonds®.

Dr. Lisa: How much of what you're perceiving has nothing to do with you at all, but you've reacted to it, which is actually the judgments of you. How many judgments of other people are you carrying for the money you have? And how much would you like to let go of that right now?

Participant: All of it.

Dr. Lisa: So how about all of judgments that judged you for the affluence, the wealth, the goodness, the ease, the joy, and glory that has been afforded to you and that you've created for you. Can we revoke, rescind, recant, renounce, denounce, destroy and uncreate that on your body that you've made true for you, that isn't.

Participant: Yes.

Dr. Lisa: Right, wrong, good and bad, POD and POC, all nine, shorts, boys and beyonds®.

Take that energy and say, "No more" on three. "1, 2, 3. No more."

Everybody can do it.

Everybody: 1, 2, 3. No more. 1, 2, 3. No more. 1, 2, 3. No more.

Dr. Lisa: Lighter, heavier, more space, less space?

Participant: Yes, more space.

Dr. Lisa: Good.

And everywhere you locked into your body the 'what' they're being from the 'who' put on them, and the lie that they wanted you to be, which had nothing to do with you – can we destroy and uncreate that?

Participant: Yes.

Dr. Lisa: Right, wrong, good and bad, POD and POC, all nine, shorts, boys and beyonds®.

Would it be okay if your body was no longer the hoarding storage container for everybody else's judgment around their lack of willingness to have money?

Participant: It would be very okay.

Dr. Lisa: It would be very okay, right?

Right, wrong, good and bad, POD and POC, all nine, shorts, boys and beyonds®.

So, when people are doing that around you and you sense that they're zinging you, you can be like, "You know what? Go make some money. Go have money. I'm going to demand for that. Stop putting your crap on me," or some version of that.

You can run the clearing statement in your head over and over again or, this is probably the easiest one – just say fraud patrol, 1, 2, 3, 4, 5, fraud patrol. 1, 2, 3, 4, 5, fraud patrol. 1, 2, 3, 4, 5, fraud patrol.

Dr. Lisa: Right, wrong, good and bad, POD and POC, all nine, shorts, boys and beyonds®.

It's like your super power shield.

Never, never, never disavow or disempower what has been gifted to you and what you have created for you. Having in this reality is an ability to receive, especially with money, at a level that most people aspire to and never achieve.

We need more beings like you.

So, keep having money and keep allowing people, like your friends, to really know, be, receive, and perceive the difference and unique capacity you be. It's a gift.

Right, wrong, good and bad, POD and POC, all nine, shorts, boys and beyonds®.

Many of you who have been here for the first six days have met my partner. She comes from money, she manages money, and she has a lot of money. She's never, ever, ever been without money.

I had my father and we had money, but I always worked for money. I've been working since I was young. There was also a lot of abuse, a lot of stories.

I have a modeling history with money that was full of pornographic things in the agency I worked for. It's too long of a story to go into right now, but I had a lot of stuff regarding money and having. I didn't want it because it was associated with abuse and things like that. I was getting paid to do something that I never saw the money for.

So being with her and learning how to have money, pragmatically witnessing brilliance, has infiltrated my reality in ways that has gotten me to think and feel and know and be and receive more money – and get better at making decisions with money just by simply being in her presence and witnessing and watching, even to the point of, "I'm not going to get Wi-Fi on a plane because it's $7 extra."

And I think, "Okay, if somebody that has money doesn't want to do that, what is that? Like, really, what is that?" It's not a judgment – not like, "She's being penurious."

I really need to look at all of this and be like, "Alright, do I need to travel first class or business class everywhere? Does my body just like it?"

Right?

It's just all these different things I've learned because of her.

Right, wrong, good and bad, POD and POC, all nine, shorts, boys and beyonds®.

Participant: The biggest thing that's coming up is, what lie did I buy when I moved to California? Because it's been like eight or nine years and, before, I had a 6-figure job making $30,000 bonuses.

Dr. Lisa: Does it have anything to do with the move to San Francisco?

Participant: No.

Dr. Lisa: Okay so everything that you're making about the good old San Francisco – can we destroy and uncreate that?

Participant: Yes.

Dr. Lisa: Right, wrong, good and bad, POD and POC, all nine, shorts, boys and beyonds®.

What is the lie that you're buying into and what's the real question here? It's not about the move, but you're noting everything about the move when everything changed.

Are you happy?

Participant: No, I wasn't happy there.

Dr. Lisa: Okay, so you made the decision because you weren't happy there. And did you know how to create happiness not there?

Participant: Yes.

Dr. Lisa: Say no.

Participant: No.

Dr. Lisa: What's lighter?

Participant: Yes, no.

Dr. Lisa: What's lighter?

Participant: I think yes.

Dr. Lisa: Look at me.

Participant: It's maybe yes.

Dr. Lisa: Everywhere you're looking outside of you that's about the source of your yes and no, can we destroy and uncreate that?

Dr. Lisa: Right, wrong, good and bad, POD and POC, all nine, shorts, boys and beyonds®.

Participant: I didn't want to move.

Dr. Lisa: I didn't want to – everything's back to the move.

Participant: Yes.

Dr. Lisa: I didn't want to when I thought I would move or whatever, but…

Participant: I just wanted to get out of there.

Dr. Lisa: You just wanted to get out of there.

Participant: Yes.

Dr. Lisa: If you just wanted to get out of there, did you actually, pragmatically, set it up for yourself to succeed?

Participant: Yes.

Dr. Lisa: Or mimic what you were already generating and creating.

Participant: Yes.

Dr. Lisa: No, you just wanted to get the fuck out of there.

Participant: Yes.

Dr. Lisa: When we're running and things save our life, there's still this pragmatic thing, even though it sucks about this reality, which is partnered neck and neck with money.

Everywhere that you run before you walk, everywhere you run and you create havoc versus perhaps instilling a little bit of order so you take care of yourself pragmatically – can we destroy and uncreate it?

Participant: Yes.

Dr. Lisa: Right, wrong, good and bad, POD and POC, all nine, shorts, boys and beyonds®.

What did that do for you? What are you seeing now?

Participant: It's lighter. You need to talk about instilling more chaos. Chaos and order, it's a double view.

Dr. Lisa: Did you not turn on the chaos to create a different possibility?

Participant: Yes.

Dr. Lisa: Would you turn that on now?

Participant: Yes.

Dr. Lisa: Right, wrong, good and bad, POD and POC, all nine, shorts, boys and beyonds®.

Truth. What do you love about being the energy of the starving San Francisco-ite or not starving, the struggling.

Participant: Struggling.

Dr. Lisa: What do you love about your struggle with money?

Going back to when I was working at the bank that almost killed me, I was getting this, that, and the other thing, but now I have to struggle, right?

So you're like the binge and purger.

Who would you be now that you know that you can create your financial reality? Who would you be? What would you be doing and how much would you generate and create? Truth.

Participant: A lot with ease.

Dr. Lisa: Right, but who would you be? Who would you be and what would you generate and create?

Participant: ME.

Dr. Lisa: When you go home tonight, write 25 things about what your financial reality is. Test yourself with the light and the heavy. Run the clearing statement and look at it everyday for the next 30 days.

Create it every day for the next 30 days. Take one action creating it for the next 30 days. Take another action, create it for the next 30 days.

Be you, commit to you, choose you and collaborate with the universe conspiring to bless, and then create from there. That's what I call radical aliveness.

Right, wrong, good and bad, POD and POC, all nine, shorts, boys and beyonds®.

Participant: There's a lie when you're in the U.S. dollar system. We need money and we use money, but the currency that they're creating and keep printing more of because of the Federal Reserve and the treasury is actually fraud perpetrated against us, because it's indebting our future and our next generation's future. It's spending out of control. We're in trillions of dollars of debt.

What is it that energy is connected to where we're receiving this paper dollars for our work, a promissory note, but that's a lie. In 1971, it was connected to the Gold Standard. But they disrupted that and print money like nobody's business, and now we're at a point in the world where –

Dr. Lisa: How much of you aligned? And how much of you resisted and reacted to the lie and has that shown up as your money flows?

Dr. Lisa: Right, wrong, good and bad, POD and POC, all nine, shorts, boys and beyonds®.

I know what you're saying, there's a lot of truth to that.

Participant: Right.

Dr. Lisa: How much of what you just said have you embodied as your resistance and reaction against receiving and showing up in your bank account?

That's how you're using that perpetration against you.

Dr. Lisa: Right, wrong, good and bad, POD and POC, all nine, shorts, boys and beyonds®.

And then, even though you're speaking about the truth, you've actually become a part of the perpetration of you by not allowing you to have what's yours and what you can contribute to dismantling that, to changing this world, to getting rid of Monsanto, if you had money.

Dr. Lisa: Right, wrong, good and bad, POD and POC, all nine, shorts, boys and beyonds®.

You've got to be brilliant with money, even though you know the truth about that perpetration. We're changing the energy, money, and the Earth and the cycle right now by you just expanding and having the affluence that is rightfully yours, by you receiving the lie and having, acknowledging, that, and realizing that you've been resisting and reacting to it, which is fucking you. Which is then the perpetration of you, which is then buying into the lie and the fraud patrol in this reality while you're fighting it, and then you're lying, and agreeing, and resisting, and reacting, but you're still not having it and you're letting them have it because you're abdicating your power and potency and yours and yours and yours and yours and yours and yours. Can we together destroy and uncreate that?

Right, wrong, good and bad, POD and POC, all nine, shorts, boys and beyonds®.

We eliminate and eradicate abuse on this planet by having and using the money, the way that the world works here to change realities. If you don't have it, you become part of the problem, not the solution.

Participants: Yes.

Dr. Lisa: Because not everybody's going to look. You guys look.

Participants: Yes.

Dr. Lisa: Right, wrong, good and bad, POD and POC, all nine, shorts, boys and beyonds®.

1, 2, 3, 4, 5. Fraud patrol. 1, 2, 3, 4, 5. Fraud patrol. 1, 2, 3, 4, 5. Fraud patrol. 1, 2, 3, 4, 5. Fraud patrol. 1, 2, 3, 4, 5. Fraud patrol. 1, 2, 3, 4, 5. Fraud patrol. 1, 2, 3, 4, 5. Fraud patrol. 1, 2, 3, 4, 5. Fraud patrol. 1, 2, 3, 4, 5. Fraud patrol. 1, 2, 3, 4, 5. Fraud patrol.

Everybody: 1, 2, 3, 4, 5. Fraud patrol. 1, 2, 3, 4, 5. Fraud patrol. 1, 2, 3, 4, 5. Fraud patrol. 1, 2, 3, 4, 5. Fraud patrol. 1, 2, 3, 4, 5. Fraud patrol. 1, 2, 3, 4, 5. Fraud patrol. 1, 2, 3, 4, 5. Fraud patrol. 1, 2, 3, 4, 5. Fraud patrol. 1, 2, 3, 4, 5. Fraud patrol. 1, 2, 3, 4, 5. Fraud patrol.

Dr. Lisa: There you go, baby.

Everybody: 1, 2, 3, 4, 5. Fraud patrol. 1, 2, 3, 4, 5. Fraud patrol. 1, 2, 3, 4, 5. Fraud patrol. 1, 2, 3, 4, 5. Fraud patrol. 1, 2, 3, 4, 5. Fraud patrol. 1, 2, 3, 4, 5. Fraud patrol. 1, 2, 3, 4, 5. Fraud patrol. 1, 2, 3, 4, 5. Fraud patrol. 1, 2, 3, 4, 5. Fraud patrol. 1, 2, 3, 4, 5. Fraud patrol.

Dr. Lisa: Open the door to a new possibility. 1, 2, 3, 4. Alright.

Participants: Yes.

Dr. Lisa: Right, wrong, good and bad, POD and POC, all nine, shorts, boys and beyonds®.

Dr. Lisa: In summary, get a crisp $100 bill, put it in your wallet. Keep adding to it, listen to it, talk to it. Rub it on your body.

I double dog dare you in front the mirror.

Love it, lay on the bed with it. Lick it, play with it. Do whatever you want to do.

I'm serious… if it makes you laugh, it's like fun.

Money comes to the party of fun.

Second thing, create your 10% account. I double dog dare you.

Third thing, write 25 things about your financial reality. Ask yourself after that, "Light or heavy?" If it's heavy, ask more questions, POC and POD. Then you can have it, because you having your reality is what this life is all about.

Dr. Lisa: Then ask yourself these questions.

Participant: You said, "Your financial reality, what does it look like?" I'm not sure about that.

Dr. Lisa: I don't know what your financial reality is, but I know that my financial reality has a generosity of spirit in it. Whatever that means to me, it's kind of a little bit like my father. It may not be the same way he showed up, but my financial reality has a kindness to it.

My financial reality takes care of my body. That's been a real big work in progress listening to my body. My financial reality is having. That's my 10%-10%-10% accounts, body, business honoring account.

My financial reality means I will go all around the world wherever I'm invited to do classes like this. My financial reality does a Voice America radio show that is a labor of love that costs somewhere between $30,000 and $50,000 a year. It's a free resource because I know when I get that call from Dubai or Pakistan or India, Australia, Hong Kong, Israel, or whatever, and I facilitate one person out of their cage of abuse to radical aliveness – transitioning their traumatic to orgasmically alive – I know I've touched that land and that country.

I know the internet is accessible everywhere, and I'm not going to stop as long as that is still part of my financial reality.

How much have I said is about money?

I haven't said one thing that's specifically about money right now.

That's me.

There's more about money. My financial reality is my 'go to San Francisco' or my next places, that there's a profit. Before I was willing to do without profit. Now there's a profit. What would I need to do to make that happen? Do I need to do a day of individual sessions or 10 days of individual sessions to make it happen? I'll do it.

I'm not afraid of working. I love what I do.

Right, wrong, good and bad, POD and POC, all nine, shorts, boys and beyonds®.

I so thank you for your time. For those of you that I've met for the first time, thank you for coming. For those of you that I know very well and you're all here, thank you for coming. I value your voices. I value your attention.

I really appreciate and honor the courage and vulnerability that it takes to ask a question and lift and look under the hood, and to play with this wacky energy called Access Consciousness™ and the tools and the clearing statement.

I hope you found this evening fruitful. I hope I was a contribution to you, and I definitely hope I get to see you again.

Bring your money to the bedroom, don't leave it on the couch.

Participants: Thank you!

Dr. Lisa: Be You! Beyond Anything! Create Magic! and Go Have Money!

Afterword

In the introduction, I told you that you had your hands on a gold mine, and I hope you can now see why.

The truth is, there's simply no reason you cannot create all the money you desire if you have the courage and willingness to look 'under the hood' of your own financial reality. And in this book, I've shown you a way and given you tools to begin the process of examining three lies of money.

The first lie is that money is god and you are less than.

The second lie is money is your perpetrator, your eternal jailor, and you can't have it.

The third lie is that money is a problem.

And, while, this is by no means all of the lies of money, it's enough to get you started.

Remember, you only need to shift 1° or 1%, right?

I'm sure you noticed there are many, many profound questions you can ask yourself to unravel whatever you've got going on around money and, I hope, that you were asking them of yourself throughout the course of reading this, or marked them to return to again.

(However, if you didn't, or feel you'd like more help with this, take a look at the Appendix where I've listed other resources I have available. There are a plethora of them, and they're all designed to help you break through to your own ROAR – your radically, orgasmically, alive reality.)

Whenever you get stuck and want to walk yourself out of it, begin asking yourself these three essential questions:

- *Who am I being?*
- *What am I being?*
- *What lie am I buying into that I've made true?*

Then, as you discover the truth for yourself and free up your energy, you'll want to move forward in your life with the "4 Cs":

- *Commit to you*
- *Choose for you*
- *The Universe is Conspiring to bless you and wants to Collaborate with you*
- *Create*

Once you begin choosing what's light and right in front of you – and follow that energy – money will follow you because of what's inside of you.

So, like I said to the others…

I double-dog dare you to be the walking, talking, tsunami or earthquake that alters reality simply by your mere presence, to be your ROAR (Radically Orgasmically Alive Reality).

Be you, beyond anything and create magic.

Appendix

The following are registered trademarks of Access Consciousness:

ACCESS CONSCIOUSNESS®

CONSCIOUSNESS INCLUDES EVERYTHING AND JUDGES NOTHING®

EASE, JOY AND GLORY™

ENERGETIC SYNTHESIS OF BEING™

HOW DOES IT GET ANY BETTER THAN THIS?®

RIGHT AND WRONG, GOOD AND BAD, POD AND POC, ALL 9, SHORTS, BOYS AND BEYONDS®

THE BARS®

About the Author

Dr. Lisa Cooney is a thought leader in the area of personal transformation. A licensed Marriage and Family Therapist, Master Theta Healer, and certified Access Consciousness Facilitator, she's the creator of Live Your ROAR! Be You! Beyond Anything! Creating Magic! An internationally recognized expert, Dr. Lisa's work has allowed thousands of people to cross the bridge from childhood sexual abuse, and other forms of abuse, to living a "Radically Orgasmically Alive Reality" (ROAR).

The magic of her work centers on core concepts that she used to heal herself, not only from early childhood abuse, but from a life-threatening disease. These essential principles, which include the 4 C's – Choosing for you, Committing to you, Collaborating and knowing that the universe is conspiring to bless you, and Creating the life you desire – are the touchstone for deep and lasting transformation.

Besides a Doctorate of Psychology, she is certified in other healing modalities that utilize all her energetic gifts: Reiki, Theta Healing, Thermometry, Breath Therapy, Psychodrama, Dream Therapy, Socially Engaged Spirituality, Heart-Centered Hypnotherapy, Depth Hypnosis based in Shamanism, and Access Consciousness Facilitation.

In addition to her own revolutionary and "revelationary" contributions to the body of transformative wisdom, she is gifted in using the creative tools of Access Consciousness to facilitate others in moving beyond all obstacles and into a place of their own knowing...that space where they have direct access to the whisperings of consciousness.

As host of her own live stream show on the Voice America Empowerment Channel, Dr. Lisa speaks to thousands of listeners each week who seek help and inspiration. Besides writing articles and being a coauthor in numerous projects, her latest book, *Kick Abuse in the Caboose: A Journey to Radical Aliveness* is currently at a major publishing house. A sought-after, dynamic facilitator, she's invited to conduct classes and workshops, as well as speak at TeleSummits and other events, all around the world.

Known for her "I'm Having It!...No Matter What!" approach to life, Dr. Lisa teaches people how to playfully engage this magical and generative energy to create a life that's light and right and fun for them.